T0341732

Wind, Life, Health

Wind, Life, Health

Anthropological and Historical Perspectives

Edited by Elisabeth Hsu and Chris Low

Blackwell Publishing

Royal Anthropological Institute

© 2008 by Royal Anthropological Institute of Great Britain and Ireland

First published as a special issue of *The Journal of the Royal Anthropological Institute* (Volume 13, April 2007)

BLACKWELL PUBLISHING
350 Main Street, Malden, MA 02148-5020, USA
9600 Garsington Road, Oxford OX4 2DQ, UK
550 Swanston Street, Carlton, Victoria 3053, Australia

The right of Elisabeth Hsu and Chris Low to be identified as the authors of the editorial material in this work has been asserted in accordance with the UK Copyright, Designs, and Patents Act 1988.

All rights reserved. No part of this publication may be reproduced, stored in a retrieval system, or transmitted, in any form or by any means, electronic, mechanical, photocopying, recording or otherwise, except as permitted by the UK Copyright, Designs, and Patents Act 1988, without the prior permission of the publisher.

Designations used by companies to distinguish their products are often claimed as trademarks. All brand names and product names used in this book are trade names, service marks, trademarks, or registered trademarks of their respective owners. The publisher is not associated with any product or vendor mentioned in this book.

This publication is designed to provide accurate and authoritative information in regard to the subject matter covered. It is sold on the understanding that the publisher is not engaged in rendering professional services. If professional advice or other expert assistance is required, the services of a competent professional should be sought.

First published 2008 by Blackwell Publishing Ltd

1 2008

Library of Congress Cataloging-in-Publication Data

Wind, life, health : anthropological and historical perspectives / edited by Elisabeth Hsu and Chris Low.
p. cm.
'First published as a special issue of The Journal of the Royal Anthropological Institute.'
Includes bibliographical references and index.
ISBN 978-1-4051-7893-8 (pbk. : alk. paper) 1. Human beings – Effect of climate on. 2. Human beings – Effect of environment on. 3. Winds. I. Hsu, ELisabeth. II. Low, Chris, 1966– III. Journal of the Royal Anthropological Institute.

GF71.W56 2007
304.2′5—dc22

2007042074

A catalogue record for this title is available from the British Library.

Set in 10/12pt Minion
by SNP Best-set Typesetter Ltd., Hong Kong

The publisher's policy is to use permanent paper from mills that operate a sustainable forestry policy, and which has been manufactured from pulp processed using acid-free and elementary chlorine-free practices. Furthermore, the publisher ensures that the text paper and cover board used have met acceptable environmental accreditation standards.

For further information on
Blackwell Publishing, visit our website at
www.blackwellpublishing.com

MIX
Paper from
responsible sources
FSC
www.fsc.org
FSC® C013604

Contents

Preface

This publication stems from an eponymous conference held at Oxford University in June 2005. The editors can claim to have met at a drinking hostelry on St Giles to discuss informally topics of interest whence the initial spark was born and momentum instigated for a wind conference. With particular backgrounds in the medical historical anthropology of southern African Khoisan and the anthropology/history of Chinese medicine, we were intrigued in our discussion of wind not only by the diversity and richness but also the fundamental congruency in the way wind has been perceived by peoples in different parts of the world. Wind is a theme central to the thinking of peoples in both contemporary and ancient cultures. The value of discussing wind lies in what it brings not only, on a theoretical level, to elucidating human relationships with one of the planet's basic aspects of life but also to exploration of how the materiality of wind shapes social practice at a number of fundamental levels. The particular sensorial relationship we have with wind has persistently led to embedding our experience of the meteorological phenomenon, and of respiration, in a web of associations concerning life and death and the cosmos at large.

The volume examines the richness of human ideas and practices surrounding wind, breath, spirit, sentiment, life, and health by seriously exploring the primordial human experience of being immersed in the winds in the environment and breathing them in. It seeks to balance detailed ethnography with theoretical insight and deliberately takes a broad approach to broach the subject from different disciplinary perspectives. The papers engage with a wide range of themes, including landscape, weather, body, perception, emplacement, climate, seasons, song, and music. They concern hunters and gatherers in the polar region, the Malaysian rainforest, the Andaman Islands, and the deserts of southern Africa, as well as stratified societies of Muslim East Africa, ancient and medieval India, China, and Greece, and historical and modern Europe, namely the Victorian English and mountain-dwelling Swiss. Each author brings out specific ways in which different peoples, physically and conceptually, have grappled with winds and spirits, their smells and sounds, the way they feel and sentiments they bring about, and how these are linked to ways of knowing about the world and being in the world. Two regrettable exceptions from the volume concern the potential contributions by Jim McNeley on Navajo wind and Carol Laderman on the inner winds amongst the Temiar, but echoes of their generous participation at the conference can be felt throughout.

We are grateful for the support received from the British Academy, the Institute of Social and Cultural Anthropology, the Wellcome Unit for the History of Medicine, and the staff and facilities of the Osler-McGovern Centre, Green College.

Elisabeth Hsu & Chris Low
Editors
December 2006

1
Introduction

Chris Low & Elisabeth Hsu *University of Oxford*

Wind, on first consideration, may be thought of as a 'natural phenomenon': 'air in motion'. Our different words for wind, including breezes, wafts, squalls, whirlwinds, hurricanes, and cyclones, tell us something about the origins, scale, and implications of the phenomenon. Cyclically or erratically winds appear and dissipate across the landscape as one of the primordial rhythms of unfolding life and part of the backdrop of life in the open. Yet wind is also experienced indoors, in the form of 'drafts' and 'currents of air', and if it is not reduced to a phenomenon of modern meteorology and the natural sciences, wind can also be thought to manifest in breathing and in the internal body winds that circulate in veins or appear in the form of sneezes and coughs. Or winds can be deities and spirits.

Wind takes on different guises when it works its way into different aspects of people's lives. It becomes a power when the sailor hoists his sail, a friend when it cools an overheating body, an enemy when the rhinoceros that you did not see, just behind the bush, picks up your scent in a capricious flirt of the breeze. It becomes an illness from a bitter relative or an offended ancestor. The English phrases 'winds of change', 'winds of war', 'to get wind of something', 'throw it to the wind', or 'three sheets to the wind' all point to different relationships with wind. The different ways in which winds interact with people lend them different identities.

In this volume, we begin with the ubiquitous external 'wind' phenomenon, which more often than not is linked to the internal experience of 'breathing', and explore the enormously rich range of ideas about wind and ways of being in wind, negotiating with, controlling and 'binding', inhaling and expulsing the winds. The volume discusses both meteorological winds and embodied experiences of wind in social and historical context, by drawing out local nuances of understanding. It presents a detailed study of intimate relationships with wind which hold the life-giving sensual phenomenon in a profound relationship with ways of conceptualizing life and death, sickness and healing.

Consideration of wind forces a return to the big questions of life that have occupied philosophers since the earliest documented records. Wind could arguably be used as a conceptual tool to inform a fundamental set of core dichotomies, often perceived as a legacy of Greek thought, through which the conundrum of life continues to be explored: being and becoming, reality and appearance, subject and object, nature and culture, mind and body. This potential capacity of wind stems from it being recruited across cultures as a way of thinking about a host of phenomena that define fundamental aspects of the physical and spiritual world. Wind is both felt and tangible, and thus physical and elusive, as is the spiritual. It comes as no surprise, therefore, that ideas of wind persistently overlap with notions of spirit, divinity, breath, smell, and shadow. These concepts work together in a family of resemblances to inform ontology and epistemology.

Wind envelops people within their environment and breathing is the basis of life. In this volume, which takes those fundamental experiences of 'nature' as a starting point for discussing their resurfacing in core concepts of 'culture', we provide a further anthropological critique of the nature-culture dichotomy that has long entrenched Western thought. At its heart is the identification of, and meaning attributed to, wind as it moves between nature and culture, body and mind. While building on Ingold, Descola, Ellen, and Rival, who since the 1990s have provided a sociological reformulation of nature that directly challenges the nature-culture dualism (Franklin 2002), this volume's interrogation of how wind moves between the domains of the perceptual, symbolic, and metaphorical owes, furthermore, a particular intellectual debt to the phenomenology of perception and the anthropology of the senses.

The strength of the ethnographic accounts in our endeavour lies in exploring, in vivid sensual terms, how wind, the environmental phenomenon, becomes socialized through practice and belief. The papers begin with Ingold's analysis of wind, which takes up his theme of 'dwelling', that is, the recursive relationship between people and landscape laid out in earlier works (e.g. Ingold 1993; 2000), and explores wind as an aspect of landscape. Parkin, Roseman, Pandya, and Low similarly develop themes of how wind, as an aspect of the sensual experience of being in a certain place with certain sorts of winds, at a certain time, informs social practice. These papers postulate, in the vein of Rival (1993; 1996), that perceptual knowledge of the landscape affects cultural choices, ideas, and practices.

Another theme intrinsic to all papers in this volume, which is not explicitly dealt with in any single one, concerns the apparent cross-cultural similarity of wind ideas. Thematic clusters can be observed in the above-mentioned ethnographic papers, in those on ancient and medieval India, China, and Greece by Zysk, Hsu, and Lloyd, and those on modern Europe by Jankovic and Strauss. The question that these apparent similarities pose concerns, ultimately, issues of biological parity in people's participation in the environment, and how this feeds into a biologically mediated set of similar ideas. Ellen (1996) pushed for an underlying 'cognitive geometry' that allows some realist crossover between different cultural conceptions of nature. Descola (1992; 1996), who works with totemism and animism as two principal agents in his discussion of how people construct continuity between the natural and the cultural, acknowledged the existence of cognitive universals but emphasized that these fuzzy templates or patterns are heavily mediated by the local environment and the types of practices through which the environment is socialized. However, as evident from the recurrent themes of wind in this volume, which resurface in disparate literate and oral, contemporary and ancient settings, the question is perhaps best answered with less geometry and more allowances for ambiguity.

Although ethnography would appear better suited to bringing out the contribution of the personal to societal ideas of wind, individual voices necessarily underpin the distillations of history, as is evident from the contributions by Lloyd, Hsu, Jankovic, and Zysk. When the textual sources are returned to, the clean historical generalizations that have fed Western popular imagination soon break down in the face of real discrepancies and inconsistencies, both within the work of one author and across authors. Such inconsistency is generally not associated with received textual knowledge, but as the authors in this volume show, who all are attending to primary source material, it is intrinsic not only to oral but also to literate transmission; the texts in question contain as much contradiction, ambivalence, and flexibility of knowledge as anthropologists have identified in contemporary settings. Regardless of previous orality-literacy debates, these studies demonstrate how wind as an overarching term holds different ways of being known that can be called upon in different contexts, making knowledge of wind seem variable, precise and imprecise at the same time.

Whilst taking a broad historical and ethnographic approach, it is hoped that this comparative exercise, with its focus on the phenomenology of wind, goes further towards a profound understanding of the relationship between the natural-turned-cultural phenomenon of wind and its role in the foundation of life. Questions posed include: who experiences wind, and how? What is the relationship of outside wind to inside wind? Who has an interest in wind and in controlling and binding the winds – doctors, priests, farmers, or ascetics – and why? What are the ways in which such binding is conceptualized and operated? This collection of essays seeks to find a meaningful way of talking about human/wind relationships more broadly.

The experience of wind

Wind as breath of life reflects a basic daily experience as much as a mythological truth. Breathing generates and ensures the continuation of life, and this has consistently been taken as evidence of divine presence, or the gift of life, by all manner of cultures, including our own. Wind touches and is felt, inside out. While there is considerable variation in the experience and the expression of wind ideas as a concept, it is hard not to be struck by the remarkable congruence in relationships understood to exist between wind, breath, and variously framed notions of life-force. Equally remarkable is the way such themes reveal themselves at work in webs of different sorts of cultural contexts.

The Navajo, for example, perceive life to have emerged from two winds in the lower worlds, a white wind and a dark blue wind, which existed in Earth's veins or roots. Male white wind lay on top of female dark wind, intermingled in the manner of sexual intercourse, and thereby generated Earth, Sky, and the plants, animals and peoples of the lower world. The two winds gave these forms the breath of life and the powers of behaviour and thought. At a later period these manifestations of life moved up to the earth's surface accompanied by the winds. These winds were placed in the east and south, and the two further cardinal winds were placed alongside them (J.K. McNeley, pers. comm., June 2005).

Cross-culturally, considerations of wind very quickly lead to overlapping ideas of breath, spirit, smell, song, sentiment and shadow. Whilst this web of relations may at first appear unfamiliar to contemporary Western intellectual traditions, similar ways of thinking have a long pedigree in Western thought and continue to operate in more everyday contexts of living in wind. In ancient Greece, Aristotle thought that life-engendering 'vital heat' was present in all *pneuma* (Lloyd, this volume). Through the early modern period and into the present, different theories of 'vitalism' or 'vital principle' have persistently associated breath and life-force. Moreover, the Western Christian theological tradition has provided an ongoing arena in which notions of wind are articulated in a distinctly un-meteorological manner. In the Bible the word *ruach* has been translated variously as air, breath, wind, divine power, and Holy Spirit. In Genesis we find: 'Then the Lord God formed man of dust from the ground, and breathed into his nostrils the breath of life, and man became a living being' (Genesis 2:7); in Job 'the Spirit of God has made me, the breath of the Almighty gives me life' (Job 33:4); and from Ezekiel (37) we learn that human bones become alive as the four winds blow on them.

In addition to links made between wind, breath, and life-force by ancient science and theology, as Jankovic identifies in nineteenth-century Britain, there has long been a parallel thrust from more mainstream corners of science, medical topography, and geography. These various research contexts have looked more towards measurable physical and mental effects of wind on people. Strauss, who combines anthropological, literary, and scientific data to explore the relationship between the inhabitants of alpine Leukerbad and the Foehn, demonstrates how a folk idiom and knowledge of wind continue to interact with modern contexts of scientific analysis. The Foehn is a down-slope katabatic wind, like the Chinook or Sant Ana. They all are hot and strong, and known to cause strange behaviour, migraines, and even fits of madness, and are a determinant of living patterns and of regional identity.

That wind affects feelings highlights the fact that wind penetrates the body at both a physical and a mental level. The ecological psychologist James Gibson, who had observed that air is insubstantial and proposed that life or activity takes place at its boundaries or points of interaction with objects, ascribed wind as *medium* and its manifestations as the result of contact with *substance*. His approach usefully draws our attention to what wind does at a macro level and where and how this might relate to biological and evolutionary development. His emphasis of surfaces is important in relation to how wind contact shapes the gross physical environment, such as sand dunes, mountains, or wind-beaten hedgerows. It is also at this level that wind feeds into human technological and economic relationships through, for example, sailing ships or building designs. Additionally, Gibson's exploration has some particularly useful insights into how animals relate to wind as the holder of tracks of smell, light, and sound (Gibson 1979: 17). Informative as his approach is, however, he does not seem adequately to take into account the penetration of wind.

In this volume, Ingold engages with feelings in his contestation of Gibson's polarization of wind and substance. He envisages that people 'mingle' with 'wind, rain, sunshine and earth'. Life, he suggests, is lived in a zone in which substance and medium are brought together. As he forefronts issues of 'immersion' and the 'environmental relationship', feelings emerge as a consciousness of connection and interaction. This conflation of mental and bodily processes, and the consolidation of humans within the world, reflects life-views of many indigenous peoples. In very different intellectual contexts, not entirely unrelated links have similarly been made by two pillars of New Age philosophy Joseph Campbell (1991: 18), the comparative mythologist, and James Lovelock (1979), the atmospheric geochemist. We live in a dynamic relationship with our surroundings, and the experience of wind lends itself well to accounting for subtle atmospheric change, regardless of whether it is seasonal, climatic, or emotionally felt. With Ingold in mind, feelings can usefully be thought of as evidence and means of participation.

From a loosely conceived co-evolutionary perspective, what seems emergent from this research is an acknowledgement that the receptivity to nature evident amongst many indigenous peoples is tied to what Bird-David (1990) termed the 'giving environment'. Within such worldviews the world reveals itself in a regular manner. Events that happen together or phenomena that are experienced in a like manner are connected and likely to recur in a similar pattern as the world continues to unfold, regenerate, and provide. A particular example of how such attention to the environment might relate to wind is the observation that the inhabitants around Lake Titicaca, in Peru, connect the colours of the lake to the strength of the wind (Orlove 2002: 35, 144-5). A further impressive awareness of such connections is also evident in the ability of Polynesian navigators to read ocean swells as indicators of the direction of and distance from land (Lewis 1973). Through a skilful reading of this patterned and revealing environment, humans are enabled to make predictions and act in ways that are beneficial to survival.

In his study of nomadic spirituality, Berman (2000) observed that when many Native Americans refer to the Great Spirit, they are talking about wind. He notes that spirit refers, in this sense, to the creation itself: 'Water coming off a leaf, the smell of the forest after rain, the warm blood of a deer' (Berman 2000: 11). His observation is linked to the wider-held ties between wind and breath as life-creator, but the Native American beliefs clearly take the understanding further. What seems to be referred to is a notion of a universal flowing force that is particularly evident in the discernible patterns of life, although it is thought to be at work in all things. Historically, such beliefs have been referred to as 'animism'. Ingold (this volume) sheds some light on what this animistic label actually deals with in his assessment that what distinguishes so-called 'animists' is their receptivity to life and their awareness of living within a current of continual generation. His recognition of the importance of such awareness confirms findings of other anthropologists, from Paul Radin and Robin Riddington working amongst Native Americans to George Silberbauer amongst southern African Bushmen.

When an awareness that all life by definition has the breath or wind of life within it is combined with this notion of connection, it becomes possible to conceive of life being underpinned by wind relationships, in which each phenomenon possesses its own wind whilst partaking in the general or divine wind. In many indigenous perspectives wind and breath stand for both the medium of connection and the marker of power and identity. While experienced as weaving a binding pattern through life, wind has an undeniably felt presence, and perhaps it is such a relationship between divine breath and materialized breath that holds wind, breath, and spirit in such a tight conceptual overlap. In this sense humans may stage themselves as participating in divine breath, the same but less powerful. Wind and breath provide both the triggering spark and the materiality that make possible this process.

Parkin (this volume) discusses the prevalence of the breath, wind, and spirit in as diverse contexts as classical Greek, Sanskrit, and Semitic thought and that of recent Australian Aborigines. In his analysis, he highlights not so much air or wind as a marker of spirit identity but smell. When one considers that wind or smell may stand for certain characteristics of an entity, and hence certain abilities, coupled with an awareness that wind and smell are fluid, the notion that wind can be channelled and used by humans to achieve powerful desired ends seems a small step. Similarly the notion that one entity can transform into another by sharing wind or smell becomes a possibility. Parkin suggests that smell, and associated smoke and fumes, is a key medium through which humans attempt to physicalize and de-physicalize spirits. The Swahili speakers he studies hold no rigid conceptual line between substance and non-substance. In a cycle of spiritual and material transformation, smell contributes to the identity of a spirit.

Roseman (this volume) outlines a Malay Temiar worldview which is congruent with the notion of wind as an all-pervasive phenomenon that coalesces in distinctive forms whilst at the same time remaining bound to a discernible chain of connection. The Temiar world, she suggests, is underwritten by a 'poetic economy' interlinking winds of landscape, winds of spirits, voices of mediums, and movements of dancers. Roseman seems to perceive a tie between an accumulation or 'density' of wind and the essence of an organism or object. '[A]ll entities', she observes, 'exhibit the potential to take shape at various levels of density best viewed as points along a continuum'. Her explorations place the smell aspect of wind, as privileged by Parkin, within a wider sensuous world, including sound and movement, and provide a sense of how wind is drawn into culture. Roseman relates how the shuddering of light and rustling sound in the foliage of tree leaves or in plastic strips hanging from the ceiling allow spirits to descend on people, become present, and in an instant, barely perceptible, vanish. In other contexts, the voice serves as much as a spirit conduit as do blowing and sucking, which affect the movements of spirit and soul components. Roseman notes that there is significant resonance with the fluidity of the world conceived by the Temiar and that of the East Africans described by Parkin. The significance of the sound of wind in leaves, plastic strips, or voices reminds us how the aural manifestation of wind through its roaring or rustling, singing or chiming instruments, widens the life-like repertoire of wind's being.

Whilst in many contexts wind and spirits seem inextricably bound, other contexts emphasize wind more as carrier than the actual spirits themselves. Whence winds blow and what they carry often relates to seasonal change. In his account of the Andaman Islanders, Pandya links experiential knowledge of the cyclical appearance of winds with the changes they bring to food resources and life-ways. Winds blowing from a certain direction cause seasonal change and thereby regulate patterns of movement, seed-sowing, food-gathering, fishing, and hunting. Pandya (this volume), in a way that modifies slightly his earlier schema of the seasons (Pandya 1993), ties the seasonal oscillation of the Ongee and Jarwas between inland and coastal camps to the consumption of food and the manipulation of smells that impinge on the movements of the spirits. In his analysis, human beings chase away the winds, and thereby create man-made windless seasons during which the islanders can eat the food of the spirits, honey and cicada grubs.

In many cultures thinking of winds in a wilful manner replete with certain characteristics has led to the association of the winds with specific sorts of spirits, or to the personification of wind. The ancient Greeks mythologized the winds into the four (sometimes eight) *anemoi*: Zephyros, Boreas, Notos, and Euros. Amongst some Bushmen, an inchoate link is made between destructive whirlwinds and sickness-causing spirits of the dead. Biblical authors singled out the east wind as the fruit-drying (Ezk. 19:12), locust-bringing (Exo. 14:21), drought-inducing (Ezk. 17:10) ship-breaker (Psa. 48:7). Perhaps, they worked a specific experience of wind in the Holy Land into a cultural trope and personified it. In contrast to Eastern understandings that associated the east wind with springtime and with the source of life through the idea of the rising sun (the west and the dying sun being associated with death), the perceived properties of the biblical east wind served as the hand of God's retribution and became symbolic of moral worthlessness (Hos. 12:1).

One recurrently encounters the link people make between wind type, landscape source, and a particular sort of spiritual encounter. Amongst the Temiar, it seems, the moist characteristics of the local mountain winds are central to their conceptions of the cool watery essence of the spirits that visit from the landscape in dreams and ceremonies. The Navajo, who identified a sacred mountain at each cardinal point, tied specific landscape features to different winds that manifested in the human body in different functional capacities. From the four cardinal mountains the Holy People sent winds that provided guidance, instruction, and strength. Wind was linked with personal spirits, in the sense that personality is made up of what enables people to do things, what inspires and motivates them. Thus, the 'Holy Wind' among the Navajo, called *Niłch'i*, which unites external nature with the internal natural human body, contributed to the powers of thought, speech, and the power of motion (McNeley 1981: 1). These various links that the Navajo made between wind and human motivation again bear strong resemblance to ideas found in many other cultures.

Similarly to the Navajo, the Khoisan associate life-wind with the power of motion (Low, this volume). As amongst the ancient Greeks, Chinese, and Indians, they link motion to the blood flow, and ideas of blood overlap significantly with wind. As the heart is recognized as a primary reservoir of blood amongst the Khoisan, so too is it the home of wind. As motivation is linked to purposeful spirit, the heart also becomes conceptualized as a seat of thought, both good and bad. The Namibian Damara accordingly massage a 'displaced' heart to realign it and treat the negative thoughts that the diseased organ sends to the head. Low emphasizes wind as an overarching concept with great explanatory power. It can explain as varied phenomena as those of Bushmen who have been reported to point at a springbok and freeze it in its path; a dog's stare which has the power to terminate a pregnancy; or a Nama patient who unknowingly 'arrows' a person while performing a massage.The wind of illness passes through the arrows to the healer, as the wind passes to the springbok and from the dog. Wind conceptualized in this manner explains not only Khoisan relations to powers of thought and speech but also ideas lying behind 'action at a distance' and witchcraft.

If wind is identified with bodily functions, it is perhaps not surprising that aberrations of wind are recognized and techniques developed which address wind pathologies or seek to enhance bodily and mental function through controlling the winds by binding them. Zysk examines the very sophisticated development of such techniques in Sanskrit texts of the Ayurvedic and Yogic traditions. In ancient India, ascetic practices of harnessing the cosmic winds comprised inhalation, exhalation, and breath retention, which in turn were subdivided into seven types each. The Yogic tradition of breath control was distinctive from medical traditions in that it involved also a meditative process for stabilizing the mind. Although the highly elaborate relationships of wind and breath in these scholarly texts stand in contrast with the more inchoate relationships of many hunter-gatherers, Zysk points out that these sophisticated practices of breath control, much like those techniques Roseman describes among the Temiar hunter-gatherers, are ultimately performed with the aim of anchoring winds in the body.

Laderman (1991) furthermore observed that among the contemporary Temiar, the inner winds, *angin*, which make possible imagination, feeling, and thinking, constitute a key component of a Malay person. Temiar shamanic ritual is directed at modulating the state of inner winds. As among the contemporary Temiar, the ancient Chinese seem to have spoken of cognitive and emotional dynamics in terms of inner winds when in the feudal Zhou they discovered the interiority of personhood (Hsu, this volume). The body was then conceived as having a form (*xing*) that was outwardly visible and could be firmed up with gymnastics and breathing techniques, and that lodged within it one's thoughts and feelings, and *qi*. When the Chinese physicians who worked in the social strata of the nobility realized that psychological states can cause illness and became interested in regulating their clientele's psychology and internal emotional processes, they made *qi* into a central concept of their medicine. While early medicine distinguished between *qi*-breath and *feng*-winds as inner and outer winds, the medicine of systematic correspondences that became well established in Han China referred to *qi* as the unifying medium that permeated the universe.

It is difficult to summarize what makes wind so salient across cultures. The repeatedly observed ways in which similar ideas and actions coalesce around the climatic wind phenomenon and couple it with the experience of breathing strongly suggest commonality in the way wind is known. More precisely, they hint at a common phenomenology of experiencing wind and breath. It appears as though the body as generative principle has worked the experience of wind-cum-breath into recurring cultural tropes. Scrutinizing these and their provenance may contribute to the growing body of literature interested in the biological constitution of culture (Lewis-Williams & Pearce 2004; Maturana & Varela 1998; Mithen 2006; Pinker 2002).

Brief reflection on a possible evolutionary benefit of being aware of the wind reminds us why we might be so receptive to it. It is often cited that in hunting, wind serves both quarry and prey by laying tracks of smell. But it is less considered, for example, that the over-exciting or, aptly termed, 'spooking' effect of a sharp skittish breeze or gale on horses, dogs, and children could well be related to the inherent vulnerability such vicarious winds place on a potential prey animal. Similarly, smell is often highlighted as an aspect of hunting knowledge, but it clearly plays a far wider role. Smell informs us of the familiar, the foreign and dangerous, the edible and drinkable, and the noxious. As any indigenous person will tell you, these aspects of wind, which do not begin to explore what wind might tell indigenous people, are not trite reminders of a hypothetical evolutionary past, but day-to-day realities. However, this acknowledgement of wind's evolutionary role raises the question why it leads to the sort of ideas of divinity, spirits, and shadows so often encountered in this volume. Precisely their allusion to the divine and to spirits, rather than evolutionary survival functions, may have led wind ideas to persist in stratified societies.

In his evolutionary analysis of religious ideas, Pascal Boyer proposed that it is the way that the mind has evolved that lies behind the recurrence of certain religious ideas and particularly the 'set of ideas concerning non-observable, extra-natural agencies and processes' (1994: 5). He has spirits primarily in mind, although wind could easily be substituted. Boyer identifies that the mind is attuned by natural selection to picking up relevant information. Of the ideas that evolve in the mind, those that are 'acquired' more easily are those that are found more widely (Boyer 2001: 4). Whilst wind ideas are not substantive universals, they are significantly consistent and widespread. Boyer's analysis suggests both that wind ideas are easy to acquire and that being attuned to wind serves an evolutionary role. However, his discussion concerns 'the mental' as an independent entity in interaction with 'natural' processes, while the family of wind ideas discussed in this volume arises from the prime experience of a body that is mingling with its environment (often a pervious body thought to be dotted with orifices).

Without further treading the slippery grounds of whether and how commonly evolutionary processes determine cultural ones, we point out here that the ubiquitous social practice surrounding wind hints at links between biological predisposition and cultural elaboration. Partly, it is the recurrent conflation of climatic outer winds with internal breathing that allows the wind experience of a mingling body to be applied in a multitude of cultural contexts. Partly, it is wind's ability to cross boundaries that makes it such a rich hermeneutic tool. Wind connects the wilderness to the hearth. It moves from beyond the body to within the body, from the dead to the living, from the quotidian to the divine. Wind connects people with people, and people with the environment, near and far. It is a connective force, causes change, triggers events, and can be attributed with all sorts of effects inside and outside of the body. It can be accumulated, passed around, pulled about, and manipulated. With these properties it becomes a means of regulating the body, treating disease, engineering wider social events, and, ultimately, a way of understanding life.

The anthropology of the senses and the phenomenology of wind

Since the development of phenomenology by the philosopher Edmund Husserl in the mid-1890s, many proponents of the phenomenological approach have brought their own nuances to the discipline. Interest in existential phenomenology has continued in recent contexts from, amongst others, Maurice Natanson, Michael Henry, and John Compton. Of all contributors, the most widely known has undoubtedly been the philosopher Maurice Merleau-Ponty and especially his *Phenomenology of perception* (1962 [1945]). Husserl sought to bring science to a point where it acknowledged that it is rooted in the same world encountered by everyday people through unaided sensory modalities. From seeking to place a scientific way of knowing the world back into the realms of feelings, he moved towards the body as the locus of self but stumbled on the self as an ultimately disembodied transcendental ego. Merleau-Ponty, by contrast, elevated the body to a generative principle through which the world is known by experience. In a sweeping resolution of Descartes's lingering separation of mind and self from the body, Merleau-Ponty asserted that without the body there is no relationship with the external world and there is no self. Every thought, every motivation, is a response of body as it participates in a sensuous world (Abram 1997).

Csordas's (e.g. 2002) writings on 'embodiment' have combined Merleau-Ponty's philosophy with Bourdieu's (e.g. 1977 [1972]) practice theory, which defined *habitus* as a disposition, as internalized history, a structured structuring device for future practice. This allows Csordas to account for the body as a generative principle of social practice in interaction with the world. As the body is immersed in the world and in wind, the notion of 'embodiment' provides a means of encompassing processes of the mental within those of perception and participation. Wind can be remembered in the body and its perceived effects transformed and reproduced.

Wind provides an exceptional sensory experience. The feeling of mingling is evoked as it is felt both on the body surface and inside the body. It can be smelt, heard and felt, if not touched, and its effects are visible. As wind, including smell and sound, sometimes in combination, is often felt but not seen, it is also a readily available causal concept for events that can be felt to occur but are not seen to occur. If we tie this appreciation of wind to the sort of understanding of the world known as 'animism', in which all things are linked and events happen for a reason, we begin to see how wind could serve as the unseeable connective medium or the invisible force that drives the action. If we make a final connection between breathing and breath as the self-evident manifestation of life, wind begins to look like the ultimate explanation for life in all its diverse unfolding.

In the following papers, immediate sensory experience has served as an entry point for the discussion of the spirit world in that all authors have related ideas about the spirit world, and practices for manipulating it, to immediate experiences of wind. In other words, their discussion of spirits and the divine is inspired by the phenomenology of perception. Some authors have also worked wind into an anthropology of the senses at a number of levels, including most conspicuously smell and sound, and to a lesser extent touch and temperature. Sound, like smell, is invisible, and hence it lends itself particularly well to relationships with the invisible and powerful. Music modulates emotion. While it is thought to nourish the soul in some cultural contexts, it chases away spirits in others. Song and music, like the odours of incense, can entice spirits or draw groups together, enclosing them in a particular kind of atmosphere.

The song-lines of Australian Aborigines map out how the landscape was sung into being by the ancestors. The Word of God spoke the earth into being. Singing and words have the creative power of breath and spirit. In parts of Polynesia there is a condition known as *fooee*. It is a state of abject listlessness induced by the noise of relentless days of rustling sun-baked palm leaves endlessly accompanied by the lapping of a gleaming sea on a sandy shore. Who is listening to the rustle of leaves or the swishing of breeze-kissed grasslands depends on who has been taught to attend to certain sounds.

Smell as smell-threads, smell-scapes, or wind-threads maps the seeable and unseeable worlds. Amongst numerous peoples, including the southern African Bushmen and Andamese islanders, the idea of wind potency overlaps strongly with understandings of smell. In these contexts, smell is envisaged as holding the essence or the personality or windspirit of an organism. It holds the attributes that make an entity what it is, or, reframing the concept, smell holds the essence of how an organism is known. The smell embedded in wind indicates where animals, people, and spirits have been and, consequently, where they are now.

Classen has observed that 'the most powerful animals also have the strongest odour' (1993: 86). Amongst Khoekhoegowab speakers of northern Namibia there is a direct overlap between the dangerous smell of 'strong people', be they healers, menstruating women, excessively sweaty men, or sick people, and their *≠oab* (*b*) or wind. Yet not merely the living but also the dead exude smells, be it the smell of corpses, mixed with that of sweet perfume among Swahili-speaking peoples, or the smell of the ancestors' bones among the Ongee and Jarwa. As spirits are guided by smells, Khoisan people endowed with witchcraft utilize directed threads of connection between the potent and the victim. To envisage that the footprint of a victim has direct access to the victim is to recruit tracks of relationships between spirits, potency, smell, and wind.

Being immersed in wind and air as a medium can also have an egalitarian aspect, regardless of the political system in which wind immersion occurs. Thus, healing potency, sometimes conceived as wind, plays a role in the binding of Kalahari Bushmen communities and contributes to what has been perceived as egalitarian behaviour. Wind potency is drawn in by Bushman healers and shared amongst the group in acts of community healing. In Han China, promulgating the notion of *qi* as a medium that permeates the universe had an equalizing effect insofar as it affected everyone. As a concept that gained in currency as a strong state administration, which produced great inequalities, established itself, *qi* proved powerful and convincing precisely because of its equalizing and unifying character, which simultaneously could be used to express the moods of locality. Among Arabs in the Middle East, the sharing of the same air can be a sign of trust and intimacy as they stand so closely to one another when speaking as to share in the often strong smell of the other's breath (Hall 1982 [1966]: 45-9). The Arabic association between intimacy and breath speaks of the overlap between smell, breath, and life. To share the breath is to share something of intimate value, to forge a bond between selves.

This aspect of wind as both an equalizing medium and a force that can explain 'action at a distance' is taken up in scholarly medical learning. Wind retains its transformative and ever-elusive qualities in that it is known to take on many different forms, dependent on particular locality and time, but it tends to be stripped of its ephemeral sensorial properties of scent, its roaring sound or listless rustling. Scholarly medical reasoning in terms of the hot and cold can be interpreted to allude ultimately to the tactile qualities of wind, which emphasize its materiality, constancy, and omnipresence. Although scholarly medical terminology may appear abstract and far removed from immediate sensory experience, once scrutinized, a case has been made that early Chinese terminology was steeped in a language of tactility (Hsu 2005). As scholarly medicines elaborate on different types of inner winds, their pathologies and treatment, the phenomenology of wind and its multi-sensorial experience promises to open up new avenues of thinking about complex medical theorizing.

Situating the field: environmental history, medical geography, and medical anthropology

There has been considerable interest in human relationships with nature over recent decades from both academic and popular authors, not least because of impending climate change. Accounts of wind from a more general stable point to the welter of ways in which wind features in human and animal life. Among this popular but none the less highly informative literature belong *Heaven's breath: a natural history of the wind* by Watson (1985), *Wind: how the flow of air has shaped life, myth, and the land* by DeBlieu (1998), and *Encyclopedia of air* by Newton (2003).

A striking theme from Watson and DeBlieu concerns parallels they draw between biological adaptations of animals and human technological relationships with wind. Watson (1985: 90) contrasts human sailing knowledge with the sailing ability of the Portuguese man-of-war jellyfish, which hoist part of their structure above the surface of the sea to take advantage of wind currents. DeBlieu (1998: 92) compares wind funnels of Near Eastern buildings with wind-channelling termite mounds and the silk-lined entrance burrows of turret spiders that provide a reservoir of distilled moisture. Both highlight how essential properties of wind become built into environmental adaptations and human behaviour.

Writing about wind and people is, of course, far from a new undertaking. In the occidental tradition, rudimentary roots of the topic can be traced back to the ancient Greeks. *On airs, waters and places* in the Hippocratic corpus from around 400 BCE accounted for the seasons and weather and their impact on the health of people, and the seven books on the *Epidemics* contain long sections entitled 'Constitutions' that record general weather conditions, followed by individual case records of pathological conditions (Chadwick & Mann 1983). Classical architectural building practices relied heavily on ideas surrounding *pneuma* (Kenda 2006), and also Aristotle took consideration of the influences of sunlight and prevailing winds as he drew up rules for the siting of cities (Illich 1986: 45).

In Enlightenment Europe, following this classical legacy, weather and people were an aspect of the landscape as it was linked to medicine and politics. The opening up of the colonial world, from the late fifteenth century onwards, played a key factor in these changing attitudes to place. Until the eighteenth century the sort of accounts that arose from new geographical and travel experiences reported people relative to places very much within the older classical idiom. In the spirit of natural history inquiry and curiosity, accuracy and first-hand experience replaced the superficial observations, epitomes, and epithets that characterized older accounts of the foreign. So too from the eighteenth century the landscape of home became subject to a new kind of attention. Out of this collective new interest, 'medical topography' emerged as a distinctive descriptive study of the conditions of health and disease of particular places, at home and abroad.

By the late eighteenth century, imperial expansion encouraged a change in the scale of the already tight binding of imperialism to medicine. As vistas and ambitions grew, 'medical geography' emerged as a complementary discipline that concerned large-scale distribution patterns of human disease in relation to environmental conditions. The pillar of imperialism, the Royal Navy, played a particularly key role in knowledge of climatic wind, both through the systematic observing of nature that was intrinsic to the new habit of ships' logs and the 1805 introduction of the first wind-scale by Sir Francis Beaufort. In colonial contexts, characteristics of local winds fed images of colonial spaces and legitimized colonial occupation as environments that needed curing (Bewell 1996: 780). Indicative of the importance attributed to climate in medicine, James Ranald Martin's various editions of *The influence of tropical climates on European constitutions* (1813-55) is conspicuous as what Bewell determines 'the most influential text on colonial medicine of the Victorian period' (1996: 779).

From the later eighteenth century, scholarly works exist concerning health, nature, and life beliefs from such diverse backgrounds as mythological, folklore, theological, etymological, and philological studies to the occultist Blavatsky's influential 1895 theosophical musings. Wind in the non-Western sciences was discussed within this rich corpus of inquiry, particularly in the work of the members of the various incarnations of the Asiatick Society of Bengal, founded in 1784 (Stocking 1987: 22), and, in the early twentieth century, Frazer's *The Golden Bough* (1993 [1922]: 80-3) includes references to wind ranging from beliefs of African Hottentots and Bedouins to those of classical mythology. In the 1930s, the historians Garrison and Sigerist both emphasized the importance of the role of climate in the European history of health. But in spite of this, climate, and wind, in particular, remained a neglected topic.

Recent interest has come largely within contexts of social history and the expanding fields of environmental history and medical anthropology. In the context of social history, interest in weather and health has persisted since the 1980s (Burton 1990; Dolan 2002; Sargent 1982). Within this arena water has received particularly perceptive attention (Illich 1986; Porter 1990), and insights concerning the study of water lend themselves to the study of wind. Illich's *H_2O and the waters of forgetfulness* draws our attention to the elusive qualities of water – where we might substitute the word 'wind' – rendering it with an almost unlimited ability to carry metaphors. Adapting Illich, wind is like 'a shifting mirror'; what it says reflects 'the fashion of the age'. Wind, like water, 'remains a chaos until a creative story interprets its seeming equivocation as being the quivering ambiguity of life' (Illich 1986: 24-5).

Simultaneously, historians of science began focusing on medical alternatives, looking beyond the historical foundations of contemporary biomedicine (Cooter 1988; Porter 1989). Historians of medicine have subsequently developed a keen sense of pre-bacteriological theories of disease and illness, including miasmata and other early theories of contagion (Bynum 1994; Cipolla 1992; Hannaway 1993; Rosenberg & Golden 1992). With ongoing interest in colonial deconstruction, social historians have equally turned to considering health in the colonies (Arnold 1988; MacLeod & Lewis 1988). Whilst earlier work tended more to concern the health of colonials and the rise of colonial medicine (Gelfand 1984; Worboys 1976), later studies examined the impact of colonialism on the well-being of local populations, including indigenous responses, medical and other, to colonial settlement, war, and dispossession (Greenough 1995; Marks & Worboys 1997; Pati & Harrison 2001; Vaughan 1991). A select group of historians have additionally sought to go beyond the colonial paradigm to identify 'indigenous' histories, some of which concern theories of illness (Low 2004; Prins 1992; Waite 1992).

One of the most remarkable testaments to the currency of 'wind' in the last few years is Strauss and Orlove's *Weather, climate, culture* (2003), which frames wind within a broad range of public, institutional, political, private, oral, and literate discourses of weather, both historical and recent, and examines how weather is described and felt on an everyday level, both within conversation and in recent, more technical discourses. There has since been a flourishing history of meteorology (Anderson 2005; Corbin 2005; Fleming 2005), and Jankovic's (2004 and this volume) contributions in particular have drawn attention to how weather might affect health.

The scholarly medical traditions have in common that they are framed as wind physiologies and pathologies. New impetus for thinking about *prana*-breath and *vatu*-wind in Ayurveda, *feng*-wind and *qi*-breath in Chinese medicine, *ki*-breath in Japanese *kanpo*, *rlung*-wind and *bla*-soul in Tibetan medicine, and other impersonal all-pervasive life-forces is found in recent medical anthropological research. These studies have detailed the different conceptualizations of wind, explored the social practices within which wind ideas are prominent, and also attempted some general theoretical hypotheses in the search for an underlying rationale of these pre-modern sciences.

The concepts *prana* (breath) and *vatu* (wind) in Ayurveda have been extensively discussed by Langford (2002), Obeyesekere (1992), Trawick (1992), and by the philologist Zysk (1993), as has *ki* in the discussion of *kanpo* in contemporary Japan (Lock 1980; Ohnuki-Tierney 1984), and *qi* in Chinese medicine (e.g. Farquhar 1994; Hsu 1999; Porkert 1974; Sivin 1987; Unschuld 1985). Mental disorders that pertain to the notion of *rlung* (wind) have been the focus of studies on Tibetan medicine (Gutschow 1997; Janes 1999) and *feng*-wind disorders of more recent research on madness in Chinese medical history (Chen 2002; Messner 2000). Kuriyama's (1994; 1999) study of wind, which is much wider in its conception, has made major inroads into the history of the body. However, it celebrates the cultural imagination of the ancient Chinese and Greeks rather than elaborating on the aspects of wind as a prime experience of a mingling body in its environment.

Zimmermann's (1987 [1982]) study on the fundamentals of Ayurvedic theory and its *materia medica* in the light of the geographic distribution of different animal and plant species on the Indian subcontinent deserves particular attention here as it represents an early recent attempt at relating in sophisticated ways the ecological to the cultural. While overlooked by general theorists like Franklin (2002), it has inspired cross-culturally relevant findings in Chinese medical circles. In her exploration of local *qi* resonating with local bodies in the bustling commercial and urbanized region Jiangnan of late imperial China, Hanson (1998) highlights how ecology was used for formulating a territorial politics of locality. And in her outline of the 'body ecologic' as an analytical medical anthropological concept, Hsu (1999: 78-83; in press) builds heavily on Zimmermann when she uses a genealogical approach for interpreting the contemporary medical terminology that relates to the ecological environment (like the hot and cold or the 'five agents').

This volume draws out the often unspoken aspects of wind relationships in scholarly medical learning and among hunter-gatherers, agriculturalists, and urbanites, and examines ancient and medieval as well as early modern and contemporary wind ideas and techniques for manipulating its manifestations in the body. It brings together approaches inspired by the history of science, medical history, philology, ethnomusicology, medical anthropology, and anthropology more generally that, with few exceptions, draw on the phenomenology of perception and the anthropology of the senses. The bodily experience of breathing, smelling, hearing, seeing, touching, and feeling is intrinsic to a body constitutive of, penetrated by, and intermingling with its environment. With its focus on the body, its being in the world and mingling with its environment, this volume aims to lead to a deeper understanding of ways in which the experience of the wind, as natural phenomenon, has shaped social practice and become intrinsic to core cultural concepts.

REFERENCES

Abram, D. 1997. *The spell of the sensuous*. New York: Vintage Books.

Anderson, K. 2005. *Predicting the weather: Victorians and the science of meteorology*. Chicago: University Press.

Arnold, D. 1988. *Imperial medicine and indigenous societies*. Manchester: University Press.

Berman, M. 2000. *Wandering god: a study in nomadic spirituality*. Albany: State University of New York Press.

Bewell, A. 1996. Jane Eyre and Victorian medical geography. *English Literary History* **63**, 773-808.

Bird-David, N. 1990. The giving environment: another perspective on the economic system of gatherer-hunters. *Current Anthropology* **31**, 189-96.

Blavatsky, H.P. 1895. *The secret doctrine: the synthesis of science, religion, and philosophy*. (Third edition). London: Theosophical Publishing Society.

Bourdieu, P. 1977 [1972]. *Outline of a theory of practice* (trans. R. Nice). Cambridge: University Press.

Boyer, P. 1994. *The naturalness of religious ideas: a cognitive theory of religion*. Berkeley: University of California Press.

——— 2001. *Religion explained: the evolutionary origins of religious thought*. New York: Basic Books.

Burton, J.M.C. 1990. Meteorology and the public health movement in London during the late nineteenth century. *Weather* **45**, 300-7.

Bynum, W.F. 1994. *Science and the practice of medicine in the nineteenth century*. Cambridge: University Press.

Campbell, J. 1991. *The power of myth*. New York: Anchor Books.

Chadwick, J. & W.N. Mann 1983. *Hippocratic writings*. Harmondsworth: Penguin.

Chen, C. 2002. Medicine, society, and the making of madness in imperial China. Ph.D. thesis in history, University of London.

Cipolla, T. 1992. *Miasmas and disease: public health and environment in the pre-industrial age*. New Haven: Yale University Press.

Classen, C. 1993. *Worlds of sense: exploring the senses in history and across cultures*. London: Routledge.

Cooter, R. 1988. *Studies in the history of alternative medicine*: New York: St Martin's Press.

Corbin, A. 2005. *Le ciel et la mer*. Paris: Bayard.

Csordas, T.J. 2002. *Body/Meaning/Healing*. Basingstoke: Palgrave Macmillan.

DEBLIEU, J. 1998. *Wind: how the flow of air has shaped life, myth and the land.* Boston: Houghton Mifflin.

DESCOLA, P. 1992. Societies of nature and the nature of societies. In *Conceptualizing society* (ed.) A. Kuper, 107-26. London: Routledge.

——— 1996. Constructing natures: symbolic ecology and social practice. In *Nature and society: anthropological perspectives* (eds) P. Descola & G. Palsson, 82-102. London: Routledge.

DOLAN, B. 2002. Conservative politicians, radical philosophers and the aerial remedy for the diseases of civilization. *History of the Human Sciences* **15: 2**, 35-54.

ELLEN, R.F. 1996. The cognitive geometry of nature: a contextual approach. In *Nature and society: anthropological perspectives* (eds) P. Descola & G. Palsson, 103-124. London: Routledge.

FARQUHAR, J. 1994. *Knowing practice: the clinical encounter of Chinese medicine.* Boulder, Colo.: Westview Press.

FLEMING, J.R. 2005. *Historical perspectives on climate change.* New York: Oxford University Press.

FRANKLIN, A. 2002. *Nature and social theory.* London: Sage.

FRAZER, J.G. 1993 [1922]. *The Golden Bough: a study in magic and religion.* Ware, Herts: Wordsworth Reference.

GELFAND, M. 1984. *Christian doctor and nurse: the history of medical missions in South Africa from 1799-1976.* Sanderton: Aitken Family and Friends.

GIBSON, J.J. 1979. *The ecological approach to visual perception.* Boston: Houghton Mifflin.

GREENOUGH, P. 1995. Intimidation, resistance and coercion in the final stages of the South Asian smallpox eradication campaign, 1973-75. *Social Science and Medicine* **41**, 633-45.

GUTSCHOW, K. 1997. A study of 'wind disorder' or madness in Zangskar, Northwest India. *Recent Research on Ladakh*, vol. 7 (eds) T. Dodin & H. Raether, 177-202. Ulm: Ulmer Kulturanthropologische Schriften.

HALL, E.T. 1982 [1966]. *The hidden dimension.* New York: Anchor Books.

HANNAWAY, C. 1993. Environment and miasmata, in *Companion encyclopaedia of the history of medicine* (eds) W.F. Bynum & R. Porter, 292-308. London: Routledge.

HANSON, M. 1998. Robust northerners and delicate southerners: the nineteenth-century invention of a southern medical tradition. *Positions: East Asia Cultures Critique* **6**, 515-50.

HSU, E. 1999. *The transmission of Chinese medicine.* Cambridge: University Press.

——— 2005. Tactility and the body in early Chinese medicine. *Science in Context* **18**, 7-34.

——— in press. The cultural in the biological: the five agents and the body ecologic in Chinese medicine. In *Holistic anthropology: emergences and divergences* (eds) D. Parkin & S. Ulijaszek. Oxford: Berghahn.

ILLICH, I. 1986. *H_2O and the waters of forgetfulness.* London: Marion Boyars Publishers.

INGOLD, T. 1993. The temporality of the landscape. *World Archaeology* **25**, 152-74.

——— 2000. *The perception of the environment: essays in livelihood, dwelling and skill.* London: Routledge.

JANES, C.R. 1999. Imagined lives, suffering, and the work of culture: the embodied discourses of conflict in modern Tibet. *Medical Anthropology Quarterly* **13**, 391-412.

JANKOVIC, V. 2004. Atmospheric constitutions: a taxonomy of issues in European medical meteorology. Unpublished paper presented at 'From Beaufort to Bjerknes and Beyond: Critical Perspectives on the History of Meteorology', July, Weilheim, Germany.

KENDA, B. (ed.) 2006. *Aeolian winds and the spirit in Renaissance architecture.* London: Routledge.

KURIYAMA, S. 1994. The imagination of winds and the development of the Chinese conception of the body. In *Body, subject, and power in China* (eds) A. Zito & T.E. Barlow, 23-41. Chicago: University Press.

——— 1999. *The expressiveness of the body and the divergence of Greek and Chinese medicine.* New York: Zone Books.

LADERMAN, C. 1991. *Taming the wind of desire: psychology, medicine and aesthetics in Malay shamanistic performance.* Berkeley: University of California Press.

LANGFORD, J. 2002. *Fluent bodies: Ayurvedic remedies for postcolonial imbalance.* Durham, N.C.: Duke University Press.

LEWIS, D. 1973. *We the navigators.* Honolulu: University Press of Hawaii.

LEWIS-WILLIAMS, D. & D. PEARCE 2004. *San spirituality: roots, expressions and social consequences.* Cape Town: Double Storey.

LOCK, M.M. 1980. *East Asian medicine in urban Japan.* Berkeley: University of California Press.

LOVELOCK, J. 1979. *Gaia: a new look at life on earth.* Oxford: University Press.

LOW, C. 2004. Khoisan healing: understandings, ideas and practices. D. Phil. thesis in the history of medicine, University of Oxford.

MACLEOD, R. & M. LEWIS (eds) 1988. *Disease, medicine and empire: perspectives on Western medicine and the experience of European expansion.* London: Routledge.

MCNELEY, J.K. 1981. *Holy wind in Navaho philosophy.* Tuscon: University of Arizona Press.

MARKS, L. & M. WORBOYS (eds) 1997. *Migrants, minorities and health.* London: Routledge.

MATURANA, H. & F. VARELA 1998. *The tree of knowledge: the biological roots of human understanding.* (Revised edition). Boston: Shambhala.

MERLEAU-PONTY, M. 1962 [1945]. *Phenomenology of perception* (trans. C. Smith). London: Routledge & Kegan Paul.

MESSNER, A.C. 2000. *Medizinische Diskurse zu Irresein in China (1600-1930).* Stuttgart: Steiner.

MITHEN, S. 2006. Ethnobiology and the evolution of the human mind. In *Ethnobiology and the science of humankind* (ed.) R. Ellen, S45-S61. *Journal of the Royal Anthropological Institute, Special Issue.*

NEWTON, D.E. 2003. *Encyclopedia of air.* Westport, Conn.: Greenwood Press.

OBEYESEKERE, G. 1992. Science, experimentation and clinical practice in Ayurveda. In *Paths to Asian medical knowledge* (eds) C. Leslie & A. Young, 160-76. Berkeley: University of California Press.

OHNUKI-TIERNEY, E. 1984. *Illness and culture in contemporary Japan.* Berkeley: University of California Press.

ORLOVE, B. 2002. *Lines in the water: nature and culture at Lake Titicaca.* Berkeley: University of California Press.

PANDYA, V. 1993. *Above the forest: a study of Andamanese ethnoanemology, cosmology and the power of ritual.* Delhi: Oxford University Press.

PATI, B. & M. HARRISON (eds) 2001. *Health, medicine and empire: perspectives on colonial India.* London: Sangam Books.

PINKER, S. 2002. *The blank slate: the modern denial of human nature.* London: Allen Lane.

PORKERT, M. 1974. *The theoretical foundations of Chinese medicine: systems of correspondence.* Cambridge, Mass.: MIT Press.

PORTER, R. 1989. *Health for sale: quackery in England 1660-1850.* Manchester: University Press.

——— (ed.) 1990. *The medical history of waters and spas. Medical History* (Supplement **10**). London: Wellcome Institute for the History of Medicine.

PRINS, G. 1992. A modern history of Lozi therapeutics. In *Social basis of health and healing in Africa* (eds) J. Janzen & S. Feierman, 339-65. Berkeley: University of California Press.

RIVAL, L. 1993. The growth of family trees: understanding Huaorani perceptions of the forest. *Man* (N.S.) **28**, 635-52.

——— 1996. Blowpipes and spears: the social significance of Huaorani technological choices. In *Nature and society: anthropological perspectives* (eds) P. Descola & G. Palsson, 145-64. London: Routledge.

ROSENBERG, C.E. & J. GOLDEN (eds) 1992. *Framing disease: studies in cultural history.* New Brunswick, N.J.: Rutgers University Press.

SARGENT, F. 1982. *Hippocratic heritage: a history of ideas about weather and human health.* Oxford: Pergamon.

SIVIN, N. 1987: *Traditional medicine in contemporary China.* Ann Arbor: Michigan University Press.

STOCKING, G. 1987. *Victorian anthropology.* New York: Free Press.

STRAUSS, S. & B. ORLOVE 2003. *Weather, climate, culture.* Oxford: Berg.

TRAWICK, M. 1992. Death and nurturance in Indian systems of healing. In *Paths to Asian medical knowledge* (eds) C. Leslie & A. Young, 129-59. Berkeley: University of California Press.

UNSCHULD, P.U. 1985. *Medicine in China: a history of ideas.* Berkeley: University of California Press.

VAUGHAN, M. 1991. *Curing their ills: colonial power and African illness.* Cambridge: Polity Press.

WAITE, G. 1992. *A history of traditional medicine and health care in pre-colonial East-Central Africa.* Lewiston, N.Y.: Mellen Press.

WATSON, L. 1985. *Heaven's breath: a natural history of the wind.* London: Hodder & Stoughton.

WORBOYS, M. 1976. The emergence of tropical medicine: a study in the establishment of a scientific specialty. In *Perspectives on the emergence of new scientific disciplines* (eds) G. Lemaine, R. MacLeod, M. Mulkay & P. Weingart, 75-89. Paris: Mouton.

ZIMMERMANN, F. 1987 [1982]. *The jungle and the aroma of meats: an ecological theme in Hindu medicine* (trans. J. Lloyd). Berkeley: University of California Press.

ZYSK, K. 1993. The science of respiration and the doctrine of the bodily winds in ancient India. *Journal of the American Oriental Society* **113**, 198-213.

2

Earth, sky, wind, and weather

TIM INGOLD *University of Aberdeen*

We all know what it feels like to be out in the open air on a windy day. Yet once we try to pin it down within established categories and conventions of thought, no experience could be more elusive. What is the open air? Does it circulate in the sky or the atmosphere? Are these the same or different? If the atmosphere surrounds our planet, and the sky arches above our heads, then in what shape or form can the earth exist in relation to the sky? And if we are *out* in the open world of earth and sky, how can we simultaneously be *in* the wind? How, in other words, can we inhabit the open? If we can do so only by containing it, then how can the wind still blow? In what follows I seek to establish what it means to be 'in the open'. Instead of thinking of the inhabited world as composed of mutually exclusive hemispheres of sky and earth, separated by the ground, we need to attend, as I shall show, to the fluxes of wind and weather. To feel the wind is not to make external, tactile contact with our surroundings but to mingle with them. In this mingling, as we live and breathe, the wind, light, and moisture of the sky bind with the substances of the earth in the continual forging of a way through the tangle of life-lines that comprise the land.

To reach this conclusion I shall proceed in four stages. I begin with what is supposed to be the objective, scientific account of the shape of the earth, an account that cannot readily accommodate the phenomenon of the sky. For in relation to the sky, the earth can exist only as a ground of habitation. Yet as I go on to show, a ground populated solely by people and objects, and a sky that is empty but for birds and clouds, can exist only within a simulacrum of the world, modelled in an interior space. The third stage of the argument is to show that in the open world, beings relate not as closed, objective forms but by virtue of their common immersion in the fluxes of the medium. The process of respiration, by which air is taken in by organisms from the medium and in turn surrendered to it, is fundamental to all life. Thus, finally, to inhabit the open is to dwell within a weather-world in which every being is destined to combine wind, rain, sunshine, and earth in the continuation of its own existence.

How to draw the sky

There is currently some controversy in the fields of cognitive and developmental psychology concerning how children learn the shape of the earth. A number of studies suggest that a correct understanding of the earth, as a solid sphere surrounded by space, challenges fundamental presuppositions that children everywhere, regardless of cultural background, initially bring to their reasoning about the world. These presuppositions are, firstly, that the ground is flat, and, secondly, that unless supported, things fall. To grasp such a counter-intuitive understanding that the earth is round like a ball and that people can live anywhere on its surface without falling off calls, it is argued, for nothing less than a complete conceptual restructuring in the child's mind, comparable to a paradigm shift in the history of science. Experimenting with schoolchildren aged between 6 and 11 years, researchers claim to have identified a developmental sequence in thinking about the earth, running from an initial mental model of an earth that is flat like a pancake to a final model of a spherical earth, by way of various intermediate models in which children attempt to reconcile their initial presuppositions with information supplied by their teachers, or gleaned from books and other sources (Vosniadou 1994; Vosniadou & Brewer 1992; see Fig. 1).

But this research is not without its critics. They argue that the problems of reconciliation that many children undoubtedly faced in these experiments have less to do with their own intuitions or 'naïve theories' about the world than with the demands of

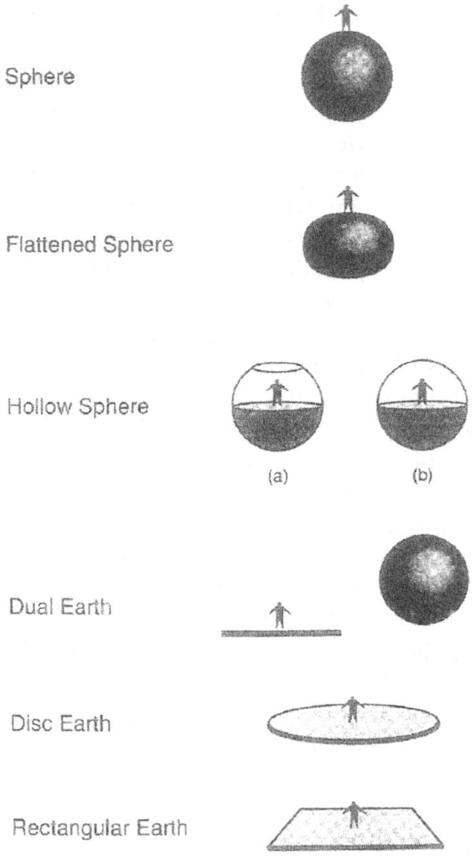

Figure 1. Mental models of the Earth. Reproduced from Vosniadou & Brewer (1992: 549) with the kind permission of Elsevier.

an experimental situation in which they are called upon to justify what they had said or drawn in response to previous questioning. In reality, these critics claim, children do not begin with any beliefs, intuitions or theories about the shape of the earth, but rather set out with an open mind. Their knowledge is then acquired piecemeal, in loosely connected fragments, through participation in a social and cultural environment that is scaffolded by knowledgeable adults such as teachers, but also by artefacts such as the ubiquitous globes of school classrooms. Since there is no initial conceptual barrier to be overcome, and given adequate scaffolding, children have little difficulty in acquiring a 'scientific' picture of the earth. Indeed, experiments involving children having to choose between ready-made pictures – rather than drawing them themselves or having to respond to interrogation – seem to show little difference in understanding between younger and older children, or even between children and adults (Nobes, Martin & Panagiotaki 2005).

I do not intend to take a stance in this debate. It is but one version of a long-standing argument in psychology about whether knowledge acquisition is strongly constrained by innate mental structures or more fundamentally dependent on socio-cultural contexts of learning. It is what the two sides have in common that interests me. For neither is in any doubt that there exists a 'scientifically correct' account of the shape of the earth, against which any alternatives may be judged more or less erroneous.[1] More remarkably, both sides seem to agree that where there is an earth, there must also be a sky. How, then, might we render a 'scientifically correct' account of the nature and shape of the sky? Let me present two examples, taken from studies representing opposed positions in the debate outlined above, of what is taken to be the 'correct' view. In the first example, 6-year-old Ethan tells the experimenter – in response to her questions – that the earth has the shape of a ball, that to see it one should look downwards, and that it is completely surrounded by space. The experimenter then asks Ethan to draw a picture of the earth, and he obliges with a rough circle, within which he draws the outlines of what look like continents. 'Now', commands the experimenter, 'draw the sky'. Ethan is perplexed. 'The sky has no shape', he protests, 'you mean space'. Nevertheless, draw the sky he must, so he proceeds to describe a ring around the circle depicting the earth (Vosniadou & Brewer 1992: 557, see Fig. 2A).

In the second example the experimenters prepared a set of picture-cards, each of which showed the earth, people, and sky in one of sixteen possible combinations of the following alternatives: earth a solid sphere, flattened sphere, hollow sphere, or disc; people all around or only on top; sky all around or only on top. Participants, who included both children (aged 5-10) and adults, were individually asked first to select the card they thought looked most like the real earth and then to repeat the procedure with all the others so as to yield a ranking from 'most' to 'least like the Earth' (Nobes, Martin & Panagiotaki 2005: 52-4). Some two-thirds of the participants in the study selected, as their first choice, the combination of solid sphere with both people and sky all around. On the card depicting this combination, the earth figures as a greeny-brown ball, with rigid, Lego-like people standing around its circumference and set against a light blue background flecked with fluffy white patches resembling clouds (Fig. 3). The selection of this card by the majority of participants, according to the authors of this study, 'indicated a scientific understanding of the Earth' (Nobes *et al.* 2005: 55-7). The picture is, however, strangely paradoxical. On the one hand, it depicts people distributed around the outer surface of a solidly spherical earth, but, on the

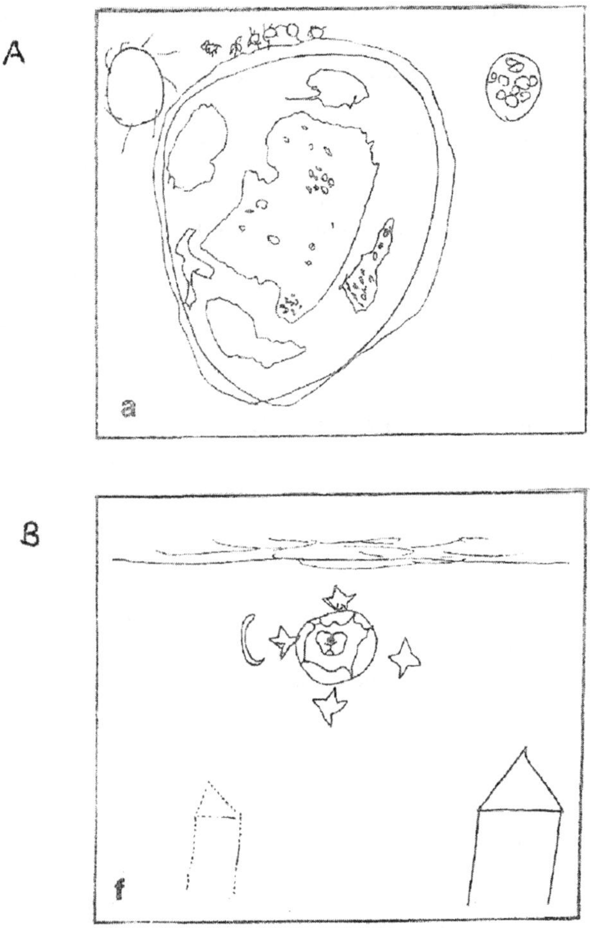

Figure 2. A: Ethan's drawing of the spherical earth surrounded by the 'sky'. B: Darcy's drawing of the sky, the ground (with houses) and the spherical earth. Reproduced from Vosniadou & Brewer (1992: 558) with the kind permission of Elsevier.

other hand, it depicts the sky in a form that would be apparent only to someone lying on his or her back on the earth's surface, gazing upwards! The perspective that leads us to recognize the earth as a ball is not one that could possibly yield an image of a blue sky with scattered clouds.

The perspectival double-take involved in the attempt to combine the spherical earth and the sky in the same picture confused participants in the first experiment, as much as in the second. Ethan, as we have seen, took the experimenter to mean not sky but space, and the gesture he made to signal his understanding that space is all around left its trace in the outer ring of his drawing. But the reaction of another participant in this study, 9-year-old Darcy, is even more revealing. Responding to the experimenter's request, Darcy has drawn a round earth, and has added the moon and some stars. The experimenter then asks Darcy – as she had asked Ethan – to draw the sky. Like Ethan, Darcy is thrown by this. 'It's icky', she says. Her solution, however, is to sketch some

Figure 3. Spherical earth with people and sky around. Reproduced from Nobes *et al.* (2005: 54) with the kind permission of the British Psychological Society.

roughly horizontal lines, looking much like a cloud-base, near the top of the paper, and above her drawing of the earth, moon, and stars. When the experimenter asks where people live, Darcy draws a house whose base lies along the lower border of the paper. The experimenter asks again, and Darcy draws another house. On the third request, Darcy eventually gives in to the experimenter's implicit demands, rubs out one of her houses, and draws a stick figure upon her round earth (Fig. 2B). But this only sparks off a further bout of interrogation. 'This house is on the earth isn't it?', says the experimenter, pointing to the sketch of the house that remains after the other was erased. 'How come the earth is flat here but before you made it round?' The following dialogue ensues:

> *Darcy:* Because it's on the ground.
> *Experimenter:* But why does that make it look flat?
> *Darcy:* Because the ground's flat.
> *Experimenter:* But the shape of the earth is ...
> *Darcy:* Round.
>
> (Vosniadou & Brewer 1992: 570)

To the experimenter it seemed that Darcy was being thoroughly inconsistent, wavering between conceptions of the earth's surface as round and flat. What she failed to observe was that Darcy was being absolutely consistent in applying a distinction between the *earth* and the *ground*. As Darcy explains, the earth is indeed round, as shown in her drawing. However, the houses people live in are built on the ground, and the ground is flat. Thus the houses in her drawing were on the ground and not on the earth's surface at all.

Of course the word 'earth' can mean many things, depending on the context. Sometimes we use it to refer to the ground beneath our feet, or even to the soil itself; at other times the word refers to our entire planet. In this case the context of the experimental interview unequivocally specified the earth in the latter sense, compelling Darcy to have resort to the term 'ground' in order to uphold a distinction she needed to make, but which the experimenter refused to recognize. In retrospect, we can see that it was the experimenter's instruction to complete the picture of planet earth by adding the *sky* that threw the whole exercise into confusion. For in relation to the sky, the earth can figure only in the phenomenal form of the ground upon which people live and on which their dwellings are built. The result, in effect, was not one complete picture but two quite separate pictures superimposed on the same page. One is a picture of our planet as it might be seen from outer space; the other is a picture of the ground, the sky and the abodes in which people live as they appear in the phenomenal world of inhabitants. Reporting on the results of their experiments, however, the authors of this study project their own double-take onto their experimental subjects (Vosniadou & Brewer 1992: 569-71). Thus Darcy, along with many others, is credited with a 'dual earth model', one of a number of synthetic models that are said to be intermediate between the naïve presupposition that the earth is flat and the mature understanding that it is round like a ball (Fig. 1).

According to the dual earth model, 'there are two earths: a round one which is up in the sky and a flat one where people live' (Vosniadou & Brewer 1992: 550). A dual-earther can stand on the ground looking up at the sky and see there not just the clouds, the sun and the moon, and the stars but also this other earth with its inhabitants stuck to the outer surface. This is of course the same view, of a spherical earth floating in a blue sky, that is represented in the 'correct' picture-card in the second of our two studies (Fig. 3). Children who selected this card, according to the authors of this study, 'already know that the people and sky are around the earth' (Nobes *et al.* 2005: 59). Scientifically speaking, of course, what surrounds the earth is its atmosphere, a gaseous envelope that peters out with increasing distance from the earth's surface. By no stretch of the imagination can the image of the sky on the picture-card be taken as even a minimally accurate representation of the atmosphere, nor did the experimenters intend it to be so. It is more likely, then, that participants who chose this card were treating the sky-design as a kind of wallpaper, characterized by shapes and colours drawn from everyday experience, upon which is mounted a quite separate image of the earth modelled perhaps on the familiar classroom globe. And just as Darcy found it necessary to distinguish the planetary earth from the ground beneath our feet, so, too, most people who are entirely familiar and at ease with the idea that the earth takes the form of a solid sphere would probably want to distinguish the atmosphere that surrounds the planet from the sky over our heads.

It is not obvious how one should draw this sky. Indeed, as the authors of the first study admit, 'asking children to draw the sky may appear strange to an adult' (Vosniadou & Brewer 1992: 544). The purpose of the exercise, they explain, was to help them distinguish children who thought the sky was on top of the earth from those who thought it surrounded the earth. In their terms, Darcy – who drew her sky above the round earth – expressed a scientifically incorrect, dual earth model, whereas Ethan – who drew a ring around his earth – was operating with a correct, spherical model. Yet Ethan, who probably lacked a notion of the atmosphere, thought the experimenter must be referring to space, and not to the sky. Darcy, for her part, realized (as the experimenters apparently did not) that the sky can be described only within a picture of the earth conceived as the ground of human habitation, and that in relation to such habitation, it can only be 'on top'. Indeed the experimenters, unlike the children they worked with, seem fundamentally confused. 'The idea that we live all around on the outside of a spherical earth', they write, 'is counter-intuitive and does not agree with everyday experience' (Vosniadou & Brewer 1992: 541).[2] Quite so. From this 'scientific' perspective, human beings are *ex*habitants of the earth. But like the ground we tread, the sky belongs to the world that people *in*habit. That is to say, it belongs to the world as it is presented to experience – to the phenomenal rather than the physical order of reality. It is in the experimenters' failure to distinguish between these orders that the confusion lies.

Furnishing the earth

How, then, might we describe the shape of the world from the point of view of an inhabitant? One possible approach to answering this question was proposed by James Gibson in his pioneering work *The ecological approach to visual perception* (1979). Gibson begins by emphasizing the distinction between what he calls the 'physical world' and the 'environment' (1979: 8). The planet earth is part of the physical world, as is the atmosphere that surrounds it. Both the earth and its atmosphere were in existence long before any life evolved in its oceans or on its terrestrial surfaces. An environment, by contrast, can exist only in relation to the forms of life that inhabit it. It is a world that exists not in and of itself, but as the ambience of its inhabitants. Though no less real than the physical world, the environment is not a reality *of* objects or bodies in space but reality *for* the beings that make a living there. Thus conceived, the environment – Gibson argues – 'is better described in terms of a *medium*, *substances* and the *surfaces* that separate them' (1979: 16).

For human beings the medium is normally air. Of course we need air to breathe. But also, offering little resistance, it allows us to move about – to do things, make things, and touch things. It also transmits radiant energy and mechanical vibration, so that we can see and hear. And it allows us to smell, since the molecules that excite our olfactory receptors are diffused in it. Thus the medium, according to Gibson, affords movement and perception. Substances, on the other hand, are relatively resistant to both. They include all kinds of more or less solid stuff like rock, gravel, sand, soil, mud, wood, concrete, and so on. Such materials furnish necessary physical foundations for life – we need them to stand on – but it is not generally possible to see or move *through* them. The status of water is ambiguous. For aquatic creatures such as fish, water is a medium; for terrestrial creatures such as humans, it is a substance. This ambiguity does not, in itself, invalidate the distinction, but only reinforces the point that the qualities of an environment can be considered in relation only to specific forms of life (Gibson 1979: 16-21).

At the interface between the medium and substances are *surfaces*. Surfaces are where radiant energy is reflected or absorbed, where vibrations are passed to the medium, where vaporization or diffusion into the medium occur, and what our bodies come up against in touch. So far as perception is concerned, surfaces are therefore 'where most of the action is' (Gibson 1979: 23). All surfaces have certain properties. These include a particular, relatively persistent layout, a degree of resistance to deformation and disintegration, a distinctive shape, and a characteristically non-homogeneous texture. As illustration, Gibson offers a series of six photographs depicting different kinds of familiar surface. One shows the transverse surface of sawn wood, another shows clouds in the sky, another a field of mown grass, another a woven textile, another the rippled surface of a pond, and another a patch of gravel. In each case, the texture of the surface immediately allows us to identify what it is a surface *of* (1979: 26-7). We can recognize the texture visually because of the characteristic scatter pattern in the light reflected from the surface. But conversely, if there is no discernible pattern or structure in the ambient light, then there is no identifiable texture, and instead of perceiving a surface we see an empty void (Gibson 1979: 51-2).

The perception of the sky offers a case in point. Comparing the textureless, clear blue sky of a summer's day with the textured earth beneath, we perceive the surface of the earth as what we usually call *ground*, whereas the sky above is perceived as vacant space without limit. The ground surface, according to Gibson, is 'the literal *basis* of the terrestrial environment ... the reference surface for all other surfaces' (1979: 10, 33). It supports things that are drawn to the earth by the force of gravity, and extends towards a horizon where earth and sky appear to meet. By contrast, the sky has no surface. However, amidst the textureless void of the sky there may exist textured regions that specify the surfaces, for example of clouds, *in* the sky. Shower clouds in the sky differ from, say, puddles on the ground formed by the falling rain in that whereas when the puddle dries out, one surface – of water – gives way to reveal another – of dry mud – in its place, when the cloud disperses, it vanishes to leave no surface at all. Likewise, if we stand in a forest and look upwards, the canopy of leaves provides an overhead texture, but in the spaces between them, open to the sky, we see only holes. 'It is into these holes', Gibson states, 'that the birds fly' (1979: 106).

Or so it seems. Gibson's account of the sky, however, is fraught with contradiction. If the sky is the epitome of emptiness, and if that is what we perceive when we gaze skywards, then is the sky a part of the inhabited environment or is it not? Can an environment have holes in it? Can it be truly 'open'? There are moments when Gibson seems to answer in the affirmative. He is insistent, for example, that an environment does *not* simply consist of objects in space, closed-contour forms suspended in an empty void. It consists, rather, 'of the earth and the sky with objects *on* the earth and *in* the sky, of mountains and clouds, fires and sunsets, pebbles and stars' (1979: 66). Thus clouds, sunsets, and stars are presented to us as phenomena situated within that part of the environment we call the sky. This is one of two parts, or hemispheres, that comprise the world of the inhabitant. The other part is the earth. The ground on which the inhabitant stands – the earth-sky interface – stretches out to the horizon, 'a great circle between the upper and the lower hemisphere separating the sky and the earth' (1979: 162).

Superficially, this cosmology resembles what Vosniadou and Brewer call the 'hollow sphere' model, which, like the dual earth model, they regard as intermediate between conceptions of the earth as flat and as a solid sphere. According to this model the earth is a ball that is solid below and hollow above, while people stand on the flat interface between the two hemispherical zones. To them, the sky appears as a dome over their heads (Vosniadou & Brewer 1992: 549-50; see Fig. 1). There is a critical difference, however, between this cosmology and Gibson's. It is that for Gibson, the 'spherical field' of the inhabitant's perception is unbounded. The horizon is not a boundary, because it moves with the inhabitant. It cannot be reached or crossed. Things do not break through a barrier when they come into view. And when you look upwards, you do not see yourself surrounded by a closed surface. Life under the sky is lived *in the open*, not within the confines of a hollow hemisphere with a flat base and a domed top. The very idea of confinement, Gibson suggests, is an artefact of the practice of outline drawing (1979: 66). But the sky has no outline, and you cannot draw it. All you can draw are the shapes of things *in* the sky, or silhouetted *against* it.

Yet at another moment, Gibson declares that 'an open environment is seldom or never realized', and that life within such an environment would be all but impossible (1979: 78). In ordinary circumstances, the environment is 'cluttered' with every kind of thing, from hills and mountains to animals and plants, objects and artefacts. Or to put it another way, the environment is *furnished*. 'The furniture of the earth', Gibson continues, 'like the furnishings of a room, is what makes it livable'. A cloudless sky, in these terms, would be uninhabitable, and could not therefore form any part of the environment for a living being. Birds could not fly in it. And an empty earth, while it might provide the inhabitant with a base on which to stand and walk, affords nothing else; 'the furniture of the earth affords all the rest of behavior' (1979: 78). It seems that so long as they are stranded in the open, Gibsonian perceivers are as much exhabitants of the world as are the figures depicted in the psychological experiments described earlier, living 'all around on the outside' of the earth's surface. Like actors on the stage, they can make their entrance only once the surface has been furnished with the properties and scenery that make it possible for the play to proceed. Roaming around as on a set, or like a householder in the attic, they are fated to pick their way amidst the clutter of the world.

Let me return to Gibson's characterization of the environment, as consisting not just of objects but 'of the earth and the sky with objects *on* the earth and *in* the sky' (1979: 66). Consider some of the things that he takes to be objects: on the earth there are mountains, pebbles, and fires; in the sky there are clouds, sunsets, and stars. Of the things on the earth, perhaps only pebbles can be regarded as objects in any ordinary sense, and even then, only if we consider each individual stone in isolation from its neighbours, from the ground on which it lies, and from the processes that brought it there. The hill is not an object on the earth's surface but a formation of that surface, which can appear as an object only through its artificial excision from the landscape of which it is an integral part. And the fire is not an object but a manifestation of the process of combustion. Turning to the sky: stars, whatever their astronomical significance, are perceived not as objects but as points of light, and sunsets as the momentary glow of the sky as the sun vanishes beneath the horizon. Nor are clouds objects. Each is rather an incoherent, vaporous tumescence that swells and is carried along in the currents of the medium. To observe the clouds is not to view the furniture of the sky but to catch a fleeting glimpse of a sky-in-formation, never the same from one moment to the next.

Indeed in a world that is truly open there are no objects as such. For the object, having closed in on itself, has turned its back on the world, cutting itself off from the paths along which it came into being, and presenting only its congealed, outer surfaces for inspection. The open world, however, has no insides or outsides, only comings and goings. Such productive movements may generate formations, swellings, growths, protuberances and occurrences, but not objects. Thus in the open world hills rise up, as can be experienced by climbing them or, from a distance, by following the contours with one's eyes (Ingold 2000: 203). Fires burn, as we know from their flickering flames, the swirling of smoke, and the warming of the body. And pebbles grate. It is of course this grating that gives rise to their rounded forms; tread on them, and that is what you hear underfoot. In the sky, the sun shines by day and the moon and stars by night, and clouds billow. They *are*, respectively, their shining and billowing, just as the hills *are* their rising, the fire *is* its burning, and the pebbles *are* their grating.

In short, and contrary to Gibson's contention, it is not through being furnished with objects that the open sphere of sky and earth is turned into a habitable environment. The furnished world is a full-scale model – a world brought indoors and reconstructed within a dedicated, enclosed space. As in a stage set, hills are placed on the ground, while stars, clouds, and the sun and moon are hung from the sky. In this *as if* world hills do not rise, nor do fires burn or pebbles grate, nor do the sun, moon, and stars shine or the clouds billow. They may be made to look as though they do, but the appearance is an illusion. Absolutely nothing is going on. Only once the stage is set, and everything made ready, can the action begin. But the open world that people inhabit is not prepared for them in advance. It is continually coming into being around them. It is a world, that is, of formative and transformative *processes*. If such processes are of the essence of perception, then they are also of the essence of what is perceived. To understand how people can inhabit this world means attending to the dynamic processes of world-formation in which both perceivers and the phenomena they perceive are necessarily immersed. And to achieve this we must shift our attention from the congealed substances of the world, and the solid surfaces they present, to the media in which they take shape, and in which they may also be dissolved. My contention is that it is in the medium – and not on the surface, as Gibson thought (1979: 23) – that 'most of the action is'.

Winds of life

In the open, the medium is rarely, if ever, still. Almost always, it is in a state of flux. Sometimes these fluxes are barely perceptible; at other times they are so strong that they can uproot trees and bring down buildings. They can power mills and send ships around the world. The general term by which we know them is *wind*. But how can we tell that it is windy? A couple of years ago, I put this question to a group of students with whom I was working at the University of Aberdeen. We had been discussing the relation between weather and land (an issue to which I return in the following section), and I wanted to test the difference between the kind of discussion we could have indoors, with reference to academic texts, and the kind one can have in the open, immersed in the weather and with the land all around us. It is one thing, I surmised, to think *about* land and weather; quite another to think *in* them. Perhaps it is because we generally think and write indoors that we have such difficulty in imagining how any world we inhabit could be other than a furnished room, or how, cast out from this interior space, we could be anything other than exhabitants. What difference would it make, to borrow an expression from Maurice Merleau-Ponty, were we to acknowledge the open world of earth and sky not as the object but as the very '*homeland* of our thoughts' (Merleau-Ponty 1962: 24)?

To find out, we went for a walk in the countryside. It was a spring day of bright sunshine and occasional showers, with a gentle breeze. We could not touch the breeze, yet as the students were the first to admit, we knew it was breezy since we felt it on our exposed faces and in our breathing. Initially, this seemed puzzling. How could we feel the wind without being able to touch it? To resolve the puzzle we were compelled to recognize that feeling and touch are not merely alternative terms for tactile sensation. Of course we are forever touching things in our everyday lives, whenever we make them, or use them, or seek to identify them. And in intimate forms of sociality we touch other people, as they touch us. The action of touch is generally delivered through particular organs, above all the hands but also the lips, tongue, and feet. Feeling, however, infuses our entire being. It is not so much a way of making bodily contact with specific persons or things as a kind of interpenetration of the self and its surroundings: a certain way the world has, as Merleau-Ponty put it, 'of invading us' and our way of 'meeting this invasion' (1962: 317). Feeling, then, lies not just in what we *do* but in what we *are*: in that commingling of the perceiver with the world he or she inhabits that is an existential precondition for the isolation both of things as objects of touch and of the perceiver as a subject who touches. Thus we could not touch unless we first could feel.

To feel the wind, then, is to experience this commingling. While we did not touch it, we touched *in* it. A moment's reflection reveals that what goes for tactile perception goes for visual and auditory perception as well.[3] Let me return for a moment to the phenomenon of the sky. No more than the wind is the sky an object of perception. It is not something we look *at*. On our walk in the countryside we could see all manner of phenomena, thanks to their illumination by the sunlight. The sky, however, was not something we saw in the light, it was luminosity itself. Just like the feeling of the wind, the light of the sky is experienced as a commingling of the perceiver and the world without which there could be no things to see at all. As we touch *in* the wind, so we see *in* the sky. 'As I contemplate the blue of the sky', wrote Merleau-Ponty, 'I am not *set over against* it as an acosmic subject; ... I abandon myself to it and plunge into this mystery, ... I am the sky itself as it is drawn together and unified, ... my consciousness is saturated with this limitless blue' (1962: 214). The mystery of which Merleau-Ponty speaks here is the mystery of vision, the astonishment of the discovery that behind the sheer ordinariness of the sight of things lies the primal experience of being able to *see*. Light is just another word for this discovery (Ingold 2000: 264-5). Similarly, the mystery of sound lies in the discovery that we can hear. And while we may touch our surroundings in the wind and see them in the sky, it is above all in the rain that we hear them. The theologian John Hull, telling of his experience of going blind in adulthood, describes how steadily falling rain 'brings out the contours of everything', bathing the world in sound just as the sun bathes it in light. 'My body and the rain intermingle, and become one audio-tactile, three-dimensional universe, within which and throughout the whole of which lies my awareness' (Hull 1997: 26-7, 120).

To inhabit the open world, then, is to be immersed in the fluxes of the medium: in sunshine, rain, and wind. This immersion, in turn, underwrites our capacities – respectively – to see, hear, and touch. Of course we are not alone in feeling and responding to the wind. So likewise do birds in flight. Nicole Revel (2005) has described how Palawan Highlanders of the Philippines have a very special relationship with birds, considering them to be their close yet ephemeral companions. Their understanding of this relationship is epitomized in the practice of flying kites. Constructed of leaves or paper with split bamboo struts, kites are regarded as the copies of birds. Flying a kite is as close as terrestrial humans can get to sharing the experience of their avian companions. Playing the wind, flyers can feel with their hands, holding the connecting strings, what birds might feel with their wings. 'Anchored to the earth', as Revel puts it, Palawan kite-flyers 'dream in the air, their thrill equal to the splendour of the whirling of their ephemeral creations' (2005: 407). Becoming like birds, their consciousness is launched on the same aerial currents that animate their kites, and is subject to the same turbulence. In an *as if* world, however, furnished only with objects, neither kites nor birds could fly. A world of objects has no room for the wind, for the simple reason that the wind is not an object. It is no more an object than is, say, fire or cloud. As the fire *is* its burning and the cloud *is* its billowing, so the wind *is* its blowing. As such it belongs to the world we inhabit, not to some full-scale model of it. Birds fly in the air, and not – as Gibson claimed (1979: 106) – in the 'holes' between trees. Moreover, every tree, in the arc of its trunk and the twisting of its branches, bears testimony to the currents of wind in which it grew.

Yet in the fields of anthropology and material culture studies there is a persistent tendency to write as though people and material objects were indeed *all there is*. Perception is then held to lie in the reciprocal interplay between embodied persons and materialized things, in which each acts upon the other. If things can 'act back', the argument goes, it is because they are endowed with agency, just as persons are. Let me return to the example of flying a kite. By way of the string, we might suppose, your earthbound hand acts upon the kite, while reciprocally the aerial kite acts upon your hand. Through these actions, each continually answers in its movements to the movements of the other. A kite does not fly, however, because it has an agency of its own that counteracts that of the flyer. It flies because it is lifted up in the currents of the wind. Extinguish these currents, and the kite would drop to the ground, as limp and lifeless as a dead bird. Only so long as the string is stretched tight by the straining of the kite in the wind can it serve as a vector of interaction. Another example might be drawn from Christopher Tilley's explorations in landscape phenomenology. Tilley invites us to imagine a painter and a tree: 'The painter sees the tree and the tree sees the painter, not because the trees have eyes, but because the trees affect, move the painter ... In this sense the trees have agency and are not merely passive objects' (2004: 18). The tree, however, is not motionless. It is blowing in the wind, and the visuo-manual gestures of the painter – who follows with his brush the tree's characteristic lines of bending and recoil – resonate to its movements. In just the same way, the gestures of the flyer resonate to the movements of the kite as it swoops in the currents of air.

It is not, then, the tree that moves the painter, any more than it is the kite that moves the flyer. Rather, the resonant movements of the flyer and the kite in the one case, and of the painter and the tree in the other, are founded in their common immersion in the currents of the medium. It is only thanks to this immersion that they can interact at all. If there were no wind, then the flyer could not interact with the kite, nor could the painter interact with the tree. More generally, in a world reduced to people and objects, interaction would be impossible. We cannot, then, restore this world to life simply by endowing these objects with 'agency'. Indeed the much-vaunted 'problem of agency' is of our own creation, and has its source in an inverted view of reality that represents the dynamic potential of the lifeworld to animate forms of manifold kinds as an interior property that is carved up and distributed among the forms themselves, whence it is supposed to set the world in motion (Ingold 2005*b*: 125). This is rather like saying that a river flows because of the interactions between eddies and banks, forgetting that there would be neither eddies nor banks to interact were it not for the flow of the river itself. Similarly, there would be neither people nor trees, nor birds, clouds, fires, sunsets, or any of the other phenomena we have considered were it not for the fluxes in the medium.

This argument has a bearing on the very meaning of life. We might agree that as well as people, birds and trees are alive. But a habit of thought that leads us to suppose that the world is inhabited by entities that are already closed in upon themselves prevents us from seeing that life can be anything other than an interior property of things. Conceived as the creative potential of a world-in-formation, however, life is not *in* things; rather, things are *in* life, caught up in a current of continual generation. The recognition that all of existence is suspended in such a current underlies the ontological commitments of many of the peoples credited, in classical anthropological literature, with cosmologies of 'animism'. According to a long-established convention, animism is a system of beliefs that imputes life or sprit to things that are truly inert. But this convention is doubly misleading. For one thing, animism is not a system of beliefs *about* the world but a way of being *in* it, characterized by openness rather than closure – that is, by sensitivity and responsiveness to an environment that is always in flux. For another thing, it is not a matter of putting life into things but of restoring those things to the movements that gave rise to them. It should come as no surprise, then, that most animic cosmologies attribute supreme importance to the winds,[4] for not only do the winds give shape and direction to people's lives, they are also creatively (and destructively) powerful in their own right. It is not that they *have* agency; they *are* agency. The wind, to repeat, *is* its blowing, not a thing that blows. Likewise, persons *are* what they do.[5] There is nothing peculiar or anthropomorphic, therefore, about the attribution of personal powers to the winds.

I have already observed that in the open world there are no insides and outsides, only comings and goings. Speaking of the work of the painter, Merleau-Ponty remarks that 'there really is inspiration and expiration of Being' (1964: 167). Breathing in and out, one alternately takes in the medium and surrenders to it. Inspiration is wind becoming breath, expiration is breath becoming wind. The alternation of coming and going, in respiration, is essential to life. The parallel, in many languages, between words for life, wind, and breath bears out this idea. Our English word 'animate', for example, from which the notion of animism is derived, comes from the Latin *animare* (to give life) and *anima* (breath), both in turn derived from the Greek *anemos* (wind).[6] Life, then, is borne – along with the forms it generates – on the currents of the medium: as David Macauley writes, 'with our heads immersed in the thickness of the atmosphere or our lungs and limbs engaged with the swirling winds, we repeatedly breathe, think and dream in the regions of the air' (2005: 307). But by the same token, inhabiting the open does not yield an experience of embodiment, as though life could be incorporated or wrapped up within a solid bodily matrix. Nor does it yield an experience of disembodiment, of a spirituality altogether removed from the material fluxes of the world. To feel the wind and breathe the air is rather to ride on the wave of the world's ongoing formation – to be forever present at the 'continued birth', as Merleau-Ponty called it, of both persons and things (1964: 168). It is as though every breath was one's first, drawn at the very moment when the world is about to disclose itself for what it is. In this, it is not so much the wind that is embodied as the body, in breathing, that is *enwinded.*

The weather-world

My concern has been to understand what it means to inhabit, that is, to dwell *within*, a world-sphere that is nevertheless open rather than contained. In this world there are no walls, only the horizons progressively disclosed to inhabitants as they go their various ways; no floor, only the ground beneath their feet; no ceiling, only the sky arching overhead; no furniture, only formations and obtrusions. I have suggested that because we generally think and write indoors, the world we describe in our writing is one that has been imaginatively remodelled *as if* it were already set up within an enclosed, interior space. In this *as if* world, populated only by people and objects, those fluxes of the medium that we experience as wind and rain, sunshine and mist, frost and snow, and so on, are simply inconceivable. This, I believe, accounts for their absence from practically all discussions concerning the relations between human beings and the material world. In the alternative view I have presented – a view from the open – what is inconceivable is the idea that life is played out upon the surface of a world that is already furnished with objects. Inhabitants, I contend, make their way *through* a world-in-formation rather than *across* its pre-formed surface. For that reason, the fluxes of the medium through which they move are all-important.

With this conclusion we return to an issue that I and the students with whom I was working deliberated at length as we walked through the Aberdeenshire countryside. What is the relation between the weather and the land? Do they belong to distinct domains, respectively of sky and earth, medium and substance, separated by the ground surface? That, in effect, was Gibson's view. 'The atmospheric medium', he writes, 'is subject to certain kinds of changes that we call weather' (1979: 19). Thus, weather is what is *going on* in the medium.[7] The substance of the earth, however, is impervious to these goings-on. The terrestrial surface, relatively rigid and non-porous, ensures that medium and substance keep to their respective domains and do not mix. It is as though in the forms of the land, the earth had turned its back on the sky, refusing further intercourse with it. Thus the weather swirls about *on top* of the land, but does not participate further in its formation. Yet as every inhabitant knows, rainfall can turn a ploughed field into a sea of mud, frost can shatter solid rocks, lightning can ignite forest fires on land parched by summer heat, and the wind can whip sand into dunes, snow into drifts, and the water of lakes and oceans into waves. As Richard Nelson puts it, in his study of how Koyukon people in Alaska perceive their surroundings, 'weather is the hammer and the land is the anvil' (1983: 33). There are other, more subtle and delicate ways in which the land responds to fluxes in the medium. Think of the pearls of dew that pick out the tendrils of plants and spiders' webs on a cool summer's morning, or of the little trails left by a passing gust of wind in the dry leaves and broken twigs of a woodland floor.

Seasoned inhabitants know how to read the land as an intimate register of wind and weather. Like the Koyukon, they can sense the approach of a storm in the sudden burst of flame in a campfire, or – as the Yup'ik elder Fred George explains – they can read the direction of the prevailing wind in the orientation of tufts of frozen grass sticking out from the snow, or of snow 'waves' on ice-bound lakes (Bradley 2002: 249; Nelson 1983: 41). Yet the more one reads into the land, the more difficult it becomes to ascertain with any certainty where the substance ends and the medium begins. For it is precisely through the *binding* of medium and substance that wind and weather leave their mark in the land. Thus the land itself no longer appears as an interface separating the two, but as a vaguely defined zone of admixture and intermingling. Indeed anyone who has walked through the boreal forest in summer knows that the 'ground' is not really a coherent surface at all but a more or less impenetrable mass of tangled undergrowth, leaf litter and detritus, mosses and lichens, stones and boulders, split by cracks and crevasses, threaded by tree roots, and interspersed with swamps and marshes overgrown with rafts of vegetation that are liable to give way underfoot. Somewhere beneath it all is solid rock, and somewhere above the clear sky, but it is in this intermediate zone that life is lived, at depths depending upon the scale of the creature and its capacity to penetrate an environment that is ever more tightly packed.

It is in this sense that creatures live *in* the land and not *on* it. There could be no life in a world where medium and substance do not mix, or where the earth is locked inside – and the sky locked out – of a solid sphere. Wherever there is life and habitation, the interfacial separation of substance and medium is disrupted to give way to mutual permeability and binding. For it is in the nature of living beings themselves that, by way of their own processes of respiration, of breathing in and out, they bind the medium with substances in forging their own growth and movement through the world. And in this growth and movement they contribute to its ever-evolving weave. The land, we could say, is continually *growing over*, which is why archaeologists have to dig to recover the traces of past lives. And what holds it all together are the tangled and tangible life-lines of its inhabitants. The wind, too, mingles with substance as it blows through the land, leaving traces of its passing in tracks or trails. We could say of the wind that 'it winds', wending its way along twisted paths as do terrestrial travellers. These paths are often likened to ropes. There is an old tradition among Sami people that by tying the ropes into knots the wind may be stopped, and that by untying them they are once more unleashed (Helander & Mustonen 2004: 537).[8] Thus the relation between land and weather does not cut across an impermeable interface between earth and sky but is rather one *between the binding and unbinding of the world*. In the open world the task of habitation is to bind the weather into substantial, living forms, and in that way to participate in weaving the texture of the land. But bindings are not boundaries, and they no more contain the world, or enclose it, than does a knot contain the threads from which it is tied.

If life binds, then fire unbinds. Rather than binding the medium with substance, in the smoke of the hearth we find the reverse transformation, a release of substance to the medium in volatile form. As it rises, smoke mingles with circulations of air in the weather-world, and can even condense into clouds. In northern Finland, where I have carried out fieldwork, every dwelling was traditionally known as a 'smoke' since it could be recognized, even from some distance, by the white column rising vertically into the sky on a still, frosty day. However, the dwelling, with the hearth at its centre, still pertains to the world of the open, as does the life that goes on within it. Just as the living body is sustained by the rhythmic movement of breathing in and out, so the dwelling is sustained by the continual coming and going of its inhabitants. Thus it is important to distinguish between the 'indoors' of the dwelling that is wrapped around its inhabitants like a warm coat, and the 'indoors' of the *as if* world, of which I have already spoken, that has been reconstructed in an enclosed space. Whereas the former is a place-holder for life, the latter is a container. It has, of course, long been the ambition of modernist architecture to build spaces for living that are fully self-contained – where the whole world has been brought inside. Part of this containment entails creating the illusion of an absolute division between earth and sky, by hiding from view those disruptions of the surface that are inevitable for the bubble to be sustained. It is perhaps in this light that we can interpret the progressive banishment of the hearth, in the architecture of modernity, from the centre to the periphery of the dwelling, along with the confinement of smoke within ever-lengthening chimneys. The tall factory chimney, belching smoke, proclaims the absolute separation of earth and sky at the same time as it hides away the points of disruption where fires actually burn. A history of the chimney, however, has still to be written.

We have come a long way from the image of earth and sky with which I began, epitomized in Ethan's drawing of a ball-like earth, completely surrounded by an outline sky (Fig. 2A). This image, supposedly representing the 'correct' scientific view, leaves people as exhabitants of the earth, stranded on its outer surface. Our question has been: what kind of world can be inhabited? Gibson's answer is to imagine the open surface of the earth strewn with objects, to which people can relate in their activities. From this point of view, the terrestrial environment becomes habitable to the extent that the world is no longer open but enclosed. Such enclosure may never be more than partial, but for just that reason, the inhabitant remains, to an extent, an exile. I have argued, to the contrary, that there are no objects in the open world. To inhabit the open is not to be stranded on a closed surface but to be immersed in the fluxes of the medium, in the incessant movements of wind and weather. Life is borne on these fluxes which, felt rather than touched, permeate the inhabitant's entire being. In this weather-world there is no distinct surface separating earth and sky. Life is rather lived in a zone in which substance and medium are brought together in the constitution of beings which, in their activity, bind the weather-world into the textures of the land. Figure 4 traces the journey we have taken in this argument, from exhabitation to inhabitation.

The Koyukon of Alaska often invoke the beings that inhabit their world by means of riddles. Taking up the subject-position of the being to which he refers, the riddler describes its characteristic movements as though he were carrying them out himself, by means of an analogy with familiar human actions. Like gusts of wind, these are fugitive movements in a weather-world in which all are immersed, and in which nothing ever stands still. This world waits for no-one. It cannot be halted to allow closer inspection, and the image the

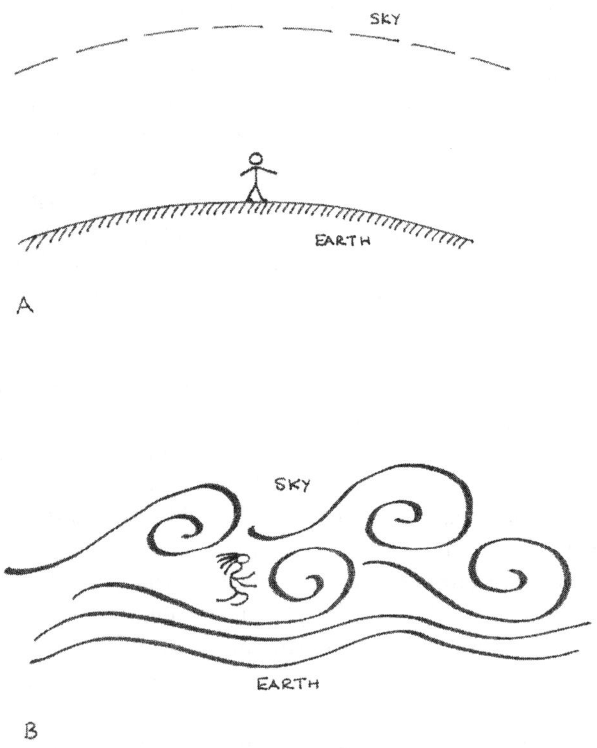

Figure 4. A: The exhabitant of the earth. B: The inhabitant of the weather-world.

riddler conjures up is one that vanishes as fast as it appears. In one such riddle, recorded by the Jesuit priest Julius Jetté at the beginning of the twentieth century, the riddler imagines himself as a tuft of grass. The literal translation runs as follows:

over-there around I-sweep-with-my-body.

(Jetté 1913: 199-200)[9]

The riddler is a broom, and the broom *is* its sweeping. He sweeps the place around him, just like the withered grasses that still poke out above the first snows of winter. In the wind the blades of grass bend over so as to touch the snow, still soft and loose from recent falls, sweeping a small circular patch around the place where they stand. Perhaps this riddle lies at the other end of the spectrum from Ethan's drawing of the earth and the sky. It concentrates in miniature the manifold of earth, sky, wind, and weather from the perspective of the inhabitant. Here, the whole world is in a tuft of grass. Grown from the earth under the summer sunshine, now frozen in place by winter frost and blown by the wind, the grass makes a place for itself in the world by creating a patch in the snow. It is by such movements that every living being inhabits the world of the open.

NOTES

This paper pulls together ideas from three separate sources which I wish to acknowledge. The first lies in the experience, over the past three years (2004-6), of working with final-year undergraduate students at the University of Aberdeen, who have taken my course 'The 4As: Anthropology, Archaeology, Art and Architecture'. Our discussions about landscape and weather, not just in the classroom but out in the hills and by the seashore, have been quite inspirational, and I would like to thank all the students for their contributions. The second source was one of a series of seminars on 'The Interactive Mind', sponsored by the Arts and Humanities Research Council, and held on that occasion at the University of Sheffield (8-9 April 2005). During this seminar I heard a presentation on 'Conceptual change in children' by Michael Siegal, and was intrigued by the psychological research he described on children's perceptions of the earth and the sky. I determined there and then to look further into this, and am grateful to Dr Siegal for pointing me towards the relevant literature. The third source of inspiration came just two months later with the Oxford conference on 'Wind, Life and Health' (3-4 June 2005). My presentation at the conference was closely based on a paper now published elsewhere (Ingold 2006). It was at the conference, however, that I first produced the sketch that now appears as Figure 4, and the comments I received encouraged me to develop the idea further. Following the conference, and thanks to the stimulus it provided, I wrote the paper entirely anew, and presented it for the first time – more or less in the form in which it now appears – at the seminar on 'Landscapes and Liminality', held at the University of Turku's research station at Kevo, in Finnish Lapland (5-8 January 2006). This seminar, along with conversations there with Kenneth Olwig, set me thinking about the significance of hearths and chimneys as sites of interchange between the substances of the earth and the fluxes of wind and weather. I presented the paper one more time, just prior to final revision, at a seminar of the Centre for Anthropology at the British Museum, on 7 September 2006. I am grateful to Robert Storrie for the invitation and to participants in the seminar for their comments. Finally, I am grateful to Elsevier for permission to reprint Figures 1 and 2 from *Cognitive Psychology* **24** (S. Vosniadou & W.F. Brewer, 'Mental models of the earth: a study of conceptual change in childhood', 535-585, 1992). I also thank Gavin Nobes for certain points of clarification and, with the British Psychological Society, for granting me permission to reproduce the image in Figure 3 from *British Journal of Developmental Psychology* **23** (G. Nobes, A.E. Martin & G. Panagiotaki, 'The development of scientific knowledge of the Earth', 47-64, 2005).

[1] I have purposefully placed 'scientifically correct' in quotation marks, to indicate that what is at stake is not people's substantive knowledge of the findings of modern science but rather the extent to which their understanding accords with formal schematic conventions consistent with a scientific worldview.

[2] Elsewhere I have characterized this idea of the solid earth by way of an image of the *globe*, and have contrasted this image with that of the hollow *sphere* (Ingold 2000: 209-18). Here, however, in order to

conform with accepted usage in the literature cited, I employ the notion of the spherical earth in both senses. The sphere may thus be understood as either solid, with people on the outside, or hollow, with people on the inside.

[3] I have explored these issues of multisensory perception in relation to the weather at greater length in Ingold (2005*a*). See also Ingold (2000: 243-87).

[4] I have discussed this issue of the wind in relation to animic cosmologies at greater length in Ingold (2006). On the personal powers of the winds, and their role in orientation, see, for example, Farnell (1994: 400) on Assiniboine; Krupnik (2004: 205-6) on Yup'ik; Fox (2002: 40) and MacDonald (1998: 180-2) on Inuit; Hallowell (1960: 30) on Ojibwa; and Nelson (1983: 36) on Koyukon.

[5] This notion of agency as the doing of the world has been proposed in rather similar terms by the sociologist of science Andrew Pickering. Significantly, he uses the example of the weather to drive home his point:

> One can start from the idea that the world is filled not, in the first instance, with facts and observations, but with *agency*. The world, I want to say, is continually *doing things*, things that bear upon us not as observation statements upon disembodied intellects but as forces upon material beings. Think of the weather. Winds, storms, droughts, floods, heat and cold – all of these engage with our bodies as well as our minds, often in life-threatening ways (Pickering 1995: 6).

[6] For examples in other languages, see Parkin (this volume).

[7] As such, weather must be distinguished absolutely from climate:

> Climate is an abstraction compounded from a number of variables (temperature, precipitation, air pressure, windspeed, etc.) that are isolated for purposes of measurement. Weather, by contrast, is about what it feels like to be warm or cold, drenched in rain, caught in a storm, and so on. In short, climate is recorded, weather experienced (Ingold & Kurttila 2000: 187).

Igor Krupnik, writing on Yup'ik weather knowledge, alludes to the same distinction when he notes that Yup'ik observation of the weather 'is primarily wind- and ocean-current oriented – unlike the scientific (that is, instrumental) observation, which is first and foremost focused on changes in temperature and atmospheric pressure' (2004: 205). Where scientists read their recording instruments, Yup'ik people observe *what is going on* in the sky and in the sea.

[8] In the course of fieldwork in the Cornish village of Boscastle, in 2003-5, anthropologist Tori L. Jennings came across an etching dating from the sixteenth century, which allegedly shows a sorcerer selling wind tied in knots to sailors. Untying the knots, it was said, would conjure up a wind from a dead calm. Having carried out my own ethnographic work among the Sami, I immediately recognized this etching: it actually comes from a well-known work by Olaus Magnus, then Archbishop of Uppsala, and was published in Uppsala in the year 1555. The book, *Historia de gentibus septentionalibus* ('History of the Peoples of the North'), is celebrated among scholars as one of the first synthetic accounts of the people and cultures of northernmost Europe. The text that accompanies the picture explains how the heathens of northern Finland would sell the wind to merchants confined to the shore by contrary winds. In return for a payment they were presented with a leather strap with three knots. Opening the first would release light winds, and the second moderate winds. But opening the third would unleash a catastrophic storm. How Magnus's picture found its way to Cornwall is a mystery, but the etching has apparently been on display at the Witchcraft Museum in Boscastle, under the title *The witches of Boscastle selling the wind*, ever since 1960, when the Museum was moved to the village by its previous Director, Cecil Williamson. It is even sold as a postcard in the Museum shop! In August 2004, Boscastle was struck by a devastating flash flood, and the Museum now has a newly painted sign, under the same title, depicting a female witch with a long pointed nose, selling a rope with three knots to a couple of bearded seamen of distinctively Cornish appearance on the shore of a rocky creek (Jennings, pers. comm.).

[9] Jetté refers to the Koyukon people as the Ten'a. This particular riddle is also mentioned by Nelson in his ethnography of the Koyukon, but is given a rather free translation:

> *Wait, I see something: My end sweeps this way and that way and this way around me.*
> *Answer: Grass tassles moving back and forth in the wind, making little curved trails in the snow.*
> (Nelson 1983: 44)

REFERENCES

BRADLEY, C. 2002. Travelling with Fred George: the changing ways of Yup'ik star navigation in Akiachak, western Alaska. In *The earth is faster now: indigenous observations of Arctic environmental change* (eds) I. Krupnik & D. Jolly, 240-65. Fairbanks, Alaska: Arctic Research Consortium of the United States.

FARNELL, B.M. 1994. Ethno-graphics and the moving body. *Man* (N.S.) **29**, 929-74.

FOX, S. 2002. These are things that are really happening. In *The earth is faster now: indigenous observations of Arctic environmental change* (eds) I. Krupnik & D. Jolly, 12-53. Fairbanks, Alaska: Arctic Research Consortium of the United States.

GIBSON, J.J. 1979. *The ecological approach to visual perception*. Boston: Houghton Mifflin.

HALLOWELL, A.I. 1960. Ojibwa ontology, behavior and world view. In *Culture in history: essays in honor of Paul Radin* (ed.) S. Diamond, 19-52. New York: Columbia University Press.

HELANDER, E. & T. MUSTONEN (eds) 2004. *Snowscapes, dreamscapes: snowchange book on community voices of change* (Tampere Polytechnic Publications, Series C, Study Materials **12**). Vaasa: Fram Oy.

HULL, J. 1997. *On sight and insight: a journey into the world of blindness*. Oxford: Oneworld Publications.

INGOLD, T. 2000. *The perception of the environment: essays on livelihood, dwelling and skill*. London: Routledge.

——— 2005*a*. The eye of the storm: visual perception and the weather. *Visual Studies* **20**, 97-104.

——— 2005*b*. Landscape lives, but archaeology turns to stone. *Norwegian Archaeological Review* **38**, 122-6.

——— 2006. Rethinking the animate, re-animating thought. *Ethnos* **71**, 1-12.

——— & T. Kurttila 2000. Perceiving the environment in Finnish Lapland. *Body and Society* **6**, 183-96.

JETTÉ, J. 1913. Riddles of the Ten'a Indians. *Anthropos* **8**, 181-201, 630-51.

KRUPNIK, I. 2004. Yupik ice and weather knowledge: some final remarks. In *Watching ice and weather our way* (eds) I. Krupnik, H. Huntington, C. Koonooka & G. Noongwook, 195, 204-7. Washington, D.C.: Arctic Studies Center, Smithsonian Institution.

MACAULEY, D. 2005. The flowering of environmental roots and the four elements in Presocratic philosophy: from Empedocles to Deleuze and Guattari. *Worldviews: Environment, Culture, Religion* **9**, 281-314.

MACDONALD, J. 1998. *The Arctic sky: Inuit astronomy, star lore, and legend*. Ontario: Royal Ontario Museum/ Iqaluit: Nunavut Research Institute.

MERLEAU-PONTY, M. 1962. *Phenomenology of perception* (trans. C. Smith). London: Routledge & Kegan Paul.

——— 1964. Eye and mind (trans. C. Dallery). In *The primacy of perception and other essays on phenomenological psychology, the philosophy of art, history and politics* (ed.) J.M. Edie, 159-90. Evanston, Ill.: Northwestern University Press.

NELSON, R.K. 1983. *Make prayers to the raven: a Koyukon view of the northern forest*. Chicago: University Press.

NOBES, G., A.E. MARTIN & G. PANAGIOTAKI 2005. The development of scientific knowledge of the Earth. *British Journal of Developmental Psychology* **23**, 47-64.

PICKERING, A. 1995. *The mangle of practice: time, agency, and science*. Chicago: University Press.

REVEL, N. 2005. Palawan Highlanders and Dayaks of Borneo: human beings and birds, their relation. In *Animal names* (eds) A. Minelli, G. Ortalli & G. Sanga, 401-17. Venice: Istituto Veneto di Scienze, Lettere ed Arti.

TILLEY, C. 2004. *The materiality of stone*. Oxford: Berg.

VOSNIADOU, S. 1994. Universal and culture-specific properties of children's mental models of the earth. In *Mapping the mind: domain specificity in cognition and culture* (eds) L.A. Hirschfeld & S.A. Gelman, 412-30. Cambridge: University Press.

——— & W.F. BREWER 1992. Mental models of the earth: a study of conceptual change in childhood. *Cognitive Psychology* **24**, 535-85.

3
Wafting on the wind: smell and the cycle of spirit and matter

DAVID PARKIN *University of Oxford*

When speaking the lingua franca, Swahili, the peoples of the East African coastal littoral distinguish four named seasons, each characterized as distinctive winds, two of which carry monsoons. Trade, political struggle, and marriage alliances carried out for centuries across the Indian Ocean in various sailing vessels have caused observers to refer to the East African littoral as having a maritime culture whose rhythm is determined by that of the seasonal winds which carry the ships to and from other parts of the northwest corridor of the Indian Ocean (Parkin & Barnes 2002). The people are therefore perfectly aware of the practical benefits of such winds as well as sometimes their danger when out in the ocean. Alongside the skills that they must develop to exploit and cope with the ocean winds, people also have a belief in spirits of the sea which have power over humans, but which can be propitiated for the good they can produce from the ocean. When, for instance, a new fishing boat is launched, the spirits will be blessed and should reciprocate by providing abundant catches of fish, but the boat launch will also entail the loss of a human life at some time to the spirits through drowning at sea, characteristically as the result of a storm, a death referred to as an offering or sacrifice (Parkin 2000: 158-60). Wind, season, sea, and spirit are, then, seen as acting together as a force for tragedy as well as subsistence and prosperity.

It is also common among peoples of the East African coast and inland to point to a sudden eddy of wind in the otherwise calm air, usually on a hot day, as evidence of a spirit. Spirits are normally invisible but can manifest themselves occasionally, as in this example of moving air or wind. Spirits are moreover expressions of a counter to human life, being evidence through their movements of an alternative world. Life in humans is evidenced by breath, which is itself often thought of as an expression of spirit and, among Muslims, can be used to give life to a creature by God. The movement of wind and breath is in all such cases brought about by divine inspiration. Thus, one way in which invisible spirit or divinity manifests itself is as the movement of wind or breath. A second way is through odour or fragrance, an association which is highly ambiguous. Spirits are sometimes propitiated through the use of incense but may sometimes exude smells regarded as intrinsic to their being. Some incenses used to invoke or please spirits produce coloured smoke or vapour and so further concretize the manifestation of spirit. As outsiders we can say that smell is the emission of molecules, an external view which parallels but does not reproduce the indigenous claim that smell gives substance to spirit by allowing one to identify it. Spirit is thus of air, wind, and breath and yet also sometimes of smell and colour. In other words this complex of wind, air, breath, and spirit may normally be invisible, a quality which imparts to the complex a special understanding and interpretation, but it stands continually on the cusp of becoming manifested as visible and accessible to the senses.

A semantic complex

Though highly variable cross-culturally, this complex of associations is globally and historically widespread. As Lyall Watson says in his popular account of smell, '[T]he ideas of life and breath and spirit and smell are intertwined in many cultures' (1999: 5). What is important here is the firm inclusion of smell within this complex of ideas. We are of course used to the idea that breath, wind, and spirit commonly go together in many ontologies. To take a recently reported example, among the Kukatja of the Australian western desert,

> the wind necessarily has both material and spiritual dimensions to it, which are intrinsically linked. In local representations of the body, when the wind penetrates any one of the human body's openings, it becomes breath; as breath, the wind could not possibly be considered intrusive ... the wind is thus consubstantial with humans: they share the same ancestral essence (Poirier 2004: 59).

Breath, wind, and spirit here constitute an interacting totality (Peile 1985: 81, cited in Poirier 2004: 59).

From a different part of the world, classical etymology reinforces this intertwining of ideas: Sanskrit *aniti* (he breathes, that which is animate) based on the root *an* (to breathe), and hence *pra-(a)na(m)* (life), and *atma(n)* (soul); Greek *anemos* (wind), *pneuma* (air, gaseousness); Latin *an-imare* (to give life to), *anima* (breath, soul), *animus* (spirit). A sense of 'airiness' appears to be the semantic template, with moving air expressed as the breath of life and hence soul and spirit. Nor is this template confined to Indo-European etymology, for it is echoed in a Semitic version with the Arabic-Jewish *nafesh* or equivalent ranging over soul, life, person, living being, blood, desire, and, related, breath and sweet odour, and with *neshama* and *ruakh* also shading firmly from 'breathing' to the idea of 'spirit'.

Its cross-cultural etymology apart, air is itself one of four Arabo-Greek elements (with fire, water, and earth) and one of five Indian (the fifth being space). Air among the Indian elements is the site where, after the existential consciousness of space, distinct energies begin to interact with each other, before being transformed through fire, defined and stabilized through water, and durably solidified through earth. In such cosmological or metaphysical systems air becomes an inextricable part of a process and cannot easily be privileged above the other elements. From its etymology, however, it is difficult not to accord it cognitive priority in human thinking on the relationship of breath to life and of life to soul and divinity. Its transition from spiritual to material, from being imagined to being felt, and from being invisible to visible, depends on people ascribing to air its property of movement as breath and wind.

In contrast to Lyall Watson, who takes smell as his starting-point, many ethnographers seem to have given little or no significance to smell in their description of the complex of wind, air, breath, spirit, soul, or divinity. I would argue, however, that it is precisely because smell wafts on the wind that it is of crucial importance. Like colour, smell may be a possible additional property of the complex of air, wind, breath, and spirit, yet, as an additional property, smell then becomes intrinsic to the complex and converts it into something more accessible to the senses and so more tangible, as well as, through colour, visible.

Returning to eastern Africa, there is a remarkably similar complex of associations. *Pepo* is a word of Bantu linguistic origin which is found as variants among Bantu speakers at least of eastern and central Africa and possibly beyond. I provide more details later but note now that the term is part of a polythetic range in the region meaning air, wind, cold, spirit (e.g. Giriama *peho*, cold (air), wind, *pepo*, spirit; Nyakyusa *imbepo*, air, wind), and, as well as carrying such connotations, has even been harnessed by Muslim Swahili speakers to refer to Paradise (*Upepo*, i.e. the great spiritual air above). In its negative effects, cold wind can enter bodily apertures and cause sickness, and a healthy body is one whose orifices and pores are closed to such wind (see also Davis 2000: 65). On the other hand, cooling processes are used as part of cure and the creation of beneficial effects, as when a Giriama herbalist blows upon leaves he is collecting and blessing for use in therapy (Parkin 1991: 177-8). Cold, wind, and spirit are, then, regarded not as unambiguously good or harmful, but as varying in their effects.

However, while the classical European etymology abridges notions of non-human and human spirit, life, soul, and breath, as do the Australian Kukatja in the example given above, the Bantu concept of *pepo* also sets up something of a division between humans and non-humans (see also Davis 2000: 95-109, 143, 148). The world of spirits or divinity it creates shares characteristics with that of humans, and in some senses offers a route between them, but stands apart. Humans and animals have breath, life, tangibility, and visibility in a way that spirits do not. Spirit and creatures thus partake of each other in a limited manner, yet paradoxically are never wholly the same and are in many respects opposed. What I want to argue, however, is that spirits threaten, so to speak, to become humans and animals through their capacity to manifest themselves not just as harmless eddies of wind but also as invisible beings having harmful or beneficial effects. Some healers employ beneficial spirits in their treatments and call them 'my people' or 'my soldiers', in explicit recognition of their human-like qualities. It is also said that evil healers, or witches, send harmful spirits to afflict people. Among Swahili-speaking Muslims, the term *shetani*, of Arabic origin (and linked to the word 'Satan'), is in many places used for 'spirit', sometimes alongside *pepo* or other terms. Given the separation of *pepo* and *shetani* from humans, to what extent do they, however, originate in humans and to what extent might they become human? Humans die and their souls leave and become ancestral spirits. Other kinds of spirits, often harmfully predatory, move in the opposition direction by possessing humans, making them sick and imposing their personalities. Their actions constitute a possible cycle of invisible and visible, non-human and human, spiritual and material, doing so often through the medium of smell and smoke as well as wind. My suggestion that the notion of smell is added, so to speak, to the *pepo* semantic complex of air/breath/soul/spirit is borne out among Bantu speakers, as largely elsewhere, through the use of quite unrelated terms (*-nuka*, to smell, *manukato*, fragrance, for example, with the Swahili language including also terms of Arabic origin, e.g. *harufu*). Extending the use of semantics to refer not just to cognate terms but also to their common sphere of references, it is clear in practice as argued above that smell (*-nuka*) and air/wind/spirit (*pepo*), while lexically unrelated, are conceptually intertwined. One way, therefore, to understand what we might call the practice of wind as metaphysical action and effect is to begin with a description of smell and smoke (and vapour) as part of its most obvious material manifestation. I argue that smell and its optional expression through smoke or vapour are half-way, so to speak, between invisible spirit and visible life-forms, such as humans. So, while spirit cannot be touched nor seen but is human-like and yet never becomes human, smell is a feature of both and is ultimately rooted in a precipitating substance which can be seen and touched. As such, smell is both part and means of a cycle of spiritual and material transformation. This claim may seem to be a far cry from Lyall Watson's general statement with which I began ('[T]he ideas of life and breath and spirit and smell are intertwined in many cultures'), yet it is more of an elaboration of than a departure from what appears to be a common feature in much human thinking. Indeed, Watson (1999: 148-9) points out that in classical times smells were associated with the gods, who were of course located within a pantheon, much as are spirits nowadays in other parts of the world. Some gods were known by more than one fragrance, and competed on this basis. The deaths of Christian saints sometimes reversed normality by being accompanied by sweet fragrances instead of deathly odour. Let me now turn to smell and smoke and vapour as entry-points into the understanding of this phenomenon.

Scent as solid and non-solid

Throughout the world over many centuries fumigation has been a widely known and used technique for cure or for expelling bodily harmful agents. During the Plague of seventeenth-century London, there was a time when people used fires to smoke out the disease, the idea being that the good air of the smoke would drive out the bad air of the infection, resonant with Hippocrates' notion that pure could replace impure air. It is an open question as to whether the smoke did reduce the incidence of bubonic plague by keeping at bay the rats later credited with carrying the fleas responsible for infection. Nevertheless, fire and smoke are often associated with expurgation. Some traditional African huts are built low, without windows and with only a narrow doorway, itself covered at night. The smoke from the hearth may damage people's eyes but at the same time repels insects and to a lesser extent rats. Fumigation using either smoke or vapour among the Swahili-speaking Muslims of the East African coast is usually through the use of a wide range of aromatic or odoriferous substances, including various kinds of incense. Incense is also sometimes used among the neighbouring non-Muslim Giriama. The curative element in cleansing the lungs and nostrils is of course recognized with regard to the use of some substances, much in the way that people inhale 'Vicks' or steam over a bowl, with their head covered. People also smoke out insects. However, as in much of the world, including that of Islam, fumigation or vaporization has been taken up in systematic attempts to drive out spirits which have temporarily possessed human victims, or as a way of invoking spirits and, as Nisula says (1999: 69), of encouraging them to appear.

In an area of the Zanzibari island of Pemba where I worked, the main idioms are of spirit expulsion or of invocation and pacification. This is not to say that people deny the possible benefits to the sick person of inhaling cleansing or sweet substances. This may resolve the acute condition. But the ongoing condition is treated as that of appeasing or exorcizing harmful spirits. That is to say, you have to do more than treat the symptoms and to deal with the spirits causing the affliction. Moreover, there is an extraordinarily wide range of aromatic substances which can be used for this purpose. The classification of different types of spirit is indeed complemented by a classification of substances whose fragrant or odorous properties are released often only by burning them.

Almagor points out that, unlike colours, which lend themselves to classification, human societies 'do not accommodate odours in their cultural classifications' (1990: 182), unlike professional perfumers, perhaps because individual persons each have distinctive and non-generalizable memories of particular smells which are not likely to be shared by other individuals. The Swahili also do not generally and explicitly classify smells as publicly representative of agreed phenomena. But they classify smells indirectly and in a limited way through the association of named gums, resins, and aromatic wood with particular spirits. Such indirect classification is perhaps analogous to the ways in which the Vedic therapeutic sequence of foods in India *ipso facto* classifies tastes and aromas (Zimmermann 1987; 1988). The different substances used are identified in terms of the spirits or kinds of spirits they treat. Put another way, different spirits demand different substances or, alternatively, different spirits are known only to retreat from the use of specific substances. There is here then a stated distinction very simply between acceptable and even friendly spirits which nevertheless expect to be offered olfactory satisfaction, and evil spirits for which the remedy is not to satisfy but to drive them out of the victim's body. Sometimes, of course, appeasing becomes a form of containment, if not actual expulsion.

This is, then, the use of the olfactory as part of fumigation and vaporization and as a means of either pacifying or expelling spirits and the sickness they bring. Complementing this usage, and indeed the obverse of it, is the use of such substances to call forth spirits which may be needed to supply medical and divinatory information or assistance.

Smells, then, wrapped up in a set process of fumigation or vaporization variously invoke, drive off, or simply appease spirits, a process that depends on a strong belief in their existence and in the availability of substances that can be used for these purposes. As Gell (1977), Howes (1987; 1988; 1991) and others have shown, smells not only communicate in this way, they also mark transition, and perhaps also help facilitate social and personal transitions.

What I want to argue, however, is that they are also sometimes part of a process by which substances come into being and life-forms are understood. I see this process as an interactive relationship. Aromas/odours/fragrance may have physical effect in the form of smoke, vapour or, as people sometimes put it, by simply being 'in the air' and/or driven by and therefore part of the wind. Alongside this capacity to become part of the visibly physical, they remain for the most part invisible or barely visible. They share these qualities with creatures of the spirit world. Spirits, too, sometimes come from the physical. For example, ancestral spirits, having emanated from a once physical, living human, in some societies eventually become merged within a non-ancestral spirit world: nature spirits are commonly associated with specific trees, caves, habitats, animals, and plants; while other spirits, such as those which possess people, are sometimes regarded as becoming part of their victim's personality, temporarily or permanently, and so part of that person in a combined mental, emotional, and physical way. It is these latter spirits in which I am here interested and which, in eastern and central Africa, are commonly called *pepo* or an equivalent.

In this interactive relationship of smell, air, wind, physical form, effect, and visibility, and of human and spirit ontology, the somewhat rigid line between substance and non-substance that is often drawn in colloquial English-speaking contexts is not one that either we or the people I study would find easy to draw. We are back into questions of substance, in which, for my present purposes, the place of smell seems especially interesting. In moving through air and in being moved by wind, smell has properties and effects which are not easily distinguished in colloquial English as either material or non-material. For instance, few people ordinarily think of smell as molecular. Indeed, such colloquial terms and concepts as material and non-material, or matter and non-matter, tell us how, in modern Western society, we divide up the world. Indigenous views elsewhere, including coastal East Africa, often approach such phenomena from the assumption that, whatever their differences of form and density, they share in some underlying vital life-force.

As Allen notes (1998: 177), in contemporary Western contexts we tend to think of matter as inanimate and as contrasted with living plants, animals, and humans. Yet, up to the early seventeenth century in Europe, and elsewhere in much of the world nowadays, this distinction between living phenomena and matter which never lived is not drawn so sharply, or in the same way, or even at all. After all, as Allen further notes (1998: 177), the European word 'matter' derives from the Latin *mater*, indicating reproductive and creative properties, and so very much inscribed in life-forms. It is also linked to words for the wood of trees, which, while hard matter when used after the death of the trees, is a product of life and, in some belief systems, may preserve or perpetuate some of that life (cf. de Boek 1998; Rival 1998). Moreover, the transformational worlds described by anthropologists which cover many continents, as in studies of shamanism, cosmology, and origin myths (Lovell 1998; Overing Kaplan 1975), are of rocks, mountains, volcanoes, rivers, rain, as well as trees and other plants, as being the elements out of which humans and other animals evolve but also which they may become. In environmentally conscious modern times, transformational worlds are nowadays complemented by a combination of modern ecological and cosmological rhetoric which argues that all cosmic matter is life, since it is out of that from which the earth and its contents derived. The biblical cycle of ashes to ashes and dust to dust has given way to the view that physical particles are in constant bio-chemical transformation and evolution. An aspect of this transformational ethos is a different status given to tactility as an index and measure of matter: to feel a rock being thrown and to feel the afflictions of a vengeful ghost or invisible sorcerer may be differentiated in many ways but are both physical in their effect. They injure, maim, or make one ill.

Obviously peoples use the distinctions of hard and soft, and of touchable and non-touchable, to indicate and interpret separate effects. The Giriama use hardwood memorial effigies for deceased important men, but use softwood ones to denote less important men and women ancestors (Parkin 1991), and they are perfectly aware that harmful spirits or demons normally do not assume tangible form as do living humans and so cannot be touched in the same way. There are therefore two inversely complementary entry-points into this transformational world. On the one hand, there are the visible and tangible wooden or other effigies such as the Giriama memorials or the *nkisi* so-called 'fetishes' in central Africa (as described, for instance, by MacGaffey 1983) which, while necessarily treated in some practical contexts as inanimate or at least dormant objects, are nevertheless sufficiently respected or feared as to provide the basis of belief in their animacy. On the other hand, non-visible and non-tangible spirits have to be identified, approached, negotiated with, and handed gifts or sacrifices, or driven out, all acts necessitating an idea of them as objects at times subject to human physical agency but as themselves also able to act upon humans. This is a transformational mode of existence that may be very evident in much of Africa but, in ways that I cannot go into here, is also implicit in some respects in so-called 'Western' ontologies which acknowledge that, in Sartre's memorable phrase, '*les choses sont contre nous*' or that, more solemnly, saints' relics are a source of blessing.

Bridging sensory gaps

Ellen (1988) has usefully suggested that a 'fetish' is evident in the ways in which humans concretize/objectify concepts and social relations, personalize/anthropomorphize them, merge term and referent for them, and ambivalently alternate between controlling and being controlled by them. Much the same can in fact be said for the invisible spirits which are the subject of so much anthropological interest. Spirits are invariably fitted into a system of spirit classification or pantheon, in which the ethnic origins, types, likes, and personalities of individual spirits are detailed. This classification goes some way to objectify and personalize spirits, while leaving them usually invisible, beyond touch and silent, except when invoked or in possessory mode. It is as if, through this kind of classification by selected criteria, spirits are almost brought into fully tangible existence, but not quite.

But can we elaborate further here on the process by which humans seem to try to overcome the gap between the visible and invisible and the tangible and non-tangible, and their apparently paradoxical unwillingness actually to bridge that gap? It is, I suggest, a process which complements that by which such physical objects as memorials and *nkisi* are given life but also have it taken from them.

I suggest that the key sense by which humans attempt to physicalize and de-physicalize spirits or demons is in fact smell. It is key in that, unlike sight, touch, and hearing, odour or fragrance is always incomplete, reaching back and bringing forth social and sensory trails which never settle. Boundaries can be placed around sights, sounds, and touching, which we sometimes call, for example, phonemes, images, and gestures of contact. Taste shares much of course with fragrance but is bounded by the simple process of ingestion, whereas fragrance and odour enter and leave consciousness often quite unexpectedly. Even the association of the olfactory with memory is provisional: the odour or fragrance may remind you vividly of the event at the time of the smelling, but, once passed, a smell cannot be re-imagined to the degree that the other senses can, and depends much more on a particular context to be remembered.

As Gell notes, '[T]he smell of an object always escapes – it is an active principle, ... smell is distinguished by formlessness, indefinability and lack of clear articulation. Smells are characteristically incomplete' (1977: 27). I suggest, however, that one way in which a smell becomes completed is when it is so concentrated as to be a substance, an element of physical matter, such as pine resin, a rotting carcass, or cooked food. Smell thus alternates as tangible substance and intangible, olfactory experience, akin to a concept. As a quasi-concept, not entirely ideational or entirely physical, it heralds and marks the passage of other events and objects, such as the preparation, arrival, and consumption of a meal, this being an example of smell's context of materialization and de-materialization, as Gell points out (1977: 28). This puts the emphasis on the physical substance, the meal, resin, or carcass, as being that from which springs forth the smell. But the obverse of this process is to take the smell back to its originating substance. This is what we do when we identify a fragrance as Chanel 19 or Diorissimo, or as the scent of a particular animal during a hunt. Is it possible to take both processes together in the single act and effect a transformation? Can we release a smell from a substance but then redirect it, so to speak, not to its original substance but to another? If smell is in fact physical particles emanating from a host substance, then do the rules of physics allow such particles to become part of a quite separate substance through some process of absorption or amalgamation? In other words, substance A (a corpse) releases smell A which, however, merges with substance B (rotting vegetation) and becomes part of it, as might elements from a mixture or even compound. Or, a supposedly pleasant incense is burned to suppress the unpleasant smell of the corpse, but in due course, in the folds of the clothes of people who attend, the scent of incense and the deathly odour merge and lose their original distinctiveness, and are thence experienced as sickly sweet by the mourners. Whether or not such a process of olfactory particle transmission is demonstrably possible in physics, it may well provide a logic underlying the use of, for example, fumigatory incense to cure, cleanse, or exorcize persons of the effects of spirit, and therefore as the meeting-point of spirit and substance.

The point here is that smell, while acting as intercalary between its originary substance and the spirit to which it is directed, never seems actually to concretize the spirit. It seems to go so far and no further. It does not cause the spirit to materialize and take physical or bodily form, such that it may then be seen, heard, touched, and, in principle, tasted. Spirits can, however, be known by their own, distinctive odours, despite lacking physical bodies. The famous Popobawa (Bat-wing) great spirit prevalent in Zanzibar (Parkin 2004) smelled foully and was associated with dirt and violent sodomy, not unlike certain European notions which associate harmful or evil ghosts with the smell of sulphur dioxide (from burning sulphur). Most commonly, other spirits in Zanzibar and elsewhere are invoked by fragrant scent, seen as pleasing to the spirit(s). Each spirit, however minor, is known to be associated with specific odours and scents. Humans can seize on this odorous or aromatic quality of spirits and burn various resins, woods, and minerals as incense to repel them or, conversely, please and attract them with regard to a human body. Griffin describes how, in Morocco, strong- or foul-smelling substances are burned or released during the vulnerable period just before and after the birth of a child in order to ward off potentially harmful spirits. Such substances include Sudanese pepper, white benzoin, gum ammoniac, gum lemon, alum, and gum sandarac. Garlic can be used to the same effect, which, while not burned, is conveyed in the breath through the air, a point of great significance, as I describe later. But at the feast at which the child is given its name, an event which celebrates the infant's journey of survival through the difficult first month of its life, sweet-smelling substances are burned or applied. These include agalwood (eaglewood) and rose-water. Some of the named spirits (or *jinn*, as they are called) are indulged at various times with a combination of pleasing incenses, aromas, and perfumes, including sandalwood, mastic, rue, black and yellow benzoin, harmel, and hasalban (Griffin 1991: 211-12). Griffin notes that in her area of Morocco (though not necessarily elsewhere) foul-smelling substances are used only to repel *jinn*. In Zanzibar, also, spirits are commonly repelled by foul odours. But sometimes a spirit is known by or associated with an unpleasant smell and will be pacified only with the same or some other prescribed foul odour. Yet other spirits are associated only with pleasant fragrances and are never prescribed foul smells. The main point here is that each spirit, and often each set of spirits, is associated with a distinctive combination of substance and class of smell, as well as with the other features mentioned.

Cyclical substance

Alongside this grid of distinctive features of spirit-associated smells and fragrances, smells have in common the fact they each constitute a kind of meeting-point between physical or high-density substance, namely the origin of the smell, and spirit itself. Thus, smell is physically metonymic of its originary substance. But, in its olfactory state, smell is also metonymic of spirit, in that both are 'of the air', as it was once put to me. That is to say, smell or scent was once substance, but now is 'air' driven by wind, as is spirit, which nevertheless strives in human consciousness to become substantive, having already acquired as a named spirit some human characteristics and therefore capable of exerting physical harm or help. Physical substance, smell, and spirit are thus part of a cycle of potential or hoped-for transformations of the solid and the non-solid, the visible and non-visible, the forceful and the ethereal.

An entwined dimension of this cycle exists in the form of the relationship of the possessory spirit and its human host. First, spirits are believed to invade the person and inflict him or her with illness. Second, a number of possessory spirits may come to inhabit the person, who increasingly becomes a kind of 'natural' habitat for the spirit or spirits. Throughout coastal East Africa, possessed humans are at this stage said to be the seat (*kiti*) in which the spirits sit. The human host may suffer periodic bouts of sickness, which is taken as an indication that the inhabiting spirit requires some attention and offerings. But this chronic condition is far from serious and in fact 'becomes' the totality of that person: the spirits and their distinctive qualities are now constitutive of the person. Occasionally, new spirits replace existing ones, but overall the person becomes made up of a relatively enduring core of the same spirits, which I have heard here referred to as part of that person's 'character' or 'personality traits' and roughly connoted by variable uses of the term *tabia* (see also Parkin 2000). The spirit or spirits thus begin as invaders of a human body, to be pacified or expunged as a response to an acute condition marked by sudden sickness, but may, in many and perhaps most cases, include a number among them who over time actually become part of the person. To that extent, also, the periodic spirit-induced manifestations of sickness requiring attention act as diagnostic barometers of the possessed person's well-being. Occasionally a chronically possessed person is judged to have the knowledge to become a diviner or shaman, perhaps after collecting necessary herbs, materials, and equipment, so continuing the cycle by which other people will through that person's divination move from acute to chronic conditions of engagement with spirit.

The cycle is one in which a non-solid, non-visible spirit that is sometimes detected only as wind takes on the solid and visible form of a human, while retaining a constitutive autonomy in the form of attachable or, less commonly, detachable personality traits.

Just as long-term possessory spirits are tantamount to the possessed person's character, so the different smells by which a spirit is known constitute part of its own character. But smell is inscribed within a more comprehensive cycle of being. Smell starts out as substance, such as an aromatic gum. The gum is burned as incense, whose odour or fragrance defines, informs, and so becomes part of a particular spirit or spirits. The spirit(s) in turn becomes part of a person's character, who is known as such. However, a kind of closure is put on the cycle when the human dies, for he or she becomes the cadaver whose worsening smell must be covered with specific kinds of incense, which do not, however, indicate a habitat, home, or 'seat' for spirits. The corpse is not, after all, for habitation, except sometimes by witches in East Africa (cf. the notion of zombie believed in elsewhere), and its life-force exists thereafter only as ancestral and not possessory spirit. At death, the high density of the living body becomes the low density of the dead person's spirit, now an ancestral spirit, a transition marked by the strong and disagreeable odours of death giving way in due course to the odourlessness of ancestral spirits.

Such closure at death indicates that it is only in life that human beings and possessory spirits (as distinct from ancestral spirits) become part of each other within a particular individual, and that smell is itself part of this cyclical transformation of substance and non-substance (i.e. of gum into smell, of smell into spirit, and of spirit into person, and of person re-starting the process).

As well as marking and enabling transition (Howes 1987) and thence transformation, I argue here that smell may be an important part of such transformation. The transformative process could be laid out mechanically in terms of a distinction between solid and non-solid. That is to say, the burning turns aromatic gum (solid) into incense (non-solid), which gives form to and contributes to the identity of a spirit (non-solid), which then enters and becomes part of a human (solid), who buys the gum and burns the incense, and so on. These distinctions between solid and non-solid are made by people themselves in, say, Zanzibar, who say that spirits cannot be seen or touched as can humans and other physical objects, and that smells share something of these qualities of spirit. But the same people say that spirits, like humans, can exert physical force just as incense and other smells can exert a physical effect. The experience of physical force is therefore common to solid and non-solid alike in this transformative process, which can therefore be glossed in a Western metaphysical idiom as an unending continuum of changing matter and non-matter in which force is always present or potentially so.

Now, while these distinctions drawn from conversation and observation satisfy general description in the community of Zanzibar, they are not watertight. What are we to make of the claim that a sudden wind eddy is evidence of a spirit? Wind itself is not thought of as visible. Yet there is visible and tangible evidence of its presence, as ground leaves and dust swirl in the unexpected gust. Similarly, incense and other smells may take the form of smoke or vapour, which is visible, if only indeterminately, and tangible, to the extent that it may be felt as some definite thing in the nostrils. Once again, despite people's claim that smell cannot be seen or touched, as can a solid object, they also say that it leaves visible trails and, like spirit, enters and exits the bodily orifices of nose, mouth, and anus, and other openings such as festering sores, and so on. Smell does, then, come across as a betwixt-and-between substance, rather like spirit. Smell comes from a solid but may also become like a solid in its physical effect. Take the case of the fumigation of a patient suffering illness. The patient sits, is covered with a blanket, and breathes in incense for many minutes as the healer invokes the spirit's assistance. The often very strong fumes, smoke, or vapour collect under the blanket as a mass of effect and conjoined matter, enveloped and delimited but not exclusively either substance or vapour, spirit or cure, but a compound of all these.

In this and other healing contexts, the idea of spirit accompanied by smell is said to give life to the human sufferer, just as the idea of life taken, appropriated, or afflicted is the obverse negative effect. But it is clearly an idea of life, appropriation, and relief which plays upon the impermanence and transitoriness of substance, of spirit and smell as both not-quite substances, and not-quite human life itself. Is this not in fact a discourse on the frailty and vulnerability of human life and its likeness to other life-forms captured in the idiom of unsettled, boundless, and transforming spirit and olfaction?

Muslims and non-Muslims

Let me here return to a number of terms used to describe spirit, human soul, and animality among both Swahili-speakers and the linguistically related Bantu-speaking non-Muslim neighbouring peoples of the East African coastal area. The terms making up this semantic complex indicate existential overlap between these phenomena, which neatly fudge absolute distinctions between life and death. It is as if the transformable nature of the terms defers the proposition that human or other life can ever reach a state of absolute non-existence.

Thus, among the non-Muslim Giriama the term *kivuri* means 'life-force' or 'soul'.

> The repetitive form, *kivurivuri*, means 'shadow'. It can only exist as part of a visible object. Similarly, only visible, living persons can have a *kivuri*, soul. While a newly born baby has a *kivuri*, a foetus in the womb does not, for you cannot see it, although it is understood that the foetus is alive and growing. By the same token the *kivuri* does not survive a person after their death. At that point they become, instead, a *koma*, or ancestral spirit (Parkin 1991: 214).

The life-force or soul of a living human being, *kivuri*, can, then, exist only as an aspect of a visible human being. It is, moreover, believed to be tangible and solid to the extent that witches may take the life-force or soul of a living person and do harm to it (i.e. practise witchcraft). 'The witch fattens it up, cuts it off from its owner, who will therefore become sick and die, and eats its flesh' (Parkin 1991: 214). Human life-force thus straddles conditions of tangibility and intangibility and is dependent for its visibility on being part of its human host. Similarly, the ancestral spirit, *koma*, is not normally visible or tangible but becomes so in the form of a wooden memorial post placed in the ground, which is also called *koma* and is addressed, prayed to, treated, and fed as a living being.

The two terms, *kivuri* and *koma*, thus complement each other, *kivuri* indicating the material transitoriness and vulnerability of human life and *koma* the immaterial permanency of ancestral life. Taken together they are about that stage of soul that lives in the living physical body and is dependent on it and that which does not actually need the human or any other body for its survival but which may simply wish to be part of a venerated wooden effigy. This betwixt-and-between position of being and not being part of substance is much like that of a possessory spirit and its human host, mediated by the place and use of invocatory or associated olfaction. The two terms, however, extend to a semantic cluster. Thus, *kivuri*, the life-force or soul of a living human being, is sometimes referred to also as *peho*. But *peho* also means windy, cool, and shady. Apart from referring to a cool temperature or something that is cold to touch, *peho* has important curative health connotations, indicating beneficial cooling foods, trees, and herbs to treat fevers, sickness, and misfortunes, and identifying, for instance, an infertile man's sperm as too cold or weak (*menye ga peho*). In referring to wind, the term is sometimes used to describe the presence of spirits, which, as mentioned before, appear as sudden gusts. But the most common term for spirit throughout the area is in fact *pepo*. Given the transformational relationship of *p* and *h* in a number of Bantu languages, including Giriama, there is no doubt that the two terms, *peho* and *pepo*, are from a common source. Given the additional use of *peho* to mean shade and of *kivuri*, meaning soul and in its repetitive form, *kivurivuri*, meaning shadow, and the occasional use of *peho* also to mean soul, the semantic cluster indicates a complex intertwining of ideas in this one society about living bodily substance and non-substance and the cosmic impossibility of ever sharply distinguishing the one from the other.

This inseparability is even more evident in another more specific term used to describe spirits among Giriama, namely *nyama*. This refers to a particular class of spirits, though it may once have had a more general reference to them. It thus coexists at present with the term *peho* to identify the spirit world. The reason that the term *nyama* is so important in pointing up the cosmic inseparability of living substance and non-substance is that it also means 'animal'. This is a remarkable semantic claim, so to speak, that the life of invisible and intangible spirits and that of visible and tangible animals are premised on some common mutable foundation, regardless of the fact that one is solid whereas the other is not. Humans come into the complex in that they may be possessed by the *nyama* or 'animal' spirits to the extent of incorporating them as part of their own human being.

The term *nyama* has not simply been appropriated by Giriama to refer to spirit as well as animal (or vice versa) in ethnographic isolation. What is further remarkable about the case of *nyama*, which in many other Bantu languages, including Swahili, means 'animal', is that it has a far wider African resonance. Somewhat speculatively I ask whether it is related to the concept analysed by the African philosopher Masolo (1994: 79-83), which is, however, a term here derived from the non-Bantu Dogon. Building on the work of Tempels (1965 [1945]), Dieterlen (1941; 1951), and Griaule (1950; 1952: 1965 [1948]), including the latter's conversations with the Dogon sage, Ogotemmêli, Masolo refers to a notion of *nyama* as soul and vital principle of all living creatures. Drawing from their and others' ethnography, he says: 'Before the appearance of death in the human world, order reigned among the spirits: humans and things created by Amma were provided with a soul and a vital principle (*Nyama*)' (Masolo 1994: 79).

Among the Muslim Swahili, a comparable semantic cluster has been reduced through the introduction of Arabic vocabulary. Thus, the term *nyama* means only animal and not also spirit. *Pepo* remains the prime term for spirit among many Swahili-speakers (especially those descended from non-Muslims), but the Arabic term *shetani*, mentioned above, has been adopted and refers to a complementary set of harmful spirits. Moreover, the term for cool or cold in Swahili is no longer *peho* but is the Arabic-derived term *baridi*. The idiom of life as wind, in the form of breath, is, however, retained, through use of the Arabic-derived term *roho*, an idiom of wider Semitic prevalence and indeed widespread in other languages. Among Muslim Swahili-speakers it is said of a person's or animal's last gasp that it is their *roho*, translated as soul for humans and life-force for animals. Thus, though there is significant vocabulary change in the switch from non-Muslim Giriama to linguistically and ethnically related Muslim Swahili on the East African coast, the idea is retained among both peoples of soul, life-force, breath, wind, and spirit as aspects of a single semantic cluster, one that, among both peoples, also includes smell.

The coastal Bantu-speaking peoples of the East African coast, both Muslim and non-Muslim, thus share a cluster of concepts and practices which link what I translate as wind, air, breath, life-force, soul, spirit, and solid substance as part of a transformational world. It is a world which holds in abeyance, so to speak, and so transcends any set or absolute distinction between solid and non-solid, spirit and human, and human and ancestor. It defers questions of ultimate death and cosmic finality by positing a transformational life-cycle of substance and non-substance or spirit. Although primarily regarded as in origin a form of Islamic healing, the use of incense in fumigation and other kinds of olfaction to appeal to spirits in both groups is a special mid-point between the breath of life and the substance of health, through the concentrated spirit and incense which are less than solid and yet more than just vapour and smoke.

Through fumigation, smell is set up by human agents and is to that extent controlled, usually by being blown in a certain direction or kept under cover. To the extent, however, that smells also waft on winds independently of human intervention, they do indeed escape human control. Like wind, smell resembles and partakes of spirit and of life itself. Humans may seek to control it and may sometimes succeed. But they are always likely to be caught unawares and subject to its effect and control. The special significance of fumigation for Muslims is that it joins Islamic medical expertise, including the idea that certain forms of incense are beneficial, with the need to curb or accommodate wayward spirits who possess and harm victims. If I may speak ethnocentrically for a moment, it is a way of bridging science and belief. On the one hand, Islamic medical science or expertise is itself believed to emanate from God's omnipotence such that only the pious can successfully practise it. On the other hand, invoking or appeasing spirits is often regarded as based on non-Islamic beliefs. Fumigation is a way of straddling the two main belief systems commonly found in Muslim society. It is significant that, through fumigation, smell plays a pivotal role in bridging these beliefs and practices, for it is itself something betwixt and between, admirably suited for cosmology in dilemma.

NOTE

The interest in the interrelationship between wind, smell, and spirit, emerged from an ongoing investigation of local systems of therapy among Swahili-speakers and other neighbouring Bantu-speakers such as Giriama and Digo living along the East African coast. Such therapy involves the invocation of spirits and their pacification and/or expurgation through the use of different kinds of incense. In describing the nature of such spirits, people consistently cited their invisibility and yet their ability to manifest their presence as wind, smell, or physical effect.

REFERENCES

ALLEN, N.J. 1998. The category of substance: a Maussian theme revisited. In *Marcel Mauss: a centenary tribute* (eds) W. James & N.J. Allen, 175-91. Oxford. Berghahn.

ALMAGOR, U. 1990. Some thoughts on common scents. *Journal of the Theory of Social Behaviour* **20**, 181-95.

DAVIS, C. 2000 *Death in abeyance: illness and therapy among the Tabwa of central Africa*. Edinburgh: University Press.

DE BOEK, F. 1998. The rootedness of trees: place as cultural and natural texture in rural southwest Congo. In *Locality and belonging* (ed.) N. Lovell, 38-45. London: Routledge.

DIETERLEN, G. 1941. *Les âmes des Dogons*. Paris: Institut d'Ethnologie.

——— 1951. *Essai sur la religion Bambara*. Paris: Presses Universitaires de France.

ELLEN, R. 1988. Fetishism. *Man* (N.S.) **23**, 213-35.

GELL, A. 1977. Magic, perfume, dream. In *Symbols and sentiments* (ed.) I.M. Lewis, 25-38. London: Academic Press.

GRIAULE, M. 1950. Philosophie et religion des noirs. *Présence Africaine* **8-9**, 307-12.

——— 1952. Le savoir des Dogon. *Journal de la Société des Africanistes* **22**, 27-42.

——— 1965 [1948]. *Conversations with Ogotemmêli*. London. Oxford University Press.

GRIFFN, K. 1991. The ritual of silent wishes: notes on the Moroccan sensorium. In *The varieties of sensory experience* (ed.) D. Howes, 210-20. Toronto: University Press.

HOWES, D. 1987. Olfaction and transition: an essay on the ritual uses of smell. *Canadian Review of Sociology and Anthropology* **24**, 398-416.

——— 1988. On the odour of the soul. *Bijdragen*, December, 144.

——— (ed.) 1991. *The varieties of sensory experience*. Toronto: University Press.

LOVELL, N. (ed.) 1998. *Locality and belonging*. London: Routledge.

MACGAFFEY, W. 1983. *Modern Kongo prophets: religion in a plural society*. Bloomington: Indiana University Press.

MASOLO, D. 1994. *African philosophy in search of identity*. Edinburgh: University Press; Bloomington: Indiana University Press.

NISULA, T. 1999. *Everyday spirits and medical interventions: ethnographic and historical notes on therapeutic conventions in Zanzibar town*. (Transactions of the Finnish Anthropological Society NRO **XLIII**). Saarijärvi: Gummerus Kirjapaino Oy.

OVERING, KAPLAN J. 1975. *The Piaroa: a people of the Orinoco basin: a study of kinship and marriage*. Oxford: Clarendon Press.

PARKIN, D. 1991. *Sacred void: spatial images of work and ritual among the Giriama of Kenya*. Cambridge: University Press.

——— 2000. Invocation: *sala, dua, sadaka* and the question of self-determination. In *Islamic prayer across the Indian Ocean: inside and outside the mosque* (eds) D. Parkin & S. Headley, 137-68. Richmond, Surrey: Curzon.

——— 2004. In the nature of the human landscape: provenances in the making of Zanzibari politics. In *Figured worlds: ontological obstacles in intercultural relations* (eds) J. Clammer, S. Poirier & E. Schwimmer, 113-31. Toronto: University Press.

——— & R. BARNES (eds) 2002. *Ships and the development of maritime technology in the Indian Ocean*. London: RoutledgeCurzon.

PEILE, A.R. 1985. Le concept du vent, du soufflé et de l'âme chez les Aborigènes dans le desert de l'Australie. *Bulletin Ethnomédical* **33**, 75-83.

POIRIER, S. 2004. Ontology, ancestral order, and agencies among the Kukatja of the western Australian desert. In *Figured worlds: ontological obstacles in intercultural relations* (eds) J. Clammer, S. Poirirer & E. Schwimmer, 58-82. Toronto: University Press.

RIVAL, L. 1998. Trees, from symbols of life and regeneration to political artefacts. In *The social life of trees: anthropological perspectives on tree symbolism* (ed.) L. Rival, 1-36. Oxford: Berg.

TEMPELS, P. 1965 [1945]. *La philosophie bantoue*. (Third edition). Élisabethville: Éditions Lovania.

WATSON, L. 1999. *Jacobson's organ and the remarkable nature of smell*. London: Allen Lane.

ZIMMERMANN, F. 1987. *The jungle and the aroma of meats: an ecological theme in Hindu medicine*. Berkeley: University of California Press.

——— 1988. The jungle and the aroma of meats: an ecological theme in Hindu medicine. *Social Science and Medicine* **27**, 197-215.

4
'Blowing 'cross the crest of Mount Galeng': winds of the voice, winds of the spirits

MARINA ROSEMAN *Queens University, Belfast*

The path led up a foothill of Mount Galeng, a peak overlooking the forests of Ulu Kelantan, peninsular Malaysia. As we reached the top, a gust whooshed up over the crest: fresh, cool, and powerful. Uda Pandak, the spirit medium walking before me, looked back over his shoulder and spoke words from one of his dream songs: '*Na-prɛdhiid num-gunung galeng*', 'It blows cool, across from Mount Galeng'. I had heard versions of this phrase in many a Temiar dream song, but never had it struck me with such force, literally, figuratively, and physically.

As we stood on the hillcrest, the valley below lent us a momentary vista, in stark contrast with the time we mostly spent immersed in thick forest growth. This is the perspective of spirits of the landscape, flora and fauna, who visit during dreams and ceremonies. There they give to human dreamers and ceremonial participants songs describing the world from the vantage point of spirit-in-motion: wide vistas, fields of flowers, the curve and lay of the land, even a bird's-eye view of a Temiar singing ceremony in process. Circling above the forest canopy, a spirit-in-motion can see long distances, *brsənywɛ̃ɛ̃d*, from whence it might find a human's lost spirit, to return it through healers to the person left ailing by its loss.

Across the valley and ringed by clouds rose Mount Galeng. The winds that blew across the horizon, funnelled by the valley into a cool blast tousling us on the foothill's crest, carried with them the cool watery essence of the spirits, *kahyɛk*, which flows with a spirit's song through the body of a healer, and thence into patients and other ceremonial participants. Uda Pandak's quote, 'It blows cool, 'cross from Mount Galeng', reveals in the symbolic economy of poetry a relationship between winds of the landscape, winds of the spirits, voices of mediums, and movements of trance-dancers fundamental to the dynamics of Temiar daily and ceremonial life.

Singers and healers bring spirits from their physical environment into their bodies and, through their voices, into people attending musical spirit séances held, in many cases, for purposes of healing. Along with healing songs received in dreams from the crest of the mountains perched high above the canopy and misted in fog (Fig. 1), or the spirit of the Rhinocerus hornbill circling high above the forest canopy, I have also recorded songs received from spirits of aeroplanes that flew above the forest during the Malaysian Emergency (1948-65) dropping strafe bombs to destroy forest swiddens the government feared would feed communist insurgents, or dropping parachutes with boxes of food supplies (Fig. 2).[1] Parachute drops began during the latter portion of the Emergency when government strategies switched toward courting Orang Asli support, and continued through the 1980s. Such spirits, whether bird or aeroplane, mountain crest or parachute, are called upon through song and dance during ceremony to address both individual and social wounds, as Temiars craft their dances of healing and survival across the proverbial winds of history.

Figure 1. Mountain crests misted in fog, viewed from the Enching River, 1991 (Mount Lobal, Kelantan). Photograph by author.

Figure 2. Parachute drops over Batek territory, Post Aring, 1971. Photograph reproduced by kind permission of Kirk Endicott.

This enclave of animists in a predominantly Muslim nation has forged ingenious techniques to convert the commodities, concepts, and technologies that assault them towards their own religious and ideological uses. Traditionally semi-sedentary horticulturalists growing rice, millet, and tapioca augmented by hunting and gathering, Temiars were once able to retreat into the montane forest running down the centre of the peninsula. Though they have long interacted with Malays, British colonists, and the Chinese and Tamils whom the British brought to work their mines and plantations, Malayan forest peoples were left with nowhere to hide when communist guerillas took refuge from government forces in the dense jungle in the aftermath of the Second World War. Small-scale, forest-dwelling groups such as the Austroasiatic-speaking Temiars live their lives under siege as they fight for land rights, maintenance of a healthy subsistence economy, and political autonomy within the Malaysian nation-state and global economy.

Thinly disguised within state policies to promote national security, national integration, and socio-economic development, most Malayan, and later Malaysian, government programmes ultimately strove towards cultural and religious assimilation of the peninsula's aboriginal peoples, now collectively termed 'Orang Asli' (Original People). Such policies imply conversion to Islam. Yet to date, less than 10 per cent, or 8,000 Orang Asli out of a population of 80,000, have converted, and in many cases that conversion is nominal (Dentan, Endicott & Hooker 1997: 149-50).

To account for the tenacity of Temiar religious ideology, concepts of person and cosmos, and performance practice, we must return to the poetic economy interlinking winds of the landscape, winds of the spirits, voices of mediums, and movements of dancers. For it is here, where the energies of wind- and fluid-in-motion through the landscape are mapped within the body, then set flowing during ritual performance, that enduring sensibilities adapt to changing circumstances.

Head, heart, odor, shadow

Let us return for a moment to the mist shrouding Mount Galeng, and cool winds rushing o'er the foothill's crest. For in this sensory image of air slightly weighted with moisture to the point of semi-visibility, brushing our faces at the brink of tangibility, we find a hint of what it might be like to live in a world continually on the verge of emergence.

Wind-in-motion, particularly wind weighted with moisture, is highly charged for Temiars. For it is both reminder and manifestation of fundamental principles of Temiar physics and cosmology, empirical science and common belief, clinical observation and religious orientation. In Temiar animistic ideology and practice, all entities exhibit the potential to take shape at various levels of density best viewed as points along a continuum. These range from mountain as mountain-crest-at-rest, to mountain-crest-in-motion in the guise, for example, of the Spirit Princess of the Crest of Mount Sewiluu'.

Mount-Sewiluu'-at-rest is highly visible and tangible: one can go hunting on it; walk on it; gather flowers in its shadow while being seen, in turn, by it; or sleep on it, as Along Indan of Belau, Kelantan, did during a hunting trip. In a dream, the Spirit of the Crest of Mount-Sewiluu'-in-motion later appeared to him in the shape of a beautiful, curvaceous young female with long, wavy hair. Now in dream-visible, dream-tangible form, she points back to her place of origin, the mountain crest. Along Indan knows then that she is a 'head-soul-in-motion' (*rəwaay*). If she had indicated a mountain cave, she would have been 'heart-soul-in-motion' (*hup, hnum, jrək*). For just as all entities can take shape at various levels of density, so, too, they may have upper ('head') or lower, interior ('heart, breath') loci. He addresses her 'Princess of Mt Sewiluu', borrowing the royal terminology from Malay in deference to the great height of the mountain crest she calls home. The song she teaches to him in his dream, and he sings as her medium during ceremonies, is recorded as Band 2 of the compact disc *Dream songs and healing sounds* (Roseman 1995).[2] In the third line of verse three, she sings: '*Cə-cii' hɛlhuul prɛdhiid 'atas 'angin*', which translates roughly as, 'I blow across in cool gusts as the wind above' (see Table 1).

We might call this spirit-substance, when back in her mountain home at rest in her most densified form, a 'soul' substance or component, and when in her more active, less dense but tangible form – even if only in the imaginal realm of dreams or the immaterial-materiality of a cool moist breeze or a vocalized song – a 'spirit'.[3] To conceive of these as points along a continuum of density and tangibility expands in significant ways upon Geoffrey Benjamin's (1967; 1979) earlier usage of the terms *bounded 'soul'*, for the potentially-but-not-yet-animated material form, and *unbound 'spirit'*, as the detached, animated form, in his Temiar ethnography.

A student of Rodney Needham, Benjamin juxtaposes bounded soul and unbound spirit in classic structural opposition. The dreams and rituals which set bounded soul into motion might then be seen as 'institutions' or processes that mediate those distinctions. This was the terminology that I followed in my earlier writings (e.g. Roseman 1990; 1991). Yet even in these publications, I showed how these distinctions, when operationalized in the performance and process of Temiar life, exhibit qualities that might better be described theoretically in post-structural terms. For there is always permeability: there is a bit of stasis or tangibility in the spirit-in-motion, and a barely settled quality to the soul-at-rest.[4] Thinking more deeply about wind weighted with water, and spirits with voices that conduct cool healing liquid *kahyɛk*, has led me to posit, here, the image of a continuum, with head- or heart-loci towards one end (the mountain crest, the mountain cave, the dew on a leaf), and head- or heart-soul-in-motion as spirit towards the other (the imaginal homunculus appearing in Along Indan's dream; the chilly wind from Mount Galeng tousling our hair; the vocalized song and cool liquid *kahyɛk* flowing through a singing spirit medium).

All entities, then, share the potential for being a locus of upper- or lower-portion souls that may be set in motion as spirit. Humans have head and heart souls; plants, leaf and root souls; mountains, summit and underground or cave souls. Each has a more 'substantial' loci at one end of the continuum and somewhat tangible, more emergent emanations at the other. Along with 'upper' and 'lower' loci, all entities, as well, share two further components, again with both substantive originary sources and emergent

Table 1.

Cə-cii'	*hɛlhuul*	*prɛdhiid*	*'atas*	*'angin*
I + reflexive	nominative hɛlnuul 'wind blowing' < *na-hul*, 'it blows'	'cool gusts blowing across'	*'atas* < Malay, above	*'angin* < Malay, wind
I	blow	across in cool gusts	as the wind above.	

emanations: odor soul substance (*ŋɔɔy*), a composite, in humans, of things consumed and carried, which emanates from the lower back; and shadow soul substance (*wɔɔg*), not unlike the Austronesian *wayang* or *bayang*, manifest in the visible shadow, or in the reflective image portrayed in photographs.[5]

'In this interactive relationship of smell, air, wind, physical form, effect, and visibility, and of human and spirit ontology', Parkin notes (this volume, p. S44) while discussing *pepo* spirits in eastern and central Africa, 'the somewhat rigid line between substance and non-substance that is often drawn in colloquial English-speaking contexts is not one that either we or the people I study would find easy to draw'. He describes ongoing cycles of transformation as entities transmute from higher to lower densities (and back again) – concentrated as 'matter' at one end of the continuum, and concentrated as 'spirit', much in the way of a precipitate, at the other. In his analysis, smells not only mark, but also enact these diffusing (or re-concentrating) transformations. '[S]mells', he notes, 'constitute a kind of meeting-point between physical or high-density substance, namely the origin of the smell, and spirit itself' (p. S47). Observing how people say that 'spirits, like humans, can exert physical force just as incense and other smells can exert a physical effect,' he concludes: 'The experience of physical force is therefore common to solid and non-solid alike in this transformative process, which can therefore be glossed in a Western metaphysical idiom as an unending continuum of changing matter and non-matter in which force is always present or potentially so' (p. S48).

Parkin may be over-privileging smell in his analysis, an artefact perhaps of his ethnographic site. I would argue, as well, that a number of sensory forms which densify or move 'air', including moisture, sound, smoke/incense, wind, smell, or even trembling leaves (as I shall discuss, below), each with potentially multiple, sensory yet elusory effects (olfactory, tactile, auditory, visual, or proprioceptive), might be called upon to enact this transformational diffusion and precipitation of matter as it morphs between stages of densification.[6] The transformational world that Parkin describes for east and central African peoples shares some similarities with that of the Temiars. The extent to which this transformational ethos is elaborated in Temiar ontology of person and cosmos, illness aetiology and medical practice, and ceremonial performance indicates not only their comfort with such fluidity, but also their concerns about the need to stabilize spirit, in order to balance the forcible flow of spirit and wind so deeply present in their lives.

As hunter-horticulturalists living in the dense foliage and vibrant soundscape of the rain forest, Temiars have benefited from a peculiarly intimate relationship to the landscape, its flora and fauna, hills and rivers. They move through it daily, hunting, gathering, fishing, and gardening, garnering cues as they travel from bird, insect, and animal sounds that cipher through the dense foliage. They cut each stalk of rice by hand (Fig. 3), dig for tubers, climb trees to gather fruits. This closeness to the land comes out in the way they think about it. The world resonates with life, with potentially animated being.

During dreams, the head- (*rwaay*) or heart/breath- (*hup/hnum, jrək*) spirit-in-motion of the dreamer meets with upper- or lower-portion spirit-in-motion of entities who express their desire to become the dreamer's spirit guide. The relationship is confirmed through the gift of a song, associated with other performance parameters (e.g. dance steps, fragrant leaf or flower props, lighting effects, gender roles) taught by spirit guide to dreamer. Later, singing that song during ceremonial performance, the

Figure 3. Cutting rice stalk. Photograph by author.

singer becomes a medium or conduit for the spirit, who flies above the forest canopy and 'returns' to the singer what s/he experiences.

This is what Ingold (this volume) might term living life 'in the open'. 'Instead of thinking of the inhabited world as composed of mutually exclusive hemispheres of sky and earth, separated by the ground', he exhorts us,

> we need to attend ... to the fluxes of wind and weather. To feel the wind is not to make external, tactile contact with our surroundings but to mingle with them. In this mingling, as we live and breathe, the wind, light and moisture of the sky bind with the substances of the earth in the continual forging of a way through the tangle of life-lines that comprise the land (p. S19)

Such a cosmological and ontological orientation would seem to be more easily born from the experience of humans living in intimate relationship with the land- and weather-scape as these, in turn, interact with one another and shift through time. 'Seasoned inhabitants', Ingold observes, 'know how to read the land as an intimate register of wind and weather' (p. S33). Indeed, Ingold, like myself, has conducted ethnographic fieldwork and lived with hunter-gatherers and horticulturalists, and is primed to experience the world 'in the open'. Animism, he concludes, 'is not a matter of putting life into things but of restoring those things to the movements that gave rise to them' (Ingold p. S31).

Such an orientation need not limit its 'open sensibilities' to what cosmopolitan EuroAmericans might call the 'things of nature', or the 'outdoors'. Temiars are as likely to dream an encounter and receive a song from the conversation coalescing in a room as they are from a forest flower, or from the bamboo tubes played during an indoor ceremony as from a tree-trunk. I have recorded songs from all these sources. Sheltered spaces are, themselves, different from open spaces, particularly because, in a sheltered space, is it less likely that the thunder and lightning spirit-cum-deity ('*ɛŋkuu*') and his younger brother (*'aluj*) will see and respond to human activities. But for Temiars, homes and sheltered spaces are themselves alive with potentially animated spirit; these are not Ingold's impoverished indoor urban dwellers living in a Gibsonian furnished world (Ingold, p. S28) with only drafts to remind them that spirit-in-motion and beings-in-emergence are conceptual possibilities.

To live in such a world is to live with what we might now term an ecological environmental awareness: the environment might indeed strike back if it is treated without respect (see Roseman 1991: 176). Temiars use such an epistemology to explain illness aetiology: pee on a divided tree-trunk and its heart-substance may emerge into motion and bite the offending human's heart, causing illness. Drop your flowered head-wreath thoughtlessly into a swiftly flowing river and your own head-soul may follow it, causing the illness of soul loss. Build your dwelling across the river from where a tributary empties into the same river and you open yourself up to a host of illnesses flowing downstream from that tributary towards your dwelling place.[7]

To extract such illnesses, or find and return lost head-souls, one must rise to the occasion, so to speak, and set spirit in motion through singing and dancing the spirit genres or *nɔŋ* ('way', 'path', 'song', 'song/dance genre') received during dreams, now performed in nighttime, roof-sheltered, healing ceremonies. The imaginal spirit world of the dream is further densified (and, yet again, released into material-immateriality) in the media of ceremony.

Head and voice: fluid-in-motion

Each time I depart from the forest, moving from villages far upstream to those further downstream, eventually to arrive at the frontier Malay villages of the lowlands, I am called before spirit mediums of each village. They call for singing ceremonies, or draw residual *kahyɛk* from their breasts to blow into my heart- and head-soul. 'I tend it like we pat and shape the earth around a young plant shoot', one medium explained his gentle manipulations of my tenuously implanted head-soul, 'and blow in the spirit's cooling liquid to strengthen you for the assaults to come'. 'You've changed now', another commented, 'you've tranced and danced with us; your heart-soul is more labile. It's dangerous, rumbling and roaring, out there. We do this to keep your heart-soul in place'.

Spirit-in-place is the condition of everyday waking life, health, safety. Spirit-in-motion is the condition of dreams, trance, and singing when ritually or temporally circumscribed, and of illness and danger when occurring unexpectedly or excessively outside the contexts of dream and ritual. Abrupt occurrences such as sudden, loud noises, thunder and lightning, voices raised in anger, may cause one to 'be startled' (*kjʉd*), thereby disentangling the head-soul from its locus in the body and setting it into motion, which could result in the illness of soul loss (*rɛywããy*). It was the increase in potential for startle embodied in jostling Land Rover rides on rutted logging roads, or in the sudden noises and flashing lights of the city, for which mediums were preparing me. Techniques for dealing with startle and concomitant soul loss, honed by forest life, are mobilized to cushion the startling sensations of mechanization and urbanization.

Yet this fluid, labile quality of head- or heart-loci, when handled with care, intent, and purposeful contextualization, is fundamental to the flow of spirit that intimately interrelates Temiars with the world around them. This interrelationship is as charged with potential joy as it is with danger. In its most powerful manifestation, when the awakened watersnake (*dangah* < Sanskrit *naga*) of the river, in confluence with the thunder and lightning deity ('*ɛŋkuu*'), unleashes fierce storms and floods (*dɛndʉk*), these whooshing winds have deadly force. Such winds are a far cry from those tousling our hair and brushing our cheeks below the crest of Mount Galeng; yet one implies the other. We often waited out such storms with packs on our backs, ready to run should a house collapse or river change course.

The head-soul *rwaay*, with probable etymological links to the Hebrew-Arabic *ruah, ruakh*, 'breath, breathing, spirit', goes forth with one's voice, particularly in the vocalization of singing (*gnabaag*). While the head-soul is the locus of vocalized speech and song, the lower-portion or 'heart' (*hup*) soul is the locus of stored thought, memory, and feelings associated with memories. Temiar distinctions differ from the Cartesian dichotomy between thought and feeling, and turn rather on the distinction between vocalized expression and inner experience.

When spirit guides sing to mediums during dreams, or sing through them during ceremonies, their head-souls manifest as *kahyɛk*, a cool, spiritual liquid likened to the colourless sap of plants, the clear waters of mountain streams, and morning dew. *Kahyɛk* arches in a watery thread from the jungles and mountains into ceremonial leaf ornaments (Fig. 4). Mediums infuse the substance into the head- and heart-souls of trancers and patients.

The winds brought cool *kahyɛk* across the valley to us from Mount Galeng as we reached the hilltop. Winds carrying fluids, voices carrying the cool spiritual liquid of spirits: a cosmos that, when set in motion, can be used for healing, or, if too excessive or intrusive, might cause thunderstorms or illness.

Duple pulsation: heart and breath

Beating a continuous ostinato, the bamboo tube-players accompanying singing and healing ceremonies produce a duple rhythm (Fig. 5). This rhythm is accentuated by drum and/or gong, alternating HIGH-low, HIGH-low in various rhythmic configurations and tempos. The tube rhythm responds to and inspires changes in the dancers' level of trance intensity. As trance deepens, tube-players subdivide their rhythmic configurations and speed up the tempo. The resulting rhythmic intensification and densification is described spatio-temporally as having become 'crowded'.

Temiars compare the tubes' rhythm – alternating high and low, changeable in pattern and tempo yet continuous – to rhythms of heartbeat and breath. The lower,

Figure 4. Leaf ornaments in performance. Photograph by author.

Figure 5. Patient between healer and chorus beating bamboo tubes against a log. Photograph by author.

interiorized heart/breath locus moving rhythmically (*hup/hnum*) and the upper, vocalized head-soul-in-motion (*rwaay*) are categorically distinct at one level, but conceptually conjoined at the level of inspiration/exhalation of breath, rhythmicity of heartbeat, and the audio-tactile motility of pulsing sound waves. They are also performatively conjoined in the immediacy of their responsiveness to changing circumstances and emotions, as heartbeats flutter, breath quickens, or tube-players hasten their rhythms while watching trance-dancers' movements intensify.

The rhythmic oscillation of tube beats, heartbeat, and inspiration/exhalation find their kinetic correlates in dance movements, several of which are compared with either strolling through space, or strolling in place. Movements executed by one side of the body are counterbalanced by the other: on the HIGH beat, for example, a step forward on the left foot is counterbalanced by the swinging forward of the right hand with the arm crossing the lower torso towards the left. This in turn is counterbalanced by a bend and slight twist of the torso through the sagittal plane from the left towards the right. On the LOW beat, as the left foot is drawn back, the movements of hand, arm, and torso revert as well. Alternate movements occur on the HIGH beat, when the right foot comes forwards. A slight bounce in both heels on every beat conjoins the alternations between right and left, gathering in and dispersing outwards.

This associative series continues into the proprioceptive realm through symbolic and loosely biological entrainment. 'It moves with my heart', a trancer comments on the commensuration of bamboo-tube percussion, swaying dance movements, and heartbeat. 'Exterior' sounds and 'interior' sensations are increasingly experienced in dynamic interrelation as trance-dancers say they are moved, in their hearts, to feel longing. With the opening of this space of longing, the possibility of the arrival of the spirit guides, and trance-dancing with the spirits, appears.

Blurring distinctions, moving energies: shimmer, shudder, and swirl

When I first began transcribing Temiar songs, I focused on melodies and rhythms. But over time, I began to transcribe what I came to realize as equally central to the soundscape of Temiar healing and trance-dancing ceremonies: the sounds of rustling leaves, of blowing to transfer revitalizing spirit liquid, or sucking to remove intrusive soul components (Fig. 6). Leaves such as those gathered from young palms to make leaf whisks and ornaments provide another conduit, along with the medium's voice, for the flow of spirit in vocalization and fluid. Particular spirit guides may request leaves with different fragrances or from different sources, but all share the potential to give songs, conduct *kahyek* through and into humans, or sweep patients clear of intrusive spirit substances.

The forest is visibly dense but acoustically transparent; a hunter is less likely to see his prey than to hear it. And if not by sound, a hunter finds his prey by seeing its motion embodied in trembling leaves. So, too, spirits are witnessed in the trembling of leaves and embodied in the shaking of a leaf whisk. In the process of leaf whisk construction, unfurled budding palm leaves are shredded to increase their waves (Fig. 7). Trembling leaves make a whooshing sound; they also tremble visually. And when they tremble, they disassemble the visual field as they quiver and scattered light shimmers.

In the Temiar community of Bihay, I came across an astounding sight. This Temiar settlement was once surrounded by the dense green growth of the forest; now, in 1994, the forest was denuded. In the headman's house, ceremonial paraphernalia hung from the rafters. But this hanging ritual ornament (*tnamuu'* < Malay, 'tamu', guest) where spirits first alight was not strewn with the usual long, wavy strands of shredded *kwar* palm leaves. Instead, it was made from shredded plastic bags, in which Temiars carry home market-bought goods to replace the forest foods no longer there to hunt or gather.

Wondering what type of spirit would feel at home among the shredded plastic, I asked: 'What kind of spirit guide requested these leaves?'

Figure 6. Musical transcription showing blowing, whistling. The spirit Sri Kelantan Kramaad Raja' Nagaa' sings through medium Abilem Lum (Med.), with chorus (Ch.), bamboo tube stampers (Tube), and *branɔ'* drum (Drm.).

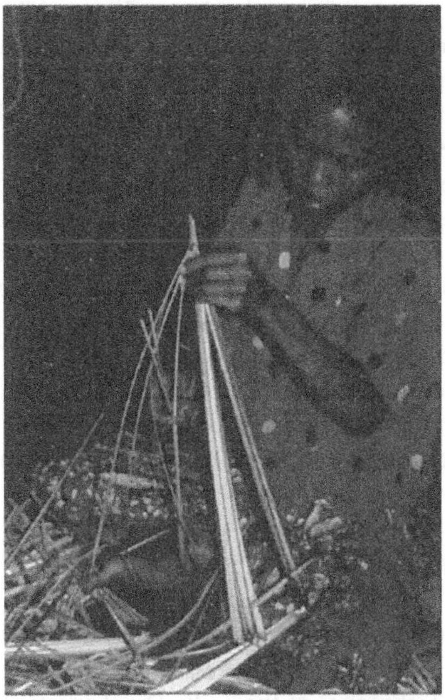

Figure 7. Shredding leaves for ceremonies. Photograph by author.

'As long as they shimmer', answered the headman's wife, implying that these plastic 'leaves' retained a quality essential for attracting and activating spirit. Her answer led me to rethink what, in a pared-down world, was absolutely necessary to enable Temiar ceremonial performances, and what the need for these shiny, winding shreds implied about ceremonial process.

'Is it still possible to heal? Can the cool liquid *kahyɛk* still flow through these "leaves"?' I queried.

A debate ensued, then the headman's wife pointed to the few *cəbaay* forest leaves mixed in with the shredded plastic bags. 'Yes', she replied, 'we can still suck out the illness, and replace it with the spirits' healing liquids. We can still dance, swaying gracefully, shuddering into trance, swirling in our hearts, as the bamboo tubes beat. As long as they quiver'. Temiars say they don't just 'see' the shimmer of the leaves, they experience a sympathetic shivering – in their hearts. When a ceremony is in progress beneath the quivering leaves, the movements of dancers progress from gentle sway into periodic shudders, which replicate shimmer in the kinetic realm.

In one ceremonial performance the medium Abilem Lum, singing a genre received from the annual fruit trees, maintains himself in the state of shuddering. His shudders are translated into the movements of the palm leaf head-wreath he wears, which brushes the hanging kwar leaf ornament. While filming his body shuddering (*kɛnroo'*) during performance, I was able to follow the shudders of his body cinemagraphically from his toes to his head, and up through his shredded palm-leaf head wreath into the hanging leaf ornament upon which spirits first alight, and through which they filter into the room. Were his shudders going up into the rafters, or down through the leaves into his body? Both, he responded later, for spirits may descend momentarily to move through mediums' voices, motions, and ministrations, while mediums and trance-dancers might ascend momentarily to fly with the spirits above the forest canopy.

In performance, then, Temiars employ a variety of tools that 'beg the difference' between sound and silence, light and darkness, motion and stillness, one bodily position and another. Some genres, such as *cincɛɛm*, received from the spirits of deceased humans, beg the difference between one tone and another through increased vibrato. This is displayed in Figure 8 in the acoustical image of spectral analysis, with the oscillation in pitch fundamental and overtones pictured in wavering lines, while the oscillation in dynamics is pictured in colours, with red indicating the loudest point along the continuum of loud-to-soft.[8] Other genres obfuscate tonal differences with melodies that wind and tug like a fast-flowing, winding river (*bar-wɛjwɛ̃ɛ̃j*). Proprioceptively, mediums and trance-dancers describe a sensation of internal 'swirling' (*lɛŋwĩĩŋ*). In this wavering, spiralling state of spirit-in-motion, trancers and mediums momentarily dance with visiting spirit guides, or take their own brief trips circling above the forest canopy in the company of the spirits.

Fluid-in-wind, wind-in-motion

I am impressed how, as sensorial anthropology, ethnomusicology, medical anthropology, and dance ethnology suggest, cultural meanings and socio-cultural changes are encoded and embodied, impressed and expressed, negotiated and transmuted through sensory experience and techniques of the body. The theoretical turns towards processual anthropology, feminist theories of the body politic, and performance theory have aided our sensitivity towards these matters. The associations that Temiars posit among

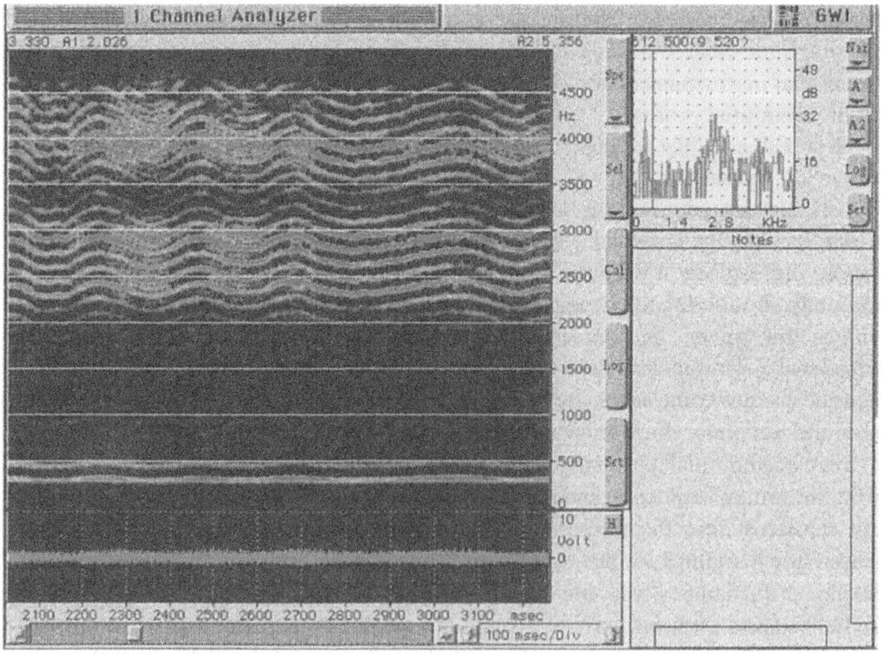

Figure 8. Spectral analysis of a 'single' held tone, showing oscillation in pitch and dynamics. Genre *cincɛɛm*, sung by Busu' Ngah.

wind, fluid, voice, motion, and rhythm constitute a sensibility they call upon during ceremonies to activate the spirits of birds and aeroplanes, river fish and canned sardines, fresh leaves and shredded plastic bags.

Winds carry fluid. Wind-in-motion energizes (and is energized by) trembling leaves and shuddering bodies, precipitating the presence of animated spirit. Leaf whisks shaken while singing distribute the dew-fluid, plant-sap, moist-breath *kahyɛk* of spirits' songs onto and into ceremonial participants. '*Na-papoh na-yelylyel rasan cno' ye*' ', sings Sri Kelantan, the Spirit Princess of Kelantan River and the state through which it wends, in the voice of medium and healer Abilem Lum (see Fig. 6, verse 13, line 2). Shaking his palm leaf whisk over the abdomen of a child with an obstructed bowel, Sri Kelantan sings through him: 'Feel your spirit blossom as my water sprays, my grandchild!' Sucking to remove the obstruction, he then sings images of dispersion and release (Fig. 7, 13-2), waving his leaf whisk to disperse the moisture of the spirits in the breeze of shredded leaves with their leaf dew-sap. Then he blows, cooling the feverish child with spirit liquid *kahyɛk* (Fig. 6, measure 2).[9]

The rhythmic alternation of inspiration and exhalation, sucking and blowing, waving of leaf whisks – like heartbeats, the duple tones and rhythms of tube percussion, and dancers' alternating movements – engenders a swirling, transformational world of excitement, healing, and momentary fulfilment. The whipping up of winds and whirling transformations can equally lead to danger, illness, and excessive longing. As forces of global capital penetrate ever more deeply into the forest, Temiars respond by spiritualizing commodities like the canned sardine, technologies like the aeroplane, and administrative units like the State of Kelantan, creatively engaging those who colonize their lands, bodies, and livelihoods. Here in ceremonial performance, Temiars craft a dance of healing and survival in the context of spirit rituals that have long been called into play when human agency, alone, seems insufficient.

NOTES

This research is based on intensive long-term ethnographic and ethnomusicological fieldwork conducted over a twenty-five-year period, in segments lasting from two years to three months, in 1981-2, 1991, 1992, 1994-5, and 2003. Research is ongoing, and conducted in the Temiar language. Research has been funded by the Social Science Research Council, National Science Foundation, Wenner-Gren Foundation, Asian Cultural Council, National Endowment of the Humanities, and the Guggenheim Foundation.

[1] Musical transcription, textual translation, and further discussion of Busu Puteh's 'Airplane Spirit Song' can be found in Roseman (1996*a*: 176-81; 2002a: 191-4).

[2] The compact disc *Dream songs and healing sounds: in the rainforests of Malaysia* (Smithsonian Folkways Recordings, SF CD 40417) is available through Smithsonian Folkways Recordings (*http://www.folkways.si.edu*) at *http://www.folkways.si.edu/search/AlbumDetails.aspx?ID=2351* and Amazon (*http://www.amazon.co.uk*).

[3] Following Henry Corbin (1966; 1972) and Barbara Tedlock (1987), I call this not quite real, not quite unreal sensory world of dream, memory, and spirit the 'imaginal world'. For further discussion, see Csordas (1996) and Roseman (1991: 54-5).

[4] My earlier writings (e.g. Roseman 1984; 1990; 1991) use the rubric 'setting the cosmos in motion' to elucidate this always-emergent quality of the Temiar life-world. I suggest an intriguing similarity between Temiar ontology and epistemology as expressed in cosmology and performance practice, on the one hand, and post-structural theory, on the other, in Roseman (2002b: 125-6) and Roseman (2000: 52-3).

[5] See Roseman (1991: 36-40) on odour, and (40-5) on *wɔɔg* and *bayang*.

[6] Sound, for example, can have tactile and proprioceptive effects, as when a teenager at a rave dances near the speakers to feel the acoustic shadow of the bass pumping through his body. For futher discussion of the multi-sensory dimensions of sound and other sensory modalities see, among others, Erlmann (2004); Feld & Brenneis (2004); Howes (2004); Panopoulos (2003; 2005); Roseman (2000: 52-3; in press); Stoller (1996).

[7] In an insightful article, Laderman (1981) investigates how empirical observations often inform symbolic classifications, blurring in interesting ways the distinctions between 'science' and 'belief'. See also Parkin (this volume, pp. S42-3) on the physical and symbolic uses of smoke and fumigation.

[8] The colour image of the spectral analysis can be found in the online version of this paper (*http://www.blackwell-synergy.com/loi/JRAI*).

[9] A detailed investigation of this song, its origin, and its use in healings both individual and social, can be found in Roseman (1996*b*).

REFERENCES

BENJAMIN, G. 1967. Temiar religion. Ph.D. dissertation, University of Cambridge.

——— 1979. Indigenous religious systems of the Malay peninsula. In *The imagination of reality: essays in Southeast Asian coherence systems* (eds) A.L. Becker & A. Yengoyan, 9-27. Norword, N.J.: Ablex.

CORBIN, H. 1966. The visionary dream in Islamic spirituality. In *The dream and human societies* (eds) G.E. von Grunebaum & R. Caillois, 381-407. Berkeley: University of California Press.

——— 1972. *Mundus imaginalis*, or the imaginary and the imaginal. *Spring: An Annual of Archetypal Psychology and Jungian Thought*, 1-19.

CSORDAS, T. 1996. Imaginal performance and memory in ritual healing. In *The performance of healing* (eds) C. Laderman & M. Roseman, 91-113. New York: Routledge.

DENTAN, R.K., K. ENDICOTT, A. GOMES & M.B. HOOKER 1997. *Malaysia and the 'Original People': a case study of the impact of development on indigenous peoples*. Boston: Allyn & Bacon.

ERLMANN, V. (ed.) 2004. *Hearing cultures: essays on sound, listening, and modernity*. Oxford: Berg.

FELD, S. & D. BRENNEIS 2004. Doing anthropology in sound. *American Ethnologist* **31**, 461-74.

HOWES, D. (ed.) 2004. *Empire of the senses: the sensual culture reader*. Oxford: Berg.

LADERMAN, C. 1981. Symbolic and empirical reality: a new approach to the analysis of food avoidances. *American Ethnologist* **8**, 468-93.

PANOPOULOS, P. 2003. Animal bells as symbols: sound and hearing in a Greek island village. *Journal of the Royal Anthropological Institute* (N.S.) **9**, 639-56.

——— (ed.) 2005. *From music to sound*. Athens: Alexandria Publications.

ROSEMAN, M. 1984. The social structuring of sound: the Temiar of peninsular Malaysia. *Ethnomusicology* **28**, 441-5.

——— 1990. Head, heart, odor and shadow: the structure of the self, ritual performance and the emotional world. *Ethos* **18**, 227-50. [Reprinted in *The meanings of madness* (ed.) R.J. Castillo, 45-55. Pacific Grove, Calif.: Brookes/Cole, 1997.]

——— 1991. *Healing sounds from the Malaysian rainforest: Temiar music and medicine*. Los Angeles: University of California Press.

——— 1995. *Dream songs and healing sounds: in the rainforests of Malaysia*. Smithsonian Folkways Recordings CD SF40417 (compact disc).

——— 1996*a*. Decolonizing ethnomusicology: when peripheral voices move in from the margins. In *Aflame with music: one hundred years of music at the University of Melbourne* (eds) B. Broadstock, N. Cumming, D. Erdonmez-Grocke, C. Flack, R. McMillan, K. Murphy, S. Robinson & J. Stinson, 167-89. Melbourne: Centre for Studies in Australian Music.

——— 1996*b*. 'Pure products go crazy': rainforest healing in a nation-state. In *The performance of healing* (eds) C. Laderman & M. Roseman, 233-69. New York: Routledge.

——— 2000. Shifting landscapes: mediating modernity in a Malaysian rainforest. *Yearbook for Traditional Music* **32**, 31-66.

——— 2002*a*. Engaging the spirits of modernity: the Temiars. In *Tribal communities in the Malay World: historical, cultural and Social perspectives* (ed.) G. Benjamin & C. Chou, 185-205. Singapore: Institute for Southeast Asian Studies.

——— 2002*b*. Making sense out of modernity. In *New horizons in medical anthropology: essays in honor of Charles Leslie* (eds) M. Nichter & M. Lock, 111-40. New York: Routledge.

——— in press. *Engaging the spirits of modernity*. Los Angeles: University of California Press.

STOLLER, P. 1996. Sounds and things: pulsations of power in Songhay. In *The performance of healing* (eds.) C. Laderman & M. Roseman, 165-84. New York: Routledge.

TEDLOCK, B. (ed.) 1987. *Dreaming: the anthropology and psychology of the imaginal*. Albuquerque: University of New Mexico Press.

5
Khoisan wind: hunting and healing

Chris Low *University of Oxford*

Wind sits at the heart of a nexus of ideas and practice among the southern African 'Khoi'[1] and San peoples. Understandings of wind tie into notions of potency – linked to identity and 'smell essence', spirits, dead people, illness, and contagion. Moving wind is offered by some Khoisan as a rationale for medical treatments, including massage, 'medicinal cuts', and the wearing of powerful animal- or plant-based necklaces and bracelets. Sharing wind essence ties people and animals together across time and space.

Because of persistent 'Western' interest in Khoisan since the seventeenth century, the material available for this discussion of wind is both rich and diverse. Little of the material I draw upon has previously been explicitly associated with notions of wind, despite the clear currency and contiguity of wind ideas across this diverse group of historical and contemporary peoples. The reasons for this, what appears to be essentially a fragmentation of Western understanding, seem to lie equally in the partiality of the ethnographic enterprise and the particularly flexible and slippery nature of Khoisan ideas.

Wind in its many guises is an invisible gift attributed to 'God' – as envisaged by Christianized Khoisan. The gift is not identical but specific. Each living entity has its own wind or smell which is a personalized expression of the breathing divinity and self evident in the act of respiration. Different winds define a particular sort of life, or person, which reveals itself to Khoisan in a 'phenomenology of encounter'. There is continuity between the wind that blows and the wind that people breathe and the winds that move between people, certain animals, and possibly some plants. Wind, often equally conceived as smell, can move between phenomena, embedding itself in the perceiver. The smell is a living connection between one organism and another, enabling one essentially to become the other.

My analysis lays out a Khoisan way of thinking that is drawn from their survival strategies and day-to-day knowledge of the environment and feeds into their ideas of cosmology, health, and the body. I additionally highlight how anthropology has fragmented Khoisan ideas, firstly, by biasing inquiry towards Western categories of interest, and, secondly, by concentrating on cultural microcosms which have disassociated particular Khoisan ideas from their wider Khoisan cultural context. What becomes apparent is the difficulty associated with linguistic representation of Khoisan ideas and how the combination of Khoisan linguistic and ideational flexibility, together with inconsistent anthropological representations, can influence the visibility of coherent Khoisan understandings. Whilst I fully recognize a need to be specific in analysis of separate Khoisan linguistic groups, I nevertheless believe the evidence points very strongly towards a consistent pattern of like thought and behaviour.

What I present is a series of associations, themes, and ideas drawn from historical and recent accounts of Khoisan alongside data and interpretations arising from eight months of fieldwork undertaken in Namibia in 2001 (Low 2004). During the fieldwork I recorded one hundred semi-structured interviews focusing on matters of healing. The interviews were supplemented by informal conversations and participant observation.

Following an outline of how Khoisan encounter wind and what it means to them at a personal level, I proceed to explore how the wind that blows becomes internalized, subsequently manifesting as the motive force behind individuals and 'personalities' in nature. It is in its personal manifestation that wind most equates with smell, and when conceptualized in this manner it becomes a powerful agent of transformation.

I begin this discussion of wind by working from macrocosmic to microcosmic associations – from the wind that blows in the trees to the wind that moves in the body. Whilst this dichotomy serves as a fluid entry point to the discussion, it also reflects an essential Khoisan recognition, acknowledged and articulated at a conversational level, that there are different winds – the ones that blow and the one that gives life. As discussion progresses I hope to illustrate how this juxtaposition dissolves in contexts of personal and group ways of knowing, thinking, and talking.

The following personal accounts of wind are revealing of its wider significance amongst Khoisan. They help illustrate the day-to-day knowledge of wind that informs behaviour and Khoisan concepts of life.

A Damara family from Puros in the northwestern Kaokoveld related how wind affects the growth of food plants and how the action of different winds thereby determines their food collection strategies.[2]

> When winter wind [*sao*: winter, *≠oab*: wind] blows it makes the *xori* fruit come out. It makes it grow and ripen because he blows and pulls the *//hao* plant off [clears the ground of everything so trees can grow]. The east wind [*ai ≠oab*] does not bring anything. He burns the plants, he blows too much and burns the plants. The west wind [*huri ≠oab*] blows and cleans the fruit outside [takes the skin off] and the winter wind makes them ripe – the wild food – and we go out and collect some fruit.

In an informal round-up of the day's work, my translator and friend Suro Ganuses, a Damara woman from Sesfontein, summarized what the wind, *≠oab,* meant to her.[3] Suro talked of relationships between wind, sickness, and animal behaviour.

> The north wind [*ao ≠oab*][4] brings flies, colds, and coughs. The west wind brings biting flies to Khowarib [a nearby settlement]. The west wind brings out snakes, scorpions, and a many-legged khaki-coloured spider-like creature, an *≠harare.* It is hairy with a body about four centimetres long and it sucks the testicles of men. Wind [*≠oab*] is bad for women and young boys up to about the age of 2.

Suro knows of an 18-year-old boy who a short time ago was cycling home to Sesfontein from the coast when he was killed by the east wind. The east wind is a summer wind and is very hot. Whilst the boy cycled, Suro was taking part in a healing dance, an *arus.* A healer at the centre of the dance smelled that something bad was happening far away. The healer knew, after having heard of the death of the boy, that this death lay behind the smell in the dance.[5]

Like Suro's account of the dying cyclist, another Damara woman believed also that the drum at an *arus* that I witnessed was 'not good'. She recognized after the dance that the wind must have been carrying bad news and preventing the drumming from working. The phenomenon of wind carrying news is part of wider Khoisan belief of wind as a transmitter of information, whether specifically concerning people and hunting or more generally.

A Hai//om/Damara man in Tstintsabis, just east of Etosha, replied to my question 'What can you tell me about the wind?' with:

> It is a thing of the God. There is the west to north wind, *//khabasi*, that is not good for hunting. He is the wind from everywhere. The north to south wind, *≠ga ≠oa*, is the best wind for hunting because he just blows straight to one side. The wind from the east, */hû!hub≠oab*, is not good. When he is blowing you are at the side of the wind, it is on your belt, you *//nâi* [*//nâi*, to put on (belt) (Haacke & Eiseb 1999: 90)] the wind so the animal gets your smell.[6]

Ju/'hoansi Bushmen related that there are two types of wind: *mà*, 'the soft one', and *da*, the bad one that twists strongly and penetrates you. Such twisting winds or whirlwinds, also referred to as *//Gauwa ≠a*, or *//Gauwa* smell, after the name of the Ju/'hoansi's chief divinity, are a relatively common feature of the Kalahari.

These various perspectives indicate a particular way of relating to environmental wind. They also demonstrate strong resemblances to nineteenth-century /Xam Bushmen comments on wind. Similar to the smell-wind revealing the death of the cyclist, a /Xam man observed: 'For the wind cries for us, that we may know that another friend is dying'. An alternative /Xam comment draws attention to the relationship between wind, people, and animals: 'Things which walk about hear the wind as it sweeps past our hut. Then the beasts of prey seem to know where we are, for they hear the wind calling to them' (D.F. Bleek 1932: 330-1). Elsewhere again a /Xam Bushman reported: '[A] story is like the wind, it comes from a far-off quarter and we feel it' (Guenther 1999: 139).

Out of her folklore studies, Biesele has presented convincing arguments for continuities between historical Cape /Xam and recent Bushmen by pointing to parallels in their respective hunter-gatherer or recent hunter-gatherer lifestyles which have informed a shared 'imaginative substrate' (1993: 13). Lewis-Williams and Dowson have further emphasized the healing dance as a key arena of continuity that draws on a persistent 'subcontinental cognitive set' (1994: 220). Khoisan relationships with wind, healing, and hunting engage with essential elements of this cognitive set. The archival /Xam material corresponds to findings amongst recent Bushmen and allows the fleshing out of broad patterns of Khoisan thought and behaviour with a significant historical dimension. Collectively the evidence indicates persistent patterns of Khoisan relationships with wind. Khoisan know that wind affects the behaviour of animals and the growth of plants. They also know wind can be dangerous both in association with the storms it brings and through its ability to penetrate people, in a physical and 'potent' sense related to personal smell. To Khoisan as current inhabitants of rural Africa who maintain proximity with the environment and wild animals, wind holds real consequences for their survival, as it has done for Bushmen in the past.

The potency of wind lies in the effects it produces, by which its existence is known. It is equally defined by its ability to connect all that exists in it. For Khoisan, the implications of these two qualities are crucial. Fundamentally, wind is tied to the phenomenon of life. A Hai//om woman, Erika Gubes, stated, 'When the wind blows the people say it is the God who is breathing'.[7] Mirroring or reproducing Christian and other beliefs, the wind or breath of God enters people and animals and gives them life. In wind, God bestows and unites life and removes the footprints of the departed from the dust.

One of my assistants, Frederick //Awaseb, a Hai//om man, gave his account of wind:

> There is a special wind blown by the God [Eloba]. We breathe it in and out from that *//hom*[?], the pipe we eat and swallow food with and the big intestine. If the wind cries inside you die. When lying down you are about to die. The wind is special because you cannot see it. It blows for our life, it is the God who is breathing, even the sun and the moon work with the wind, even the clouds also, they move also with the wind and the rain comes with the wind. Now there is no rain wind but at rain time you see the wind change and it can blow sunrise to sunset and everybody knows it is the time of the rain. The two bad winds *//khabisi ≠oas, ≠nabi ≠oas,* bring sickness but the *sore ≠gâs ≠oab* does not.[8]

Frederick's comments point to the subtle layering of conceptions of wind. In different contexts wind becomes differentiated into special God-given and life-giving wind or wind of a particular nature or identity with particular consequences, such as rain.

The idea of breathing in a life-giving, God-derived wind overlaps with notions of soul. A number of Nama women explained to me that when we breathe in and out we are breathing in and out */om*, soul. It is the wind that works with the heart. In Khoekhoegowab (mainly Nama, Damara, Hai//om) the same word, */om*, is used for breath and soul.

The wind that God gives people and animals is a specific gift of life. The gift is a personal wind that underlies an organism's form and action and constitutes its potency. The gift of life is visible in the breathing, standing, and participation of people and animals in a shared environment. Standing as a synonym for life is a particularly significant idiom amongst the Khoisan.

Lévy-Bruhl provides a helpful way of conceptualizing Khoisan ideas of personal wind. Following Cushing's work on Zuni Indians, he highlighted a link made by 'primitive' peoples between what something does and its form. The form of something both gives it its power and restricts its power (Lévy-Bruhl 1985: 38). The form defines the potency in strength and nature. An elephant is big and strong; it therefore does big and strong things. A bird flies because it has feathers and wings. In human terms personal potency relates to the form of someone – the stock of what they are and what they can do. In a sense, their form is their wind and it is moveable.

In certain contexts the idea of wind/soul/potency runs to plants, but this usage is rare. Smell is more commonly the way plant properties are conceptualized. It is, for instance, the smell of a plant that removes sickness from a body, whereas in treatments that involve human healing or animal medicine, wind or smell tend to be used to describe the active principle.

Wind, environmental awareness, and tracking

A comment from the /Xam Bushmen reiterates the very real role that wind played and plays amongst Khoisan: '[T]he crying of the wind tells the beasts of prey where to find people; and when it blows strongly they can approach the dwelling unheard' (Lloyd 1889: 203). When listened to, or smelled, wind tells Khoisan where animals are. It also tells animals where Khoisan are. The direction of wind must be known if a hunter is to avoid alerting his prey to his presence. Wind connects the hunter with the prey like a thread leading from one body to another. The relationship is a deeper one founded in a wider co-evolution. Wind or smells and pheromones draw and repulse organisms to their mutual ends. When the wind of an animal or plant enters a Khoisan body there is a unity between the two phenomena. Wind smells lock participants into a web of relationships. The essence of one organism connects with another. The consequences can be powerful. The hunter links to the prey; the wind potency of the healer cures the sick; the wind of the sick person transmits his or her illness.

Many animals, and particularly ones of consequence to Khoisan, including predatory lions, hyenas, and strong-smelling aardwolves, clearly spray or rub powerful scent over their respective territories. These markers serve as an anchor of encounter and influence between the animal and the Khoisan who smell them and watch them rubbing and spraying. The scent marker binds the one who encounters them into a powerful relationship of consequence, in a similar bind as that existing between the tracker, the track, and the animal. Potency is both a bound quality of the potential consequences of connection and the formal essence that lies behind that connection. Khoisan use certain animal remedies, particularly from strong-'smelling' animals or animals, which bring significant consequences, because their strong smell carries the essence, wind, or potency of the animal. A person with the medicine becomes potentized and takes on the wind of the source, thus both absorbing the power of the source and serving as a means of protection against it.

The idiom of connection that lies behind wind is particularly evident in relation to the tracking of animals. To my fanciful question, loosely informed by Wilhelm Bleek and Laurens van der Post, of whether or not he knew where animals are without seeing them, a Ju/'hoansi (!Kung) man, Cwi Cucga, answered with the pragmatic comment, 'If I see the footprints I know where they are. You can also use the wind. You cannot go with it, you must turn and start at the end, come through the wind so the animal cannot smell you'.[9] As Cwi's comment suggests, there is a very real sense in which wind is a scent thread. Khoisan tap onto the scent threads that riddle the natural environment and many are very aware of the role that scent plays in survival.

Tom Brown, an American tracker mentored in his youth by an old Apache scout, is highly informative concerning apposite ways of thinking about threads and tracking. The parallels between his Apache-inspired thinking and Khoisan thinking are striking. Brown relates that:

> The first track is the end of a string. At the far end, a being is moving; a mystery dropping a hint about itself every so many feet, telling you more about itself until you can almost see it, even before you come to it. The mystery reveals itself slowly, track by track ... Further on, it will tell you the intimate details of its life and work, until you know the maker of the track like a lifelong friend (1979: 1).

By standing in the path of a track or within the smell of an animal one is joined to that animal. The odour communicates the qualities of the source (Classen 1993: 98) and engages the smeller within the realm of the scent-provider. Through tracking one can know where an animal is, where it sleeps, where it hides, and when it drinks. It is possible to tell what it reacts to and what it ignores, its likes and dislikes, and its interactions with other animals (Brown 1999: 8). Knowing an animal's smell is a part of this knowing of an animal. It is not trite to remember that smells operate amongst people as they do amongst animals. Smells serve as a means of recognition, alerting the receiver to possible threats; they mark territory, attract and repulse. Smells reveal the presence of water and help identify good and bad food. The identification and mapping of a smell in relation to a Khoisan person sits within a constant process of natural awareness. Smells have very real consequences and they constantly feed into Khoisan perceptions.

Tom Brown's Apache mentor did not distinguish between tracking and awareness. Ingold observes that learning in aboriginal contexts is not a transmission of knowledge but an education of attention (2000: 167). As aboriginal peoples extend their awareness, they follow roots of connection and learn links that they perceive between environmental phenomena. Brown talks of the skilled tracker unfolding the tracks and becoming profoundly intimate with the creature at the end of the path. Some !Xõ Bushmen trackers describe how they feel the presence of particular animals before they see them. When a burning sensation develops in their central forehead, just above the eyes, they know their quarry is just ahead of them. The feeling is sometimes accompanied by perspiration under the arms (Liebenberg 2001: 93). The historic /Xam similarly described what Wilhelm Bleek translated as 'presentiments'.

> They feel in their bodies that certain events are going to happen. There is a kind of beating of the flesh, which tells them things. Those who are stupid, do not understand these teachings; they disobey them, and get into trouble, – such as being killed by a lion, etc. – The beatings tell those who understand (1876: 17).

Khoisan ideas have developed from listening to a revealing world. In persistent Khoisan ways of thinking, wind, as mover of scent and potency, tracks through the air that binds together the person with the experiential evidence and events of life. Tracking is intimately tied to how Khoisan think about wind. Like wind, tracks connect with the invisible source.

The notion of threads of connection inherent in tracking and smell plays into the invisible world of the Khoisan shaman. A Ju/'hoansi healer, Kxao ≠oma, described *tsso*, a floating yellow and green string or rope that he sees in the healing dance. The string goes to many places. Khoisan follow it to the dead people.[10] Cwi Cucga sometimes followed the string or rode on the back of animals to the village of the dead people.[11] A Hai//om healer, Gaarugu //Khumob (1904-87), told Ilsa Schatz that when he was lying as if dead on the ground in a trance-like state, his 'soul' would go up to the god, //Gamab, on a long string (Schatz, pers. comm., 3 September 2001). Lebzelter reported that the !Kung god /Nawa similarly moved between heaven and earth on a string (Lebzelter 1934: 49). /Xam Bushmen spoke of ringing strings that vibrated inside them and connected them to the physical and cosmological world. The shaman would hear the string when calling forth the mythical 'rainbull'. The strings snapped at death and the ringing ceased (D.F. Bleek 1936: 134).

Internalizing wind

Khoisan simultaneously hold multiple understandings of wind. Different aspects of wind are conceptualized depending on the context. There is the wind that blows – it is both a normal and everyday wind but at the same time it is special as God's life-giving breath. Whirlwinds are special because they hold dead people who can cause harm. Winds of healers, animals, strangers, and people in dangerous or liminal states can also cause harm. There is wind that enters people with food, particularly fizzy drinks. At the same time, winds are known by their effects, which give them a form or identity – a rainwind or a hot person-killing wind. Ingold observed that in aboriginal cultures causality is personal, not mechanical or biological, and wind is thought of as being like a person (2000: 48). To the Khoisan, wind is like a person or an animal, and as such can be talked to and negotiated with. But regardless of the differences between these various winds, they all have the potential to enter people.

How wind enters the body varies in relation both to the sort of wind and to personal and group perspectives. Most of those whom I encountered said that life-wind entered through the nose and mouth. Many included the ears and some the sexual orifices and the follicles of body hair. Very few seemed to distinguish a trachea from the oesophagus. The life-giving wind, they would say, enters where the food goes down and runs to the stomach. As will be seen, wind in the stomach is a commonly mentioned problem.

In an uneven cognitive step many Khoisan believe that the heart is the principal holder of life-giving wind. In this capacity the heart is home of the soul – the wind gift from God that bestows personality. How the wind gets to the heart as opposed to the stomach is not clear. The heart is believed to activate the lungs and cause them to breathe. The lungs hold wind, but less than does the heart. To address serious illness Khoisan healers travel to God, who is thought in such instances to have stolen the sick person's heart and hence their life-wind and soul. They plead with God for its return. If the heart is given back to the victim, via the shaman, he or she will survive. If not, he or she will die. The idea of the heart moving and causing sickness has a wider context in Khoisan concepts of disease. Many illnesses are attributed to moving organs, although it is only the heart that is envisaged as being taken outside the body.

Similarly to my findings, Guenther observed that amongst Nharo the key organs of the body, the lungs, liver, kidneys and heart, are all 'kept alive and integrated by soul, (*≠i*) ... The heart is the central organ of the body and holds the strongest concentration of *≠i*'. He elaborated that breath, *≠a*, which also means wind, is closely linked with *≠i* and believed by some Nharo to be the embodiment of soul, which is otherwise an immaterial substance (1986: 234, 241).

As noted earlier, the Ju/'hoansi think of whirlwinds as *//Guawa ≠a*, which has been translated as *//Gauwa* smell, although Marshall added that *≠a* 'is not an ordinary odour, which one can actually smell' (1962: 239). '//Gauwa walks in the whirlwind and his smell is in it and death is in it. If a wind passes over the person, the ≠a goes into him, and he will get sick and die' (Marshall 1976: 42). Snyman lists Ju/'hoansi (Žu/h'õasi) regional dialect variations that include both *mà ≠'à*, meaning 'wind' or 'wind with smell in it', and *≠'a*, meaning 'any wind' (1997: appendix 1).

Establishing relationships between different Khoisan languages is a difficult task, in part owing to the inconsistency of Western orthography and the variation in pronunciation and flexibility of ideas that seem characteristic of being Khoisan. Somewhere in the *≠a* and *≠i* complex of ideas lies the relationship of external wind to notions of internal wind, potency, and smell. Guenther has observed that different people have different *≠i* which enables them to do things specific to their *≠i* (1986: 242). This resonates with Lévy-Bruhl's ideas of 'form' and buttresses my link between form and personal wind or potency.

The Nharo association of thought, feeling, or soul with breath and wind was mirrored in beliefs current amongst all the Khoisan groups that I encountered. They linked personal thoughts and motivation, or soul, with their personal God-given wind, which is self-evident in respiration or life. Continuities were further envisaged between personal God-given wind and 'God's breath', or climatic winds.

Snyman established a link between wind and smell amongst Ju/'hoansi. This adds to the complex of ideas in a Ju/'hoan context, but is again applicable across the Khoisan. Smell accordingly also sometimes correlates to form, personal wind, or potency. In view of the relative homogeneity of this complex of ideas, and Nharo being a dialect of Khoe, it also seems quite possible that *≠ai*, meaning 'to think' amongst other Khoe speakers (Nama, Damara, Hai//om; Haacke & Eiseb 1999: 261), echoes the meaning inherent in Nharo *≠i*. Furthermore, despite the linguistic distance between nineteenth-century /Xam and recent Khoisan, Wilhelm Bleek's listing of /Xam *≠i*, as 'to think' (1911: 154), might hint at where a historical ideational continuity might lie, although, in view of the lack of wider evidence, such a conclusion must remain circumspect.

Guenther's interpretation of Nharo beliefs supports my findings concerning the notion of God wind manifesting in people as their mental and physical motivating force. He observes that amongst the Nharo, thought comes originally from the god N!eri, but, once in the body, it 'loses its metaphysical and eschatological aspects and becomes the quintessential substance of the body ... ≠i is the force in man that causes a person to think, wish and act' (1986: 242).

With the immanence of wind in the body, wind or soul motivation becomes tied to physical mechanisms of motivation or action. Many Khoisan recognize a role for blood as something that keeps the body alive and moving. Very often wind is tied to this understanding as something combined with blood or something that runs in blood vessels that enables physical movement (very few Khoisan whom I encountered differentiated between veins and arteries). The idea of bodily movement is accordingly tied to movement of wind. No Khoisan I encountered revealed an indigenous concept equivalent to nerves. A few Khoisan envisaged that the wind moved in the tendons of the body and strong-looking tendons were thought to derive their strength from the wind that filled them. There does not seem to be a clear idea of illness originating from wind stagnating, sticking, or being depleted, but sickness was attributed to the inappropriate moving of the 'wind' of certain organs and what was termed 'sticking pains'.

The complex of ideas surrounding wind, including the gift of life, soul, breath, and personality or individual characteristics, stretches further than being located centrally in the heart and peripherally in the blood. The smell, wind, and breath of someone is held in an essential form in personal smell and sweat, including the 'dirtiness' scraped off a person's skin. Personal wind is also frequently thought to be held in urine and menstrual blood and sometimes in other bodily excretions and secretions. These physical holders of personal wind become vehicles of personal influence beyond the human body. Encounters with wind in these manifestations play a profound role in Khoisan culture.

It is the personal wind of an organism or phenomenon that is envisaged as a powerful force potentially for good or bad depending on the susceptibility and disposition of the recipient. For certain age ranges and genders particular foods are deemed to be sickness-causing because of their potency or smell. They are, accordingly, treated as 'tabooed'. Lee was bewildered that !Kung did not eat zebra because they 'smelled bad', *//'o /'xau* (Lee 1979: 233). This makes sense when one thinks in terms of bad potency, or potency that these people considered too strong for themselves. Namibian Khoe speakers term food taboos *sõxa*. The chest meat of the eland is, for example, deemed *sõxa* for children. If they eat it, the meat is believed to induce coughing sicknesses. The postpositional *xa* of *sõxa* means 'from' or 'rich in' and 'full of' (Haacke & Eiseb 1999: 47;

Hahn 1881: 132). It could well be significant that in Khoe, *sō.b* means 'lung' (Haacke & Eiseb 1999: 203), the prime organ of wind alongside the heart. The meaning of *sōxa* could therefore be construed as 'full of the organ of wind' and essentially full of the wind or essence of the organism. The archival legacy of the Bleeks and Lloyd holds many examples of /Xam beliefs concerning food taboos (e.g. Lloyd 1889: 23), although, without further evidence, why foods were forbidden remains obscure.

Possessing the wind of animals and rain

The Khoisan relationship between personal vehicles of smell, well-being, and their wider environment is well illustrated by consideration of snakes. Snakes hold an important position in Khoisan life both conceptually and pragmatically. The python, cobra and the mamba seem of particular cosmological and epistemological importance. Amongst both 'Khoi' and San there is a tradition of 'poison doctors'. Such doctors have been recorded since Campbell in the early nineteenth century (Schapera 1930: 217) and the phenomenon seems to have persisted continuously into the present. Poison doctors are people who take increasing amounts of snake or scorpion venom mixed with other substances such as urine until such time that the animals will not harm them. The poison can be swallowed or rubbed into incisions cut specifically on the recipient. Importantly, whilst this taking of poison confers immunity, it would be muddle-headed to think of this process in terms of immunization in a scientific 'Western' framework. Protection of Khoisan comes from affinity with the snake; with its smell and its wind.

Laidler, a Cape doctor with ethnographic interests, observed that snakes run away from the smell of 'Hottentot' poison doctors. This smell is held in both sweat and spittle (Laidler 1923(?): 180-1). The Austrian ethnographer Lebzelter (1934: 47) reported that !Kung Bushmen who are not 'poison doctors' can help prevent snake-bite by making cuts on the lower thighs into which they rub grated bits of 'bisob' root. The snakes smell the plant and remain hidden. Laidler has more to say of snakes. At the spot where a snake lives, a cement-like slimy patch develops that can be used as a remedy against all poisonous bites (Laidler 1923(?): 181). Laidler notes that in 1835 Alexander mentioned a great snake he had seen which, when curled up, was as large as a cart-wheel. 'Its presence in the grass was known by its smell, which was offensive to cattle'. If the smell of the great snake was wafted by the wind it could kill a person unless they immediately vomited. The smell of men always made the snake cross (Laidler 1923(?): 127). One of Wilhelm Bleek's informants related similar details:

> An ignorant man having gone to dig up shs-iss, is discovered speechless and motionless, sitting among serpents, by the hole where he had been digging. By a skilful application of sho-iod, the snakes are driven away, taking with them the scent which had injured the man, but leaving the other scent with the plant in the hole. The man is ... restored to speech and motion (1876: 18).

The potency that poison doctors grant themselves through application of snake or scorpion venom sits within a context of a widespread belief that animals, plants, and people are born or *given* specific but transferable characteristics; essentially their 'life-wind' linked to their form. Although the poison doctor undergoes a procedure to become resistant to poison, there is a strong sense in which this process remains a divine gift of a specific animal quality. Amongst historical and recent Khoisan the role of the shaman, healer, or medicine person is perceived as being a bestowal of, possession of, and, in the sense of *sōxa*, being full of a particular potency, received as a gift.

Hewitt notes that amongst the /Xam there were rainmakers, medicine-men and -women, and 'those with a magical influence over certain animals'. He observes that 'rainmakers were said to "possess" rain and game "magicians" to "possess" certain animals' (Hewitt 1986: 287), such as a mantis man possessing a mantis (Lloyd 1889: 22). Hewitt interprets this 'possession' not as control 'but ownership of powers capable of influencing these things' (1986: 287). Both 'Khoi' and San have historically and recently had people who possess or 'work with' rain, animals, and other phenomena. The Bleek archive clearly pointed to people 'possessing' rain and similarly wind, *!khwe*. Schapera concluded from this material that certain /Xam magicians had power over wind and were protected by it (1930: 180). The same applies to possession of the wind of any animal or entity.

Katz observed that Ju/'hoansi healers who are very learned are said to be 'masters or owners of num' (meaning *n/um*, healing potency) (1982: 41). In a real sense they possess potency. Katz, Biesele, and St Denis point to the Ju/'hoan word *kxao* when used in post-positionals as meaning 'ownership' allied to a concept of stewardship, as in the case of *!gukxao*, meaning literally 'owner of water' and having a meaning of a person who cares for a water resource (1997: 16). They add that 'this concept of ownership extends to many commodities and activities in Ju/'hoan life that benefit from stewardship ... healers are stewards and masters'. The Ju/'hoan post-positional *kxoa* seems to overlap ideationally with the Khoe post-positional *xa*, in the sense of being full of potency.

A notable example of Khoisan possessing a phenomenon, or rather the wind of an animal, is the ability of some Khoisan to change into the animal they possess. The phenomenon has been reported since Grevenbroek in 1695 (Schapera 1933: 213). In recent contexts Bushmen have told of changing into lions (e.g. Katz 1982: 227) and leopards (Guenther 1992: 86). The /Xam also changed into jackals and little birds (Lloyd 1889: 22). Amongst /Xam, lions were even noted for turning into other animals, including humans (Lloyd 1889: 206-7). Such fluidity speaks much of the way Khoisan envisage a world of interrelationship where 'all objects are considered to have a measure of similarity' (Silberbauer 1981: 132). The notion of possession and movement of form and qualities between organisms is an expression of how wind moves through and anchors within a body. The /Xam envisaged an essential wind gift that characterized their living form. At death it fluidly left their body to re-engage with the cosmos: 'The wind does thus when we die, our wind blows; for we who are human beings, we possess wind; we make clouds, when we die' (W.H.I. Bleek 1911: 426).

One of the most ethnographically visible examples of possessing, owning, or working with a type of wind can be found amongst the Damara around Sesfontein, where there exists what are known as */nanu aob*, or rainmen. Rainmen are envisaged as possessing what a Damara translator termed the 'rain, spirit, wind thing'. Her difficulty over this translation points to a lack of direct fit with Euro-American concepts. Rainmen typically receive the rainwind or rainspirit by being struck by lightning. Being born with the caul intact or being the child of a rainperson can also bestow the gift. A rainman has something of the rain inside them and hence they can communicate with rain and storms and to this extent control them. If a storm approaches a rainman they will turn to it and say something along the lines of, 'I am one of you, do not harm me'.

Amongst Khoisan whom I encountered, phenomena of poison 'immunity', transformational abilities, or talking to rain all sat within a far wider context of potency movement and anchoring. A host of different attributes or potencies were either given to healers, like the rainwind as a gift at birth, or variously bestowed through an event or deliberately transferred from one healer to another in a ritual. A range of internalized winds or attributes were conceived of as dormant entities which lodged in particular places within a person and awoke under particular circumstances. Similarly to other African peoples, amongst Khoisan these attributes were sometimes referred to as 'spirit helpers' and often thought to be animals such as elephants or certain birds.

Khoisan healers sometimes expressed their strength in terms of how many such entities or talents they were thought to possess. The Damara and some Hai//om refer to these entities as *gaib(s)* or */gais*. One Damara rainman reported possessing thirteen *gais*, including *gais* that enabled him to dance and heal. One healer suggested twenty-one *gais* was the maximum a healer could possess, although such figures proved highly variable. *Gais* are believed to live in particular key areas of the body, including the chest, solar plexus, and the temples and centre of the forehead.

During a healing ceremony I was given the *gais*, or wind, of the mamba, and told afterwards that if I come across a mamba when walking in the bush I must not be afraid but must look at it and say, 'I am one of you, I have the mamba', and with this the snake will let me pass. This way of possessing a *gais* is intimately related to the manner in which a poison doctor possesses resistance to snake-bite. He is one of the snakes and therefore snakes will not harm him. There is much to suggest that this sort of relationship is what lay behind /Xam Bushmen with 'power over' rain or particular animals. By having or owning the wind of an entity, wind binds the source and the host in an intimate relationship. The receiver has the potency of the giver and can negotiate with them, be they snake, lion, or storm, should they need to.

The *gais* within healers communicate as either voices, pictures, or feelings that come to them whilst asleep or awake. Healers describe active *gais* as having 'woken up'. They equate this to the entity standing. At the heart of many Khoisan ideas seems to lie a fundamental juxtaposition between the dead, sleeping, and horizontal and the alive, breathing, standing, and rising. Hahn observed that in Khoikhoi the root *//o*, meaning to die, is related to *//o.b*, illness and disease, and *//om*, to sleep (1881: 127). In Khoisan thought this seems contrasted to what is expressed in Khoe as *Suris*, the sun, and a derivative *sai*, to boil (Hahn 1881: 141). Boiling is tied to life rising, grass growing after the rain, and plants ripening. Laidler similarly noted Nama associations between the sun rising and well-being, growth, and strength, and the sun setting and tiredness, failing strength, and death (1923(?): 135, 152). A strong standing eland is full of wind; the death rattle is the cold, dry, horizontal expiration of life.

The *gais* phenomenon seems closely tied to the widely known concept of Bushmen healers working with a healing substance, termed *n/um* amongst Ju'hoansi and *tsso* amongst Nharo. The substance is said to rest dormant in regions of the abdomen, often thought near the spine and termed variously *//gabas* or *//gebesi* in Ju/'hoansi. The 'healing energy' is sometimes conceived by Bushmen as arrows and the *//gabas* as the home of arrows. At a healing dance Bushmen healers dance until the energy wakes up, grows hot, like a boiling sensation, and moves up their body. Lee noted that *n/um* is symbolically related to *n!um*, which refers to boiling water, ripening plants, and, in a joking manner, the ripening of young maidens (1967: 33). Depending on the context and the aim of the ritual, either *n/um*, its equivalent, or ethereal arrows are said to be moved between healers, patients, divinities, dead people, or 'lay' people for mainly good but also bad intention. The invisible *n/um* and the ethereal arrows share in wind's elusive but effective nature. Boiling and ripening echo the generative properties of wind. There is a collective sense in which each idea feeds and supports the other.

Wind feeds not only into ideas of moving powerful arrows but also into the unseeable moving power of witchcraft, which, like wind, is known by its effects. Although witchcraft is not typically associated with Bushmen, contexts have been recorded since the /Xam in which potency or ethereal arrows have been deliberately directed at others for ill effect (e.g. Vedder 1966 [1938]: 88). Whilst such accounts may be attributed to acculturative influence, there is a broad context of shooting potency to kill or freeze game, including, for example, the springbok and dassie (Lewis-Williams 1986: 249), or, amongst the Damara, of a stare of a person inadvertently transferring harmful wind, or bad thoughts, *≠ais*, to another person, and having the effect of clogging their throat. Drawing on similar understanding, some Damara also believe a dog's stare may terminate a pregnancy (Low 2004: 237). As the alive and divine have wind that can deliberately or otherwise harm Khoisan, so too do the dead. The wind or smell of dead people, known as *//gauwasi* amongst Ju/'hoansi, is often thought a cause of sickness.

The notion of the smell or essence of dead people blowing into and lodging within others has strong parallels with ideas of spirit possession. Anthropologists have typically not associated the Khoisan with possession beliefs, although the idea has some currency (Barnard 1979: 72). When one contextualizes the notion of dead people entering a body and operating within it within the concepts of *gais* and spirit helpers, the spirit possession beliefs of other Africans do not seem essentially different from those encountered amongst the Bushmen. The difference seems to be more a matter of degree and cultural emphasis than a distinct difference of belief structures.

Anthropologists and archaeologists of Bushmen have long acknowledged the important role of 'potency' in Bushman contexts of hunting and healing. But to date potency has not been tied to ideas of wind. Marshall observed that the word *gaoxa* was used by !Kung both for the omnipotence of the great God 'which he was so mysteriously able to create for himself', and 'the special potent "spiritual" medicine which the great God puts into the medicine men, the curing power' (1962: 227). *Gaoxa* seems to reflect a wider Khoisan belief in the power of life and the power that feeds through as a gift to the medicine-men. This power speaks of the wind of life. The breath of God becomes immanent in people and abundant or of a particularly powerful nature in healers.

Medicinal cuts

Different forms of wind enter the body in different ways. Besides the anatomical routes, which primarily concern the entry of 'breathing wind' or illness-causing winds, potent winds have their own means of entry. Winds that bring potency to healers may enter via a lightning strike into the body, by hereditary means or birth circumstances, by eating smelly and *sõxa* food, and by specific rituals of 'putting in' *gais*. As we considered with poison doctors, potency can, like *gais*, also be deliberately transferred. Many Khoisan still treat sickness by introducing potency medicines into the patient. Similarly, potency medicine is used to give certain attributes to people. Better hunting skill is one of the most common instances when potency is used in this manner.

Potency may be given to someone by rubbing the potent source into a small cut or series of cuts in the body. The potent source is usually a part of a potent animal. Often this is the skin or hoof of a kudu or eland. Making 'medicinal cuts' in this manner to transfer wind properties should not be confused with bleeding. Bleeding is a common health-related practice amongst Khoisan, and is linked to notions of 'dirty blood' needing to be expelled (Low 2004: 218).

To improve hunting skills a Ju/'hoansi healer, /Kunta Bo, related, similarly to other Khoisan, that one must take small slithers of an animal's para-spinal muscle and bicep tendon, burn them until black, mix them with fat, and rub the mixture into three small cuts on the bow-drawstring-pulling arm.[12] One cut is about an inch proximal to the elbow on the bicep tendon, another about two inches in line with the first cut, towards the shoulder, and a third on the central lateral border of the shoulder, in the deltoid muscle. /Kunta Bo elaborated that the bicep tendon of the animal is used 'to make the bow arm good' and the para-spinal muscle because, 'if the animal stands up you see him. If you come near he will not feel you coming'. It would seem that what is inserted is some of the bicep muscle that is responsible for the running legs of the animal, which makes it both strong and evasive, as well as the back muscle, which allows it to stand up and makes it easier to hunt. The hunter thereby takes in those abilities of the animal, conceptualized in terms of its winds or particular potencies.

There is some variation in the position of the cuts used to improve hunting skills, as there is in medicinal cuts. Another Ju/'hoansi man, Boo Sakambanda, used the hair of animals, particularly the kudu or eland, taken from the area where the neck meets the shoulders. He burned the hairs, powdered them, and mixed them with powder from the root of a *≠nuar* plant and a *≠nae ≠nay* tree. The mixture was then rubbed into cuts on the wrist and elbow.[13]

Medicinal cuts into which substances are inserted are made for many reasons, including a 'traditional' idea of children's sicknesses, leg pain, back ache, and abdominal problems. A key example of a cut made for health reasons concerns the use of variously kudu skin or eland skin or horn being rubbed into cuts made in the pectoral muscle, just above each nipple of a child, to 'make them strong'. Parents try to ensure that their children are protected from other strong, dangerous playmates who already have been treated in this manner by carrying out the procedure on their own children. I encountered this phenomenon amongst Nama, Damara, and Hai//om. As an alternative to cutting, a child may wear a piece of the animal skin, either as a necklace or tied diagonally from shoulder to waist. This latter way of wearing the skin is termed *//hobe* amongst the Damara and Nama. One Nharo Bushman suggested they used eland skin in a similar manner for similar reasons. That one 'strong' child could make another ill whilst playing with them was attributed to the wind of the kudu or eland being too strong for the unprotected child. The wind is thought to pass between the children. The medicinal cut or wearing of the animal part bestows protective wind.

The broad idea of wind of one entity entering into another and sharing its essence, power, or identity transforms slightly in the context of plant extracts being introduced into medicinal cuts. As noted, these are said by some Khoisan to work because of the smell of the plant entering and working inside the body. A suitable plant will go to the site of sickness because it smells it, or alternatively the smell of the plant takes out the sickness. This identifying and locating sickness by smell is an idea that runs throughout Khoisan healing practices. Lebzelter noted that Bushmen treated a poison dart wound by applying a glowing piece of wood to the body. He observed that Bushmen believed the poison would 'smell' the warmth and gather around the heated area. The poison could then be released from the body by cutting at the heated area where the poison had accumulated (Lebzelter 1934: 47). Ju/'hoansi Kunta Bo, like other

Khoisan healers, knows who is sick around the healing fire because he smells them. He stated that 'you cannot ask them anything, you must just go up to them and heal them'. He knows two sickness smells, one like blood and one that 'is not good, like a rotten thing'.

In healing dance scenarios, once Khoi and San healers have focused on a sick person, they often try to remove the sickness by rubbing their head on the spot, stroking the area, or 'snoring', 'sniffing', 'sucking', or 'snorting' the sickness up and out. The nuances of the procedure vary amongst different groups. Damara rainmen whom I encountered sucked up a sickness and snorted it out into a fire, where it was destroyed. These healers danced to waken the rain- or windspirit within them. If it became too strong for one healer, he or she might collapse or release the build-up by blowing the windspirit into the ears of another healer. Bushmen healers similarly sucked out illness with their mouths. Dorothea Bleek recorded that Bushmen healers, *t/o k?au*, from central Angola extracted evil by smelling and snoring (1928: 124). In the 1770s Gordon reported that he encountered a Bushman snorting out an evil spirit or devil from her son that looked like a cobra (1988: 216). The /Xam healers 'snored' sick people with their noses and claimed to snore out illness-causing entities, including miniature lions, butterflies, and sticks (D.F. Bleek 1935: 3, 5). Often this was accompanied by a bleeding nose. In these episodes of moving sickness, the disease-causing entity is conceptually given the insubstantial quality of wind, which can settle, become dormant, move, and be moved.

Sometimes healing amongst Khoisan involves an invisible and voluntary and involuntary exchange of arrows between the healer and the afflicted. Many Khoisan believe that sickness is caused by arrows fired by a divinity into people. These invisible arrows again share wind's invisible quality for moving potency. Unlike wind transfer, arrows suggest a precision in their direction. A Hai//om medicine-man told Ilsa Schatz that he sneazed out //Gamab's harmful arrows when he treated people (Schatz, pers. comm., 3 September 2001). Some Khoi massagers reported that their patients sometimes involuntarily 'arrow' them, or similarly that the wind of the patient will go into them. Both the arrows and the wind must be expelled from a healer's body. The invisible arrows shot between healers, other people, animals, and divinities are intimately related to notions of moving wind, smell, and potency.

In the same manner that medicinal cuts introduce healing potency of animals or plants into Khoisan bodies, the personal vehicles of Khoisan potency are also part of the arsenal of Khoisan healing. Anthropologists have long observed that Khoisan shamans rub sweat on one another or on patients during healing rituals. Guenther interprets this sweat as therapeutically efficacious because it is an exudation of *n/um* (1999: 184). Another way of thinking about this entails recognizing that sweat, like the smell often intrinsic to it, carries a person's essence or potency. Similarly, in certain healing contexts patients are smeared with the healer's skin scrapings or dirtiness, termed */urib* amongst Khoe speakers, or it will be rubbed into medicinal cuts, or they might be instructed to wear an article of clothing imbued with the healer's dirtiness. Dirtiness, like sweat, transfers potency. The link with potency runs further still to the use of urine and spittle. Treatments involving urine have been observed amongst Khoisan since the late seventeenth century (Schapera 1933: 243) and spittle since the early eighteenth century (Kolben 1731 [1719]: 305). Like these other body fluids, blood is also exchanged between people and people and animals to transfer healing potency. It was recent practice amongst Sesfontein Damara to treat children's sicknesses by administering a drink of a spoonful of blood from a dog's ear. Some Damara treat gonorrhoea by inserting goat blood into medicinal cuts or rubbing the body with a mixture of goat and monitor lizard blood.

In contrast to the beneficial purpose of medicinal cuts, the idea of poisons and *sōxa* foods indicates the way in which potency can be not only a healing substance but also a harmful substance. The dangers of menstruation are a clear example wherein personal wind is specifically envisaged as being harmful. The dangers of menses have been recorded since Kolben (1731 [1719]: 147). Sleeping with menstruating women or even being near them can induce sickness because of their strong-smelling wind. According to Salphina Janjies, a Damara woman in Swakopmund, normal menstruation, *//khâ/ aesen* (*/ khâ*, moon, month sickness) is termed *≠au !gâ*, or slow, not smelly, menses. Strong, smelly menses that makes a person feel 'drunk' is termed *//ho!gâ*. It is the strong menses that can make a child or adult sick. A woman, or her smell, will *nā* the men, meaning to 'bite' them.

That there is a distinction between normal and strong and smelly menses suggests that why a menstruating woman is dangerous might be more related to the extent of her pain and sickness or smell than simply her state of menstruation. The fact that strong-smelling men are also known to make others sick reinforces the role that the actual smell seems to play. Less clearly, in other contexts it does not seem to be the smell that is the important factor but a more abstract wind-smell. /Kunta Bo related that if one's partner dies and is buried, a Bushman must cut themselves and put in the plant *!Gube* mixed with water and wash themselves so that the smell of their dead partner will not make others sick. Additionally, he reported that smelling a woman who gives birth to a child that imminently dies, or is dead, could induce neck pain, *pa deh*. Ju/'hoansi Debe Dam explained that it is the smell that goes on the wind and into the neck that is the problem.

More abstractly still, the Khoisan, like neighbouring Bantu speakers, believe that if a bird passes overhead, or particularly casts its shadow on the head of an infant, the shadow or the smell of the bird, travelling on the wind, may enter the child or person and cause illness. In children this is typically associated with the sinking or sticking of the anterior fontanel of the skull.

In addition to these arenas of negative wind and smell influence, there is a related concept that simply being exposed to unfamiliar winds of people can cause sickness. Salphina Janjies suggested that the increased mobility of people and subsequent exposure to so many different people's winds lay behind increases in disease statistics in recent Namibia. Her observation relates to the anthropological identification of smell as a marker of identity and reinforcer of 'otherness'.

Wind and moving organs

There is a widespread awareness amongst Khoisan of problems that arise from a more general wind entering the body, wherein specific organs become afflicted and consequently move. Amongst Bushmen the belief of organ movement seems mainly limited to heart movement, whilst many Khoi would also include the liver, gall bladder, uterus, placenta, intestines, testicles, and the *!arab*. The *!arab* seems to equate to the aortic artery palpable through the abdomen. Certain organs, particularly the *!arab* and the heart, are often referred to as 'standing'. Standing is a way of expressing organ over-excitement or physical prominence. Khoekhoe women relate that if the uterus moves into the intestines the uterus will stand up. Massaging must be used to correctly relocate moving and standing organs to their proper positions. The standing idea seems connected to similar notions recorded by Dorothea Bleek amongst later nineteenth-century Cape /Xam Bushmen. A /Xam healer reported that when she took illness-causing entities out of a sick person's body into her own it agitated her arteries. She had to return home for a massage to make her arteries 'lie down' (D.F. Bleek cited by Hewitt 1986: 294).

Some Khoi believe that if wind enters the body and meets the uterus it can 'turn the face' of a woman and make the tendons hard. Healers will massage the 'spastic' tissue and muscle to restore mobility. Breathing too much or consuming certain foods, especially fizzy drinks, may give the stomach too much wind. Many Damara women exercise judicious wearing of headscarves and substantial undergarments to prevent the ingress of wind whilst riding in cars. Women are particularly vulnerable to wind shortly after giving birth. If they are exposed to a cold wind and they are not sufficiently wrapped up they may develop *//khas ≠oab*, placenta wind. There is a variable understanding that either the placenta or the wind of the placenta then moves into the head and renders the woman mad. The treatment entails placing the warm lid of a cooking pot on the woman's head. The warmth drives the placenta back to its normal position. In a list of 'traditional' sicknesses an elderly Nama woman included *≠oa ≠gaa* literally, 'wind put in' or 'going mad'.

When Khoisan massage, they do so not only to attempt to relocate organs but also to examine the hardness of tendons. This is related to too much wind and functional stiffness. Some Khoisan expressed an explicit desire to move the blood around the body away from 'dry' points. This indicates the possibility of the idea of sticking wind, although this was not an expression that I encountered. After many Khoisan massage, they crack their knuckles, which they say ensures that a patient's sickness 'goes out and stays out'. This joint-popping fits into a wider context of massage procedures that channel the patient's sickness out from the massage practitioner and seem to relate to movement of wind.

When the Damara and Nama massage, it is customary to release loud long belches – referred to as *!gai*. This is envisaged as the sickness wind of the patient being released through the practitioner. Some Khoekhoe will also pop their cheek with their finger, which is referred to by the verb *abu*. This helps relocate a dislocated organ. Similarly, some Khwe massagers draw their hands off a patient's body and click their fingers to release the sickness. The idea of the healer pulling wind sickness out and expelling it through him- or herself has parallels amongst other Bushmen healers who pull arrows of sickness and release them through the top of the skull or their cervico-dorsal junction, or by flicking out their arms.

Conclusion

The Khoisan are known for the particularly inchoate nature of their ideas. There is, however, an identifiably consistent set of ideas linked to wind that operate at the heart of their worldview. Like many other peoples, they merge notions of wind, breath, and smell. The Khoisan face of the wind phenomenon is, however, distinctive in regard to their concepts of potency and movement of potency. Working from linguistic principles, Silberbauer suggested that *G/wi* Bushmen do not make the structural distinction human versus non-human and animate versus inanimate. He indeed went further to say that all objects are considered to have a measure of similarity (Silberbauer 1981: 132). This perspective, which seems pertinent to the thinking of Khoisan broadly, operates alongside an education of awareness that has historically alerted Khoisan to what is special and meaningful in different forms of organic and inorganic life that they encounter. There is a link between the sort of idea proposed by Lévy-Bruhl concerning animal forms dictating their identity and power and Khoisan ideas of potency, wind, and smell. A phenomenon is known for what is special about it, and that speciality, be it 'windness' or 'lionness', and so on, is held in both secretions and excretions of an organism or the effect it can have on the world around it. The power of the phenomenon to influence the world around it is conceived as potency. In Khoisan idiom, active potency is conceived as being 'awoken' and 'standing', as opposed to dormant and lying.

Wind, smell, and, to a lesser extent, arrows and shadow are the means through which Khoisan envisage potency, or the ability of one thing to affect another in a particular manner, moving between phenomena. That all phenomena share a measure of similarity gives licence to potency to enter, merge with, and transform the recipient. Wind, or potency, is a gift of life that lodges in the body. A Hai//om healer once told me that each person must 'dance their own dance'. The abilities different people hold are conceived by Khoisan as gifts, lodged in the body and reflected in the body. The first gift is the gift of life-wind. A person's wind develops as they participate in a world of winds and smells and their own wind reaches out to ripple the world beyond them. Healers can control wind to transform themselves. They can follow the tracks of wind and smell through the physical and spiritual world and pull and push wind through themselves and into others to restore the gift of life.

My research began with an attempt to identify and explain healing strategies. Perhaps not surprisingly, it soon became apparent that although medicine was a useful entry point and category of inquiry, the edges of what constituted healing as opposed to other life-enhancing strategies were distinctly hazy. Similarly, the explanations behind medical practice were tied not to intimate knowledge of metabolic function and recognizably 'medical' means of interaction but to observations, actions, explanations, and rituals played out in the far wider field of Khoisan life. For the Khoisan issues of health are intimately related to issues of potency. Potency is a word long applied to the healing 'energy' circulated at trance healing dances and to the power thought inherent in certain animals or other phenomena, particularly rain. Potency is shared and exchanged during healing dances. The dances involve significant proportions of communities and sometimes people from different groups. This movement of potency has been envisaged as an egalitarian binding together of people who need one another to survive.

Wind is not something readily talked about by Khoisan. They do not have a clear conception of wind as a binding or connecting force but then neither do they of potency. Potency is a theoretical abstraction for diverse substances and events attributed with power in the lives of Khoisan. An underlying role for wind does, however, come out in many explanations of powerful actions and events, including those that involve potency. Wind provides a Khoisan way of explaining invisible action at a distance. Depending on the event, different qualities of wind are drawn upon in different explanations: its ability to chill, overheat, howl, and smell, and to bring and carry things, including rain and illness. At times wind is dance potency. There is a sense in which people working together are bound together in moving air and, furthermore, that wind is deliberately shared in actions of mutual support. At other times again, wind is diminutized climatic wind or God-breath, 'the same but different'; at other times still, its meaning and role overlap with arrows, shadows, and personal smell essence. The multivalent sensual quality of wind and its boundary-crossing powerful nature give it a 'good to think with' status among the more and less inchoate ideas of these recent hunter-gatherers.

NOTES

I am very grateful to the Economic and Social Research Council for the funding of my D.Phil. research, which provides the background to this paper. The permission was sought and obtained for the presentation of personal names of interviewees mentioned in the paper.

[1] I use the artificial construct 'Khoi' to refer to Nama and Damara, as opposed to 'Khoe', which as a linguistic category includes certain San peoples as well.

[2] Interview: Elizabeth Tauros, recorded Sesfontein, 19 July 2001.

[3] Noted Sesfontein, 6 June 2001.

[4] Haacke and Eiseb (1999: 166) list this as the east wind.

[5] Noted Sesfontein, 6 June 2001.

[6] Jan Serengboom, recorded Tsintsabis, 1 August 2001.

[7] Recorded Tsumeb, 6 August 2001.

[8] Recorded Tsintsabis, 3 August 2001. Dom(mi) is the usual Khoekhoegowab word for throat.

[9] Recorded //aru (Xaru), 23 August 2001.

[10] Recorded //aru, 21 August 2001.

[11] Recorded //aru, 23 August 2001.

[12] Recorded Tsumkwe, 26 August 2001.

[13] Recorded Tsumkwe, 28 August 2001.

REFERENCES

Barnard, A. 1979. Nharo Bushmen medicine and medicine men. *Africa* **49**, 68-80.

Biesele, M. 1993. *Women like meat: the folklore and foraging ideology of the Kalahari Ju/'hoan*. Bloomington: Indiana University Press.

Bleek, D.F. 1928. Bushmen of central Angola. *Bantu Studies* **3**, 105-26.

——— 1932. Customs and belief of the /Xam Bushmen. *Bantu Studies* **6**, 323-42.

——— 1935. Belief and customs of the /Xam Bushmen. *Bantu Studies* **9**, 1-47.

——— 1936. Customs and belief of the /Xam Bushmen. *Bantu Studies* **10**, 131-44.

Bleek, W.H.I. 1876. *Second report Concerning Bushman researches*. London.

——— 1911. *Specimens of Bushmen folklore collected by the late W.H.I. Bleek and L.C. Lloyd*. London: George Allen & Co.

Brown, T. 1979. *The tracker: the story of Tom Brown, Jr. as told by William Jon Watkins*. New York: Berkley Books.

——— 1999. *The science and art of tracking: nature's path to spiritual discovery*. New York: Berkley Books.

Classen, C. 1993. *Worlds of sense: exploring the senses in history and across cultures*. London: Routledge.

Gordon, R.J. 1988. *Cape travels, 1777 to 1786* (ed.) P.E. Raper & M. Boucher. Johannesburg: Brenthurst.

Guenther, M. 1986. *The Nharo Bushmen of Botswana: tradition and change*. (Quellen zur Khoisan-Forschung **3**). Hamburg: Helmut Buske Verlag.

——— 1992. Not a Bushman thing: witchcraft among Bushmen and hunter-gatherers. *Anthropos* **87**, 83-107.

——— 1999. *Tricksters and trancers: Bushman religion and society*. Bloomington: Indiana University Press.

Haacke, W.H.G. & E. Eiseb 1999. *Khoekhoegowab-English/English-Khoekhoegowab Glossary/Mîdi Saogub*. Windhoek: Gamsberg-Macmillan.

Hahn, T. 1881. *Tsuni-//Goam: the supreme being of the Khoikhoi*. London.

Hewitt, R.L. 1986. *Structure, meaning, and ritual in the narratives of the southern San*. (Quellen zur Khoisan-Forschung **2**). Hamburg: Helmut Buske Verlag.

Ingold, T. 2000. *The perception of the environment: essays in livelihood, dwelling and skill*. London: Routledge.

Katz, R. 1982. *Boiling energy: community healing among the Kalahari Kung*. Cambridge, Mass.: Harvard University Press.

——— M. Biesele & V. St Denis 1997. *Healing makes our hearts happy: spirituality and cultural transformation among the Kalahari Ju/'hoansi*. Rochester, Vt: Inner Traditions.

Kolben, P. 1731 [1719]. *The present state of the Cape of Good Hope*, vol. **1**. London.

Laidler, P.W. 1923(?). Manners, medicine and magic of the Cape Hottentots. University of Cape Town. TS.

Lebzelter, V. 1934. *Rassen und Kulturen in Südafrika: wissenschafliche Ergebnisse einer Forschungsreise nach Süd und Südwestafrika in den Jahren 1926-1928*, vol. **2**. Leipzig: K. Hiersemann.

Lee, R.B. 1967. Trance cure of the !Kung Bushmen. *Natural History* **76**: **9**, 30-7.

——— 1979. *The !Kung San: men, women and work in a foraging society*. Cambridge: University Press.

Lévy-Bruhl, L. 1985. *How natives think*. Princeton: University Press.

LEWIS-WILLIAMS, J.D. 1986. Paintings of power: ethnography and rock art in southern Africa. In *Past and future of !Kung ethnography: critical reflections and past perspectives. Essays in honour of Lorna Marshall* (eds) M. Biesele, R. Gordon, R. Lee, 231-73. (Quellen zur Khoisan-Forschung **4**). Hamburg: Helmut Buske Verlag.

——— & T.A. DOWSON 1994. Aspects of rock art research: a critical retrospect. In *Contested images: diversity in Southern African rock art research* (eds) T.A. Dowson & J.D. LEWIS-WILLIAMS, 201-21. Johannesburg: Witwaterstrand University Press.

LIEBENBERG, L. 2001. *The art of tracking: the origin of science*. Claremont, South Africa: David Philip.

LLOYD, L.C. 1889. *A short account of further Bushman material collected by L.C. Lloyd*. London.

LOW, C.H. 2004. Khoisan healing: understandings, ideas and practices. D.Phil. thesis, University of Oxford.

MARSHALL, L.K. 1962. !Kung Bushman religious beliefs. *Africa* **32**, 221-52.

——— 1976, *The !Kung of Nyae Nyae*. Cambridge, Mass.: Harvard University Press.

SCHAPERA, I. 1930. *The Khoisan peoples of South Africa: Bushmen and Hottentots*. London: George Routledge.

——— (ed.) 1933. *The early Cape Hottentots described in the writings of Olfert Dapper (1668), Willem Ten Rhyne (1686) and Johannes Gulielmus De Grevenbroek (1695)*. Cape Town: The Van Riebeek Society.

SILBERBAUER, G.B. 1981. *Hunter and habitat in the central Kalahari Desert*. Cambridge: University Press.

SNYMAN, J.W. 1997. A preliminary classification of the !Xuu and Zu/'hoansi dialects. In Namibian Languages: Reports and Papers, *Namibian African Studies 4* (eds) W.H.G. Haacke & E.D. Elderman, 21-106. Cologne: Rüdiger Köppe.

VEDDER, H. 1966 [1938]. *South West Africa in early times: being the Story of South West Africa up to the date of Maherero's death in 1890*. London: Frank Cass.

6
Time to move: winds and the political economy of space in Andamanese culture

VISHVAJIT PANDYA *DA-IICT, Gandhinagar, Gujurat*

Winds which flow through any given space at any given time invariably bring about changes in social structure and social practice. Felt as an invisible force, winds exert compelling powers over the human body's sensory system, producing culture- and context-specific discourses. For us, expressions such as 'winds of change' that are 'inevitable' or the more foreboding 'calm before the storm' are indicative of the range of ideas about wind, which make it symbolic and metaphorically a rich field of human experience. Winds in a sense constitute a significant index of both seasonal transformations and corresponding changes in bodily and social practice. The human body and winds together form a field in which cultural strategies are evolved, in relation to given meteorological and anemological conditions that often have a discernible structural pattern. For most humans, the concern is vulnerability to wind conditions and efforts to minimize it. As a result, aerodynamics is a design issue for various forms of material culture in our world.

A longitudinally arranged cluster of islands in the Bay of Bengal (6° to 14° north latitude and 92° to 94° east longitude) forms India's union territory of the Andaman Islands. Today the total area of 6,408 square kilometres has a population of more than 356,000 and about 85 per cent of it is covered by forest. From 1788, attempts to explore and colonize the islands were met with resistance from the tribal people, who were the sole occupants of the large territory, identified by various dialect groups. The situation changed from 1858, when the British finally set up control of the islands and Andaman islanders experienced a major decline in their number in relation to an increasing number of non-tribal settlers. Today not more then 450 individuals are identifiable as descendants of the Andamanese, located in four different parts of Andaman Island. Contemporary cultural contexts and social situations for the Andaman islanders have dramatically transformed from the classical ethnographic accounts such as given by E.H. Man (1932 [1882]) and Radcliffe-Brown (1964 [1922]). None the less, as in the classic monograph on the islanders (Radcliffe-Brown 1964 [1922]: 142, 147-8, 157, 178, 195), aspects of winds and spirits (Leach 1971) continue to occupy a prominent place among the Ongee and Jarwa tribal groups. This paper aims to analyse how the Ongees and Jarwas design their practices in relation to winds and spirits, and, furthermore, how these practices structure the relationship of humans with winds and spirits.[1]

For the Andamanese, winds are indexical of the powerful presence of spirits. The arrival and departure of winds from specific directions are indicators of the traffic of powerful and angry spirits moving within the Andamanese space, a space that Andamanese also share with spirits and animals (Pandya 1993; 2005). For the Andamanese, the differentiation of places becomes possible by recognizing the presence of different winds flowing through each place. Both the winds and spirits are not visible but felt in the form of changing temperatures and smells. The experience of winds and spirits, brought together by smells, is culturally made visually concrete by smoke and clay paints on the body that either release or confine the smell of the human beings (Pandya 1993: 105-163). For the hunters and gatherers of the Andaman Islands, specifically the remaining 95 Ongees and 282 Jarwas among whom I have been conducting field research, time is experienced in the form of the varying motion of winds and spirits through places in which they move. Conceptually the two basic seasons that the islanders experience in terms of wind direction bringing rains and its effect on the islanders occupying the resource areas to hunt and gather can be represented as shown in Figure 1.

The question is how the Andamanese strive to create periodically what could be described as the structure of a 'windless space' in between the two durations associated with two distinct directions of winds that 'fill up the space'. By culturally creating

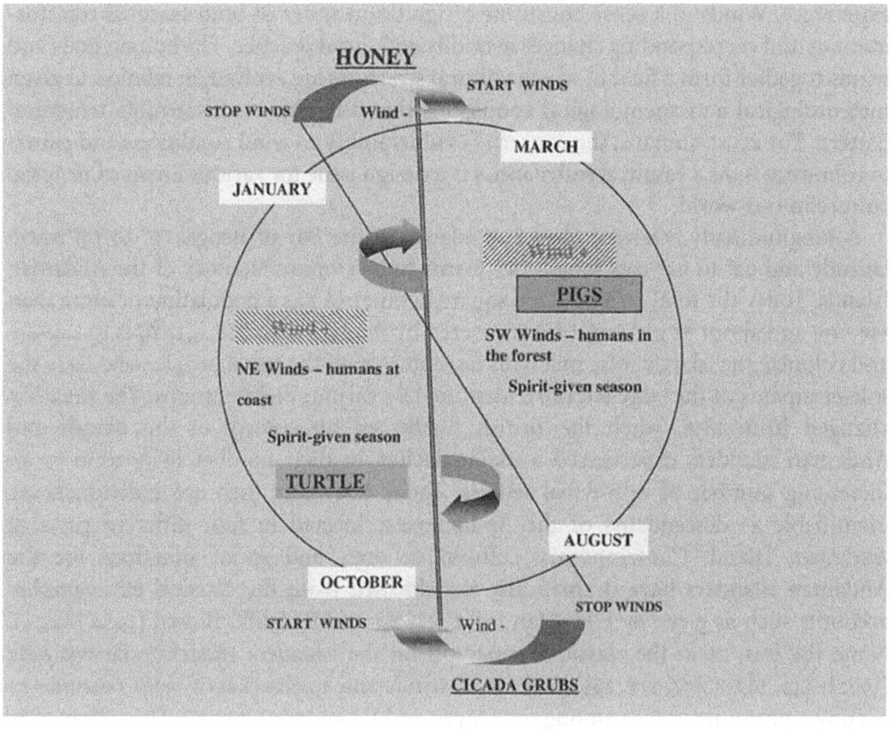

Figure 1. Andamanese seasonal cycle showing activities in relation to 'windful' and 'windless' places.

'windless space', Jarwas and Ongees effectively try to shift specific seasons and the movement of spirits associated with them. This, in brief, forms the analytical and ethnographic focus of my paper.

Winds are ritually stopped from flowing into a place to create different temporal orders. In order to explain how winds are stopped by the islanders, I will first introduce the worldview of the Andamanese, in which winds play a crucial role, and then address the 'how' and 'why' aspect of wind cessation. I will thereafter consider some ethnographic details of how winds are stopped and started by the islanders as part of a larger effort to create alternating cycles of a 'spirit-given season' of winds and 'human-made seasons' that are windless. In the concluding section, I will touch upon the issue of power implicated in the ritualized act of 'stopping winds' and 'regulating the traffic of spirits' within the confines of Andamanese space. I intend to show in my analysis the implications of the intervention of human agency in the natural and spiritual aspects of Andamanese space, and how winds and spirits have a bearing on the assumptions underlying the state-imposed political economy for the hunters and gatherers of the region. There is an inherent contradiction between the state's requirement of a fixed territorial location for the Andamanese and the Andaman islanders' own political-economic concerns informed by their specific understanding of wind and spirit movements and olfactory politics.

For a brief moment let us keep aside the Andamanese and consider our clocks, analogue or digital, as devices designed to indicate the ceaseless flow of time. This conceptualization helps us to grasp the ritual of stopping winds among the Andamanese. Chronometric instruments have to be set at a point from which these can record the flow of time. This act of setting time involves a brief but critical moment of 'timelessness' that makes the 'time-setter' in a sense the 'time-maker', too. It is through the act of transposing 'given time' into 'constructed time' that modern societies convey the inherent instrumentality of their relationship to time. This ritual of stopping, adjusting, and starting time is done in most industrialized societies at least twice in a year for summer and winter to create what could be called an effective political economy of energy consumption. These time adjustments are basically structures of practice that in turn condition our practice of structures in relation to the seasonal cycles of summer and winter. In our movements across space, too, we adjust time in accordance with longitudinal variations in order to make the transition to a place meaningful.

Homologous to this contemporary engagement with time is the Andaman islanders' practice of stopping and starting winds, as part of a complex engagement with capricious spirits pervading the islanders' space – a space that is shared between animals, humans, and spirits, who all live and move and practice hunting and gathering with each other.

Muroi, one of the most accomplished Ongee spirit communicators, explained his experience of winds in the following manner:

> When we walk through the forest our bodies touch the plants around, and we keep cutting them down along the trail, so that the plants do not tell the animals where the Ongees are moving to in the forest. While we walk through the jungle we must breathe deep and remain quiet to ensure minimal trace of us is left! Invisible spirits cannot be seen by all humans but are constantly around us. They move around everywhere and as they move they create winds along the paths they move. Wind is the experienced form of the invisible spirits all around us! Like the plants can feel us, we feel the spirits by experiencing winds.

Similar concern is reflected by a group of Jarwas near Kadamtall to whom I posed the question of why they move from place to place when the administration wants them to settle down (much like the non-tribal people). The Jarwa men collectively expressed that:

> We have to be behind the *Aholey-kwhada* [southwest winds], in the forest while the winds and spirits are at the coast and sea! But that also makes us in front of the *Mahey-kwhada* [northeast winds and spirits] that come to the forest and we move to the coastal area for gathering! Our shelters are always between the two winds but your homes stand in one place and are surrounded by winds and spirits that keep coming around. We change locations and avoid the spirits and winds.

The Andamanese world and its view

In the worldview of the Andamanese, winds flow from places, carrying along various smells that guide the movement of spirits. For the Andamanese, this makes the world both dynamic and in a state of constant flux. Human beings as source of smells and as smell-manipulators are subject to constant interaction with powerful and malevolent spirits. Proximity to spirits and the propensity to being hunted by spirits is a possibility for all and something that is regularly experienced during temporal transitions such as between dawn and dusk, between ebbing and flowing tides, and in moments when it rains during sunshine. Spirits are also associated with spatial categories that are ambivalent, like the mangrove forests, where seawater and fresh water mix. Consequently, the Andamanese remember not to be in an ambivalent place, particularly in times of transition.

Andamanese have to humanize the space around them, in which the balance of power is in a constant state of flux. In their worldview, the condition of being human is indicative of a decline from the capacity of or state of being a powerful spirit. With the inevitable transition of seasons and winds, the encounter with spirits becomes unavoidable, in particular when the spirits are believed to enter the Andamanese habitat by plotting a careful course of movement along winds and smells. Toothless spirits are known to enter human space by consuming soft food substances or become contained in living human beings in conditions of pregnancy or sickness. From the perspective of the Andamanese, the human form is actually a transformed spirit body. They are mindful, however, that as humans they can be hunted and transformed into spirit form. This makes pregnancy, sickness, and death conditions that are invariably related to the movement of winds. These, in other words, are conditions which place the human body in an ambiguous and vulnerable position. The structure of Andamanese taboos and transformative rituals makes it possible for humans to revert back for certain durations to the position of spirits so that they can continue to exist as humans in the natural world (see Pandya 1993: 211-80). This transition and shift in identities makes it possible for Andamanese to distribute the relative power of humans and spirits within their ritualized space. The humanized space is continuously 'charged' with the forces of 'spirit power' existing within the campground as well as the forests. For the Andamanese, the forest, campground, and coasts make up the space wherein they negotiate their complex relationship with spirits.

In the Andamanese world, humans constantly degrade from being human as smells are carried away by winds. So rituals become ways for humans to re-calibrate relations with spirits and endow themselves with 'spirit-like' powers. Throughout their lives humans have to constantly keep changing their conduct by being 'spirit-like', so that the order of the world continues. In doing so, the whole community can continue to be human. The difference between the 'spirit power' and 'spirit-like power' is that spirits generate wind movements and humans restrict wind movements. Winds are restricted by significant rituals that focus on the breaking of certain taboos, making the object of taboo acquire what Radcliffe-Brown called 'social value' (1964 [1922]: 264, 270, 353, 397). The breaking of the taboo causes angry spirits temporarily to move out from a place where humans can move in and avoid the chance of being hunted by spirits. So rituals that have social value are essentially assertions and reifications of the basic power relations. In order to understand the complexities of the Andamanese worldview it is necessary to recognize the fact that our notion of spirits is part and parcel of a dualist formulation that is by and large inapplicable to Andamanese thinking. For us there is an ontological opposition between spirits and matter, and a moral opposition of spirit and god and often, more radically, of numerous spirits and a single god. The former opposition implies that spirits are immaterial. Their substance is 'breath', most invisible in the visible, most immaterial in the material. Spiritual existence is understood as the existence of an animating principle without a body or outside body. But no spirit in the Andamanese world has this disembodied existence, nor is it reducible to such an existence.

This is exemplified by the fact that the closeness of spirits causes a shivering of the human body. Intense heat that generates sweat and releases odours attracts spirits to the source of smell. If the bodies are weak and light in weight they fall prey to the hunting spirits. This for the Andamanese creates a world where spirits and items hunted by them all are interrelated by a dynamic of winds, smell, temperature, and weight. The world of the Andamanese is set in motion by 'aero-, thermo-, and aroma-dynamics'. Lack of olfactorial distinctions in space makes all living and non-living things in space subject to spirits exercising power over them. Within this world the Andamanese seasonal cycle is made up of two durations, the northeast monsoon and southwest monsoon, that are associated with 'place being filled with wind' by the presence of spirits. These are the two 'spirit-given' seasons when humans are concerned to avoid being in a place where spirits are.

June to September (southwest winds) is the season (*Kwalakangney* [Ongee], *Aholey-kwhada* [Jarwa]) when it is tabooed for Andamanese to hunt and gather from the sea. Islanders have to remember that this is the time when the spirits are hunting out in the sea. This makes it imperative that Andamanese only hunt in the forest, as in the sea they themselves may get hunted. Hunting (pig) in the forest is tabooed from October to January, as at this time of northeast winds (*Mayakangney* [Ongee] *Mahey-kwhada* [Jarwa]) spirits hunt and gather in the forest. During this season the only safe place for the Andamanese is hunting and gathering (turtle) in the coastal area. From an ecological viewpoint, such transhumance ensures for the Andamanese that the natural resources of one place are not over-used.

In order for humans to survive, power over the spirits becomes an essential requirement. It is generated by rituals of stopping winds in the Andamanese world. For a brief duration, Andamanese stop the winds and appropriate the powers of and become like the spirits themselves, creating entirely windless places. Islanders expel the angry spirits from a place, an inducement, until spirits come back with winds to another place. This ensures that, like spirits, humans move to places where they can hunt and gather, without getting hunted by spirits. So, apart from the two 'spirit-given' seasons experienced in a seasonal cycle, human beings make conditions of no winds and no spirits, brief periods of human-made seasons. During these human-made seasons islanders replenish the power that has been lost in the form of smell that has been dispersed or dissipated, and find respite from sickness, misfortune, or death that is brought about by winds and spirits.

To deal with winds that take away and scatter the smells in space, islanders carefully restrict the scattering of vulnerable body odours by elaborate clay paint. Cooling white or heat-inducing red clay paint is applied in accordance with traditional designs on the body. The other technique is retaining bones: the most condensed form of body smell from dead relatives and hunted animals (Fig. 2). These retained bones constantly release the smell of the bodies that are no longer living within the natural world. The human capacity constantly to release a dead body's smell actually deceives the spirits and animals by transmitting a smell message that nothing is missing in the world of the Andamanese.

This strategic manipulation of smells in relation to the medium of winds and recipient spirits keeps spirit tempers calm and ensures safety in humanized places. These practices related to winds and smells make it possible for spirits, humans, and animals to coexist. If the spirits receive information about things being killed by the humans, particularly categories of food that spirits prefer, angry spirits come down to humanized space, which humans experience in forms of devastation caused by powerful storms and strong gusts of winds.

So the complete seasonal cycle is a process set into motion by winds and spirits coming to the place of human beings, and through rituals expelling spirits and stopping the winds. This creates a seasonal cycle in which places in a space are distinguished. Distinction of places is brought about by temporal durations that are spirit-given and durations that are made by Andamanese themselves. Windful, spirit-given seasons and windless, human-made seasons secure the transition from the forest to coast and back (Fig. 3).

The spirit-given season ends by breaking a taboo which causes *tototey-maa inangamey nanchugey*, 'windless time in a place'. Reimposing the taboos starts the

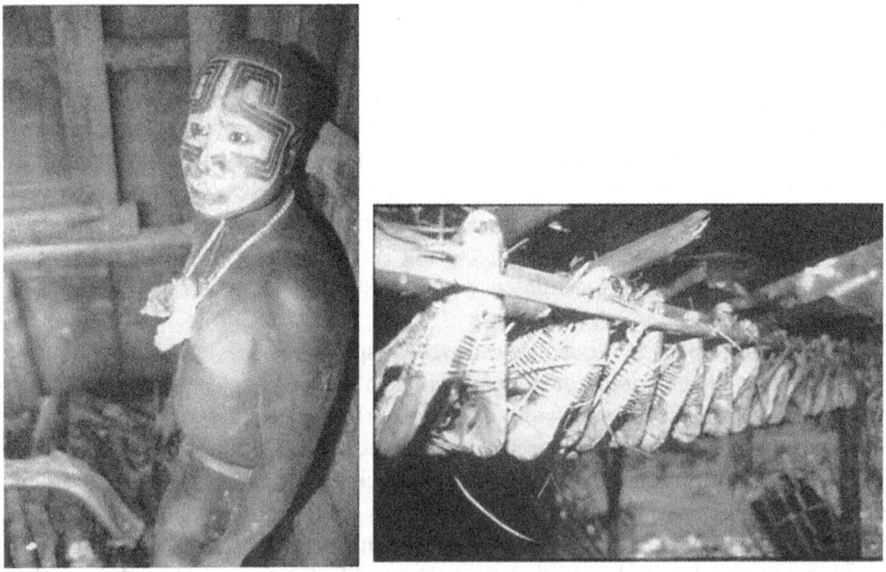

Figure 2. Typical example of body painting and bone ornament made out of dead relatives' bones.

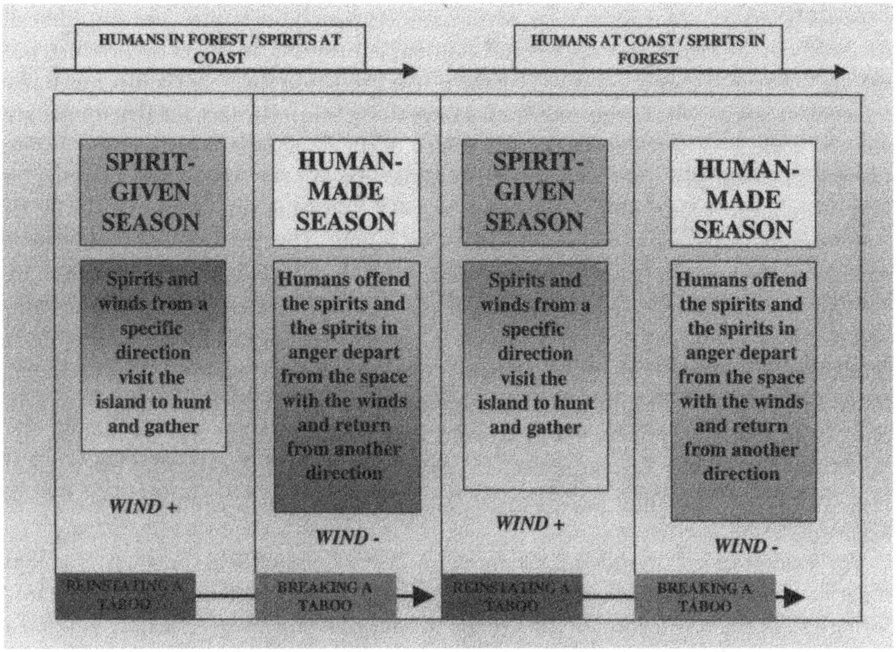

Figure 3. The Andamanese seasonal cycle represented as a sequence of seasons and taboos.

experiencing of the spirit-given season. Taboos are placed in Andamanese culture to keep the spirits calm and humans safe, but by breaking the very same taboos humans become like spirits and induce a state of windlessness, as spirits in anger leave the islands along with the winds.[2] So the ritual of breaking a taboo is like operating a 'cultural switch' that releases or restricts power in the form of angry spirits. Powerless humans for a certain period become like powerful spirits.

Let me consider a concrete case of taboo and its breaking. According to the classical account of Radcliffe-Brown (1964 [1922]: 152, 155), the cicada is protected from being killed and similarly beeswax may not be burned. However, these restrictions are specific to spirit-given seasons within the seasonal cycle. The cicada is killed during September, and beeswax is burned during February, in order to push the winds and angry spirits from one place to another (Radcliffe-Brown 1964 [1922]: 357-9). So the seasonal cycle is a sequence of interludes of spirits affecting humans and humans manipulating spirits, both of which are experienced in terms of wind conditions.

During southwest winds, as the spirits are out at sea, the Andamanese depend only on forest food. When they need to get to the sea to gather resources, the islanders need to move by changing the winds from southwest to northeast. The wind conditions are switched off and on during February and March, known as *toraley*, or *laheyteye* (extraction), when the islanders consume the proscribed, prime spirit food of honey.

Windless space to make time

During February and March, in order to satisfy their hunger, the toothless spirits enter honeycombs. As consumption of honey needs no mastication, it is the favourite food of spirits. The presence of the spirits in the honeycomb induces the bees to reproduce and produce honey as a by-product. So, when islanders search for, gather, and consume all the honey in the forest, they are not just humans consuming an insect by-product, but during this season they are consuming the spirits present in the honeycomb, much like malevolent spirits who gather and hunt humans. By mid-February the dry forests are still and eerie with only the dominating sound of the honeybees' buzz and the shrikes waiting to catch their meal around the honeycombs. All the Andamanese bands, till mid-March, move frantically from place to place following the shrikes to cut down honeycombs. All effort focuses on gathering honey. The significance of honey is reflected in the carving of the exclusive wooden honey container. Honey containers are one of the few items of material culture that islanders decorate carefully and arduously. The eating of honey at the wives' campsite is obligatory, as is a cooling dip in water or the application of cooling white clay paint after every such session.[3] All this angers the spirits as they realize that humans are taking advantage of the situation, and to make sure that the human intent is communicated to the spirits successfully, the honeycombs are set on fire and melted beeswax is collected. In this process the smell of the consumed honeycomb is released to be absorbed by the remaining spirits and to aggravate them.

For nearly a month islanders predominantly depend on honey as the staple food that must be shared by frequent inter-band visitations. Sharing honey ensures the transformation of the spirits into foetuses in the wombs of women who consume it. In fact, in Andamanese language fertile women who have experienced frequent pregnancy are often referred to as *tanjayebuley*, a word also used for the honeycomb. This culturally significant consumption of honey ensures the reproduction of human children, who are spirits trapped inside the honeycomb that are transformed in the woman's womb. Thus consumption of honey not only produces a windless situation, but also facilitates reproduction. *Torale*, honey-gathering, is a time when, in a way, humans hunt or appropriate the spirits contained in honey. During spirit-given seasons, by contrast, humans can be potentially hunted by spirits and made into fellow-spirits. Windless time multiplies the human community and windful time causes losses to the community in the form of deaths and addition to the spirit community.

By the end of March all the honeycombs have been gathered. Andamanese can now get ready to set up camps in the interior forest. Men prepare the arrows for the pig-hunting season while children make spinning-tops. Wild fig fruits have a twig inserted through them, which is twirled around to set them in a whirling motion on the ground. These tops, known as *tikitiki* (Ongee) or *tuutuhu* (Jarwa), are launched by groups of excited children shouting '*tototey tototey konyuney rotonka!*' (Wind, wind where are you now?). Only the parents who teasingly say to children 'It is not *tototey*, (winds) you can never see it, it is yet to be felt' subdue all this noise. It is time to move as forest places are now more conducive. Realizing what humans have been doing with honey, angry spirits with winds will descend to the coastal areas, but the humans have left to set up camps in the forest to pursue pig-hunting. For the islanders it is of course a desired outcome of them breaking the taboos about honey.

By April the southwest winds arrive at the coastal areas with the spirits. These shake the jackfruit tree loaded with semi-ripe fruits. Jackfruits (*buludangey* [Ongee] *Aabdangey* [Jarwa]) drop and get scattered on the forest floor for humans to gather and wild pigs to feed on. For the Andamanese this is a sign that spirits have come to the sea and the forests are ready for pig-hunting. Until August islanders do not venture out to the proscribed coastal area, as spirits are present there. The presence of the spirits out in the sea is marked by rains and rough swells, which are responding to winds that accompany the spirits hunting for turtles and fish. Subsiding storms indicate to the islanders that the spirits are moving into the forest to feed on yet another prime soft insect by-product, a delicacy for the spirits, the cicada grubs (*tombowagey* [Ongee], *payethen* [Jarwa]).

Spirits enter the rotten tree-trunks, decaying after months of the heavy downpour of the southwest monsoon. To be safe and assured that spirits will move into the forest, spirits and winds have to be moved from the sea to the forest. This constitutes the start of second short duration *Dare* (Ongee), or *Totahey* (Jarwa),[4] a human-made season when the winds are restricted and have to be started again to create the season of northeast winds, when islanders reside at the coast. To achieve this altered condition in space Andamanese rituals focus on killing the cicada grubs. Much like the honeybee larvae confined in the honeycomb, cicada grubs concealed in the rotten tree-trunks become the focus of the ritual breaking of taboo.[5]

In Andamanese mythology, cicadas are regarded as constantly complaining to the spirits by the loud sound they make at dawn and dusk. The contention is that in spite of having wings like birds they are unable to fly high and away. This ambiguity of the cicada also makes them the prime signifier of the ambivalent time of dawn and dusk when it is neither day nor night. According to Ongees, cicada should therefore never be hurt. Cicadas communicate to the world the need to differentiate and change activities from daytime to night-time.

From August to September, as the southwest monsoons subside, the fallen, decaying tree-trunks become rich nursery-beds for cicada grubs. The soft, succulent little morsels are prime food for the spirits. As the spirits feed, winds are not experienced. Spirits in the process of devouring the grubs also reduce the insect noise that irritates them and caution humans about temporal changes and associated dangers. Groups of Andaman islanders with machete set out each day to split open every possible rotten tree-trunk and extract the grubs. Cicadas are loosely packed in a green leaf and lightly grilled on an open fire. This grilling is essential as heated grubs swell up and burst open, releasing smell for the spirits to absorb, thus increasing their anger and motivating powerful winds from the northeast.

Here we have the parallel of burning honeycombs and grilling grubs. This not only transforms raw to cooked but also sends a 'smell-signal' via winds to the spirits. As the winds start again, spirits shift from the sea to the forest, where humans have consumed cicada, prime spirit food. This movement of the winds from the northeast caused by the angry spirits is induced by the Andaman islanders breaking the taboo on killing the cicadas. All this makes it possible for the islanders to move from the forest to coastal areas, whereas the winds and spirits have moved in the opposite direction. From October to January the Andamanese camp along the coastline collecting resources from the sea. Time is formed into space by movement of winds, spirits, and humans. Spirits hunt humans and animals; humans avoid spirits and hunt animals. Animals remain relatively powerless in this hierarchical relationship. Within this shared space and these power relations, consumption of the tabooed honey and cicada creates a position of power for humans where not only the winds affect humans but humans also affect the winds. Coastal residence during the northeast winds and forest residence during the southwest winds is an Andamanese 'practice of structure' in relation to winds, but the utilization of a windless situation, when spirits themselves are gathered and consumed in the form of restricted insect-derived food, is a 'structure of practice' that sets the very practice of structure into a dynamic state. From February to March and August to September, it is the humans who dominate over the spirits.

As space changes due to the presence and absence of winds, time, too, changes. Andaman islanders make possible the very essence of moving as hunters and gatherers without getting hunted and gathered in 'timespace'. Conceptually the seasonal cycle therefore acquires yet another dimension where the presence and absence of winds is connected with categories of food gathered, hunted, and consumed.

Conclusion: cultural implications and political-economic considerations

No wonder early colonial surveyors of the Andaman islanders at the turn of the twentieth century enumerated the indigenous hunters and gatherers as practitioners of animistic religion, listing them as 'Storm Worshippers'. Consequently, early ethnographers of the islands, such as Man (1932 [1882]), Portman (1899), and Radcliffe-Brown (1964 [1922]), were engaged in arguments about the animistic world focusing on Puluga, a divinity that played a significant role in generating northeast and southwest winds and different seasonal conditions (Leach 1971; Radcliffe-Brown 1910; Schmidt 1910). In the Andamanese animistic worldview there is really no differentiation and demarcation between sacred and profane, pure and impure, natural and supernatural, visible and invisible, powerful and powerless. In fact much of the world around is subject to taboos and is created so that they can be broken. For the majority of the time, spirits and winds dominate in the power relations with humans, but to deal with this asymmetry, for a short time humans do to spirits what spirits do to humans. The Andamanese culturally construct a season within the so-called 'naturally given' flow of time.

Andaman islanders oscillating between coast and forest also posed a major problem for the expanding colonial administration and its control of space. Early accounts elaborated on the breaking of 'taboos' that would cause a major imbalance in the availability of specific prescribed forms of game in prescribed seasons. However, my own ethnographic recording of Andamanese ideas about food in relation to winds and seasons considers another dimension. Radcliffe-Brown interpreted the food taboos of the Andamanese as expressions of the belief that 'food may be a source of danger unless it is approached with circumspection', that is, by respecting certain prohibitions and practising certain avoidances (1965: 272). He avoided the term 'taboo' and preferred the idea of 'ritual prohibition', a rule of behaviour that is associated with a belief that an infraction will result in an undesirable change in the ritual status of the person who fails to keep that rule. But, collectively, Andamanese rituals of breaking food prohibitions dealing with honey and cicada bring about the desired change of wind conditions and seasons for the whole community (cf. Radcliffe-Brown 1965: 135, 207).

By consuming things that anger the spirits and affect the wind conditions, Andamanese reduce the very notion of danger to that of the 'socially valuable'. Their cultural notion of winds and spirits and related ritual ensure season after season of safe hunting and gathering. Food culturally articulates a specific form of subject in Andamanese culture, a subject that is constituted in the discursive predications made possible by the very symbolic order of culture that fears loss in terms of smells caused by spirits and winds that haunt the cultural space. Andamanese culture is constituted by standing against the inarticulated flow of winds and resisting power of spirits by articulating the unseen spirit bodies that move with winds and transforming human body smells.

For Andamanese, the body is not only a substance to be legislated upon but it is also a subject that is constantly symbolically constituted by experiences of the body's resistance to the subject's symbolic ordering of self in relation to winds. One could say that the rule of avoiding contact with spirit becomes ritual where the symbolic aspect becomes completely objectified morality. Thus, Andamanese act morally, not because they follow rules for their own sake, but because they are afraid of certain putative consequences of not following them. In the same vein, many people under the rule of law obey it because they are afraid of punishment and see no other reason for lawful behaviour. However, for Andamanese it would be essential to 'disobey' law and be 'punished'. This is because Andamanese have never forgotten that humans actually exist as a form of spirits. As a result the structure of taboos and ritual makes it possible for humans to revert back for a duration to the position of spirits so that they can continue to exist as humans in the natural world. This is essentially an assertion and reification of the basic power relation whereby spirits hunt in the world of humans and animals and humans hunt animals by avoiding the spirit hunting them.

Today groups of Ongees and Jarwas are classified as 'Primitive Tribes' by the Indian administration in relation to the nation-state. Only since 1998 have indigenous groups like the Jarwas come into full contact with and ended their resistance to the increasing number of outsiders on the island. Ongees, on the other hand, have been in contact with outsiders since 1892 and exhibit a degree of acculturation. But from the days of colonialism to the present, post-independence, the major concern for the administration has been to make the tribal people settle down in one place and not allow them to translocate.

An implicit vision in the thrust of developmentalist and welfare activities headed by the nation-state is that hunters and gatherers should stay put in a place so that they can be provided for. The translocating hunter-gatherer is a problem in the eyes of the state and its vision of the political economy. The administration's major problem is to convince the Andamanese that lack of movement would bring 'winds of welfare and modernization' to them. Time and space is a given, non-changing construct in the worldview of the nation-state and its political economy. Restricted movement is the very essence of the exercise of power by the political economy that has carved out forest territories as tribal reserves. The tribal should not be seen and entertained in any way by the non-tribal.

These demarcations and restrictions, particularly in relation to a major road passing through the tribal reserves, are not really understood by the tribal people and the non-tribal people, who regularly, legally or illegally, move in and out of the bound areas (Pandya 1999*a*; 1999*b*; 2002). This worldview of the state is in direct conflict with the political economy of space as conceived by the Andamanese. For the Andamanese, space cannot be demarcated as a fixed territorial unit, as winds continue to flow and unify places into a large space. Spaces are subject to change, and time itself is a creation of movement in and out of space. For the Andamanese, the relations of power that structure their political economy are based on movements of smells, spirits, and humans, all affected by winds. In the act of stopping and starting winds, the experience of time for them becomes place-specific. It is not just *a* time, but also the experience of different *times* in different places that distinguishes the spatio-temporal conception of the Andamanese. In the structure of the state's political economy the Andamanese propensity to move and their specific experience of winds are issues best ignored. Yet the Andamanese sense of political economy continues to be based on negotiations with spirits and smells and power is exercised by moving in relation to winds. The administration's strident refusal to acknowledge this was evident in February and March 2005 when during honey-gathering season it spent an extra $15,000 to keep the Jarwas from moving in different parts, particularly in the direction of the middle and south Andamans, by posting extra guards, signs, and patrol jeeps. The justificatory logic offered was that it was not safe for the 'naked tribals' to be seen on the road passing through the reserve forest.

The administration fails to realize that the imperative of movement will continue to drive the Andamanese as long as they experience the flow of winds and feel the presence of spirits in their lives. Some administrators feel that the answer lies in the introduction of pig farming and apiculture, which should be taken up by the 'Primitive Tribes'. I have doubts about my ability to 'translate' the administration's vision of the future to the Andamanese, but I did pose a counter-question for a senior administrator on the island by saying, 'How about you dropping the idea to take leave in the summer and cruise off to cooler climes? Maybe then the "native", too, could be persuaded to stay put in just one place!' I am still waiting for the administrator to respond, as he is on his annual summer break, while the winds continue to flow in and out of the Andamans.

NOTES

I would like to thank the editors and workshop participants for the discussions and comments; Dr Madhumita Mazumadar, who made it a point to think about the wider implications within the Andamanese context; and Prof. Ralph Nicholas, who originally inspired me to start studying winds in 1983. All the years of fieldwork on the Andaman Islands would have been impossible without the kind co-operation and goodwill extended by the Andaman Nicobar Administration and Andaman Adim Janjati Vikas Samiti office at Port Blair, particularly Mr S. Awaradi, Mr B. Das, and Mr A. Mondal.

[1] Ongees of the Little Andaman Island and Jarwas are now confined to Jarwa reserve territory on South and Middle Andaman Island. In spite of the geographical distance between the two groups, historically they used to have exchange relations, linguistic affinity, and a common material culture. My fieldwork on the Andaman Islands started in 1983 when I spent a year with the Ongees in the forest of Little Andaman Island. Over the years I continued visiting an Ongee settlement at Dugong Creek. Since 1997 the Andaman Nicobar administration has permitted me to visit the Jarwa reserve territory, and with the kind assistance of the Andaman field staff I established contact with the Jarwas. Unlike the prolonged participant observation that has been possible with the Ongees, work among the Jarwas was undertaken in short trips to the reserve territory. This was primarily because the Jarwas were resistant to outsiders and to sustained contact with the outside world until 1998. The Ongees, by contrast, were hostile until 1892. Historically, culturally, and linguistically, Jarwas and Ongees share many aspects of their respective worldviews, and this paper has emerged out of years of conversations and moving with the groups of Andaman islanders and reflecting on the parallel cultural practices and thoughts among them in a space they share as hunters and gatherers.

[2] Ever since Frazer (1928) and Robertson Smith (1959) turned taboo into a subject of inquiry, it has remained a classic concern for anthropologists. However via Radcliffe-Brown's work on the Andaman Islands (1964 [1922]), a rich context was provided to question the possibility of correlating the prevalence of taboo with certain social forms or social situations. For instance, it is a 'taboo' to mention and talk about the dead and eat certain foods (Radcliffe-Brown 1965: 147). But then the mourner, like the expectant parents, are both subject to similar acts of avoidance and ritual value (cf. Radcliffe-Brown 1964 [1922]: 111, 288).

[3] Application of white clay paint on the body restricts the release of body smell and is also used after death in a family as well as after consumption of hunted animals.

[4] In both Ongee and Jarwa language *tototey* means 'winds'. They distinguish *aeoyey* as a term that implies air, something that is around but does not flow or move as *tototey* does. *Dare* in Ongee language is also a verb that means 'to bring'. In Jarwa language *Totahey* is a verb to express 'coming of'.

[5] It is significant to note that both the insects are appropriated in a form when they have yet to achieve their capacity to fly, a capacity associated with the flow of wind. Ongees in particular avoid killing birds in the forest as they can fly and are closely associated with wind, and both Ongees and Jarwas insist that things that really fly should not be made into food.

REFERENCES

Frazer, J.G. 1928. *The Golden Bough: a study in magic and religion*. New York: Macmillan.

Leach, E. 1971. *Kimil*: a category of Andamanese thought. In *Structural analysis of oral tradition* (eds) P. Maranda & E.K. Maranda, 22-48. Philadelphia: University of Pennsylvania Press.

Man, E. 1932 [1882]. *On the Aboriginal inhabitants of the Andaman Islands*. London: Royal Anthropological Institute Publication.

Pandya, V. 1993. *Above the forest: a study of Andamanese ethnoanemology, cosmology and the power of ritual*. New Delhi: Oxford University Press.

——— 1999*a*. Contact or not to contact: questions about Jarwa of Andaman Islands. *Cultural Survival Quarterly*, Winter, 59-65.

——— 1999*b*. *Hostile borders and friendly contacts: Jarwas of Andaman Islands*. (Working Paper 3). Asian Research Institute, Victoria University, Wellington, New Zealand.

——— 2002. Jarwas of Andaman Islands: their social and historical reconstruction. *Economic and Political Weekly*, 14 Sept., 3830-4

——— 2005. When land became water: Tsunami and the Ongees of Little Andaman Islands. *Anthropology Newsletter*, March. Washington, D.C.: American Anthropological Association.

Portman, M. 1899. *A history of our relations with Andamanese*. Calcutta: Superintendent of Government Printing Press.

Radcliffe-Brown, A.R. 1910. Puluga: a reply to Father Schmidt. *Man* **X**, 33-7.

——— 1964 [1922]. *The Andaman islanders*. Glencoe, Ill.: Free Press.

——— 1965. *Structure and function in primitive society*. New York: Free Press.

Schmidt, W. 1910. Puluga, the Supreme Being of the Andamanese. *Man* **X**, 2-7.

Smith, R. 1959. *The religion of the Semites*. New York: Meridian Books.

7
The bodily winds in ancient India revisited

KENNETH G. ZYSK *University of Copenhagen*

In an article written some years ago, I examined the notion of respiration and the bodily winds in the Indian tradition. In that paper, I traced the doctrine of the bodily winds from the earliest literature to the classical medical treatises, noticing that a bifurcation in the doctrine occurred between the schools of medicine and of Yoga (Zysk 1993).[1] In this paper, I would like to pick up where the other left off, and, using what A.L. Basham called a 'controlled imagination' (1959: 44), investigate more closely the historical development of the doctrine of the five body winds in the early Sanskrit medical literature of classical Āyurveda and its relationship to the Indian ascetic tradition of Yoga.

Already from the time of the Ṛgveda (*c.*1500-1000 BCE), there is evidence that the ancient Indians conceived the wind in nature and the breath in living beings to be one and the same thing, imbued with special life-giving powers. Two hymns of creation reflected their basic ideas about wind and breath.

The first speaks of a time when nothing of the living world existed. There was only an inert entity, The One, which was self-sustaining and existed without breathing. It was a primordial time before life, when wind and breath were unnecessary:

> Then even nothingness was not, nor existence.
>   There was no air then, nor the heavens beyond it.
> What covered it? Where was it? In whose keeping?
>   Was there then cosmic waters, in depths unfathomed?
> Then there was neither death nor immortality,
>   nor was there then the torch of night and day.
> The One breathed windlessly and self-sustaining.
>   There was that One then, and there was no other.[2]

Another version of the world's creation, conceived to have taken place when a cosmic man was sacrificed, connects nature's wind to the cosmic man's breath. When discussing the origin of various elements in the natural world, the author of the hymn states that when the cosmic man's body was cut up and its parts divided, as in the case of the immolation of a sacrificial animal, his breath (*prāṇa*) became the wind (*vāyu*).[3]

In this way, these myths of creation established wind (and breath) as one of the essential elements of existence and life in the manifest world. Throughout the religious literature of the early Indians, wind and breath played a central role in their understanding of the difference between life and death. Like so many peoples of the ancient and contemporary worlds, they worshipped wind and recognized that by harnessing, restraining, and controlling that which by its very nature is unrestricted and unrestrained, they could effectively control life and death.

For the ancient Indians, central to the control of the natural forces was knowledge, which involved a process of particularizing through naming and isolation through defining in order to create order out of the chaos around them. Like the boundaries round the sacrificial altar, knowledge defined the limits of the natural world, and thereby facilitated its restraint and even its control. With these basic ideas in the background, we can begin to unpack the history of the doctrine of the bodily winds in Yoga and Āyurveda.

As an idea, wind ranks paramount in the epistemology of ancient Indian medical thinkers, for it was not only one of the basic elements which made up the world, but it was also the principal empirical indicator of the existence of life in human beings. When it was witnessed in living beings, there was life, and when it was absent from living beings, life ceased. Since wind was so closely connected to life and death, it obviously held special powers, so it was given a name to distinguish it from other forces in nature. It was called *vāta* and *vāyu* in nature[4] and *prāṇa* in living beings. On the one hand, wind was revered and worshipped as a powerful deity, so that it would bestow its life-giving powers on humans, and on the other hand, if fully understood, its cosmic potential could be harnessed and controlled for humankind's benefit. Nature's wind was limitless and unrestricted; it could only be worshipped as a mighty, untamed deity. However, that same force in humans was limited: when it entered the body it was confined there until it left to reunite with its source, the cosmic wind. It could, therefore, be contained while in the body; and with that potential, it could also be controlled and manipulated during its bodily residence. However, it first had do be fully understood. Hence, from earliest times, the ancient Indians set upon the task of acquiring knowledge of the human breath.

From the time of the *Ṛgveda* and *Atharvaveda*, human breath, or *prāṇa*, was understood to be a manifestation of the cosmic wind (*vāyu*); and, furthermore, this *prāṇa* was present when there was life and absent when there was no life. Hence, it was considered to be the 'life-breath'. Like the daily rising and the setting of the sun, the life-breath was twofold. Probably by observing the rising and lowering of the chest during respiration, the Indians considered that the life-breath was divided into two parts: inhalation, *prāṇa*, and exhalation, *apāna*, which were often written as one word, *prāṇāpāna*, indicating both respiration and life, which were synonymous. The metaphor of sunrise and sunset was the first attempt to understand and define the bodily wind and its power.

It would appear that a deeper understanding of the life-breath came with early experiments with asceticism and meditation. In the *Atharvaveda*, there is mention of a group of ascetics known as the Vrātyas, who are known for their knowledge and practice of the special ascetic technique of *prāṇāyāma* or breath-control. In the sections that deal with the Vrātyas and their knowledge of the breaths, mention is made of three breaths, *prāṇa*, *apāna*, and *vyāna*, which refer respectively to inhalation, exhalation, and retention. These are the three fundamental activities in the ascetic practice of breath-control. Each of these three is further divided into seven types which deal with anatomy and physiology, worship and ritual, and macrocosmic correspondences. Three levels of understanding come from the ascetics: the microcosmic or physical level locates wind in the body; the macrocosmic or natural level locates wind in the natural world; and the religious level focuses on the worship of a powerful force. The deeper knowledge of the bodily winds in the early period came rather from techniques of breath-control practised by ascetics than from priests, who specialized in ritual procedures, or from specialists, who had knowledge of medicine and healing.

In the period immediately before the advent of the first Sanskrit medical treatises, information about the bodily winds derived predominantly from the Sanskrit treatises, known as *Upaniṣads*, which are largely philosophical works, dating from about 800 to 200 BCE. They were composed by reflective thinkers who actively engaged in ascetic practices that included breath-control. Knowledge of the bodily wind reached a stage in which it was divided into five distinct types based on its anatomical location and its physiological function. These five breaths became the standard number of bodily winds found in the subsequent literature. Two *Upaniṣads* in particular offer the earliest attempts to locate the five winds in the body and describe their functions. *Praśna Upaniṣad* (3.5-7) provides their locations:

Prāṇa is located in the eyes, ears, mouth, and nose.
Apāna is located in the organs of excretion and generation.
Samāna is located in the middle of the body and distributes digested food.
Vyāna is located in the numerous channels of the body, all of which originate from the region of the heart.
Udāna rises up from one of the central channels and functions in moral actions.

The *Maitrī Upaniṣad* (2.6) gives their functions:

Prāṇa is the wind that passes upward.
Apāna is the wind that passes downward.
Vyāna is the wind that supports *prāṇa* and *apāna*.
Samāna, being a higher form of *vyāna*, is the wind that brings the coarse element of food into the *apāna* and distributes food's subtle elements in the limbs.
Udāna is the wind that is between the *vyāna* and *samāna*. It belches forth and swallows down what is drunk and eaten.

The fundamental notions about the five bodily winds or breaths found in these *Upaniṣads* testify to an ongoing process of discovery, definition, and control by means of the ascetic practice of breath-control (*prāṇāyāma*), which was a central technique in the ascetic tradition of Yoga.

Towards the end of the time that the information about the bodily winds was being recorded by the upaniṣadic mystics, the system of Yoga was being codified by the sage Patañjali in his *Yogasūtra* (*c.*200 BCE). Patañjali described a system of Yoga consisting of eight steps which result in a condition of the mind and body in which human consciousness is wholly independent of the body. One of the key steps in this process involved the mastery of *prāṇāyāma*, breath-control, which came directly after the perfection of the postures (*āsana*), aimed at controlling the body, and before the fixing of the mind (*dhāraṇā*), aimed at controlling mental activity. In this way, *prāṇāyāma* served as the link between body-control and mind-control.

According to Patañjali, *prāṇāyāma* is the suspension of the movement of breath after both inhalation and exhalation and has four operations. The first three, external, internal, and suppression, become long and subtle when practised according to space, time, and number (Ys 2.49-50).[5] The external and internal operations are the suspension of breath respectively after exhalation and after inhalation; and suppression is the stopping of both inhalation and exhalation. They become long and subtle when respiration is controlled by a method that utilizes space, which involves the gradual shortening of the distance of exhaled air; time, which involves the gradual lengthening of the period of each of the three operations (i.e. inhalation, exhalation, and suppression); and number, which involves the gradual increasing of the number of respirations. It is said that a subtle form of exhalation occurs when fine cotton wool held at the tip of the nose does not move when a person breathes. The fourth *prāṇāyāma* occurs when both the internal and external operations are completely transcended (Ys 2.51). This *prāṇāyāma* involves a gradual process that leads to a complete control of the breath so that it can be suspended at will. Key to the practice of *prāṇāyāma* is both breathing and meditation, during which there is the visualization of air moving in the body and the experience of tactile sensations connected with the image. The dual technique of breath-control and meditation results in a form of mental fitness which Patañjali calls *dhāraṇā*. It facilitates the fixing of the mind on an internal region of the body.

The technique of controlling and outright suspension of the process of respiration in the human body developed in India over a long period and involved not only breath-control but also a meditative process whose aim was the mind's stabilization and fixation on a part or parts inside the body. It is, therefore, not unreasonable to imagine that the ongoing practice of focusing on a part inside the human body while concentrating on the movement of air within the confined space of the trunk and limbs eventually led to life-breath's standard definition consisting of five bodily breaths with their appropriate anatomical locations and physiological functions. As the different schools of Yoga developed in India, experiences of the bodily breaths became ever more refined, so that subtle nuances in the five standard winds gave rise to the identification of countless breaths in the body. However, when the medical authors appropriated knowledge of the bodily winds, they adopted the same five winds as the norm. The medical authors applied a different methodology to the basic definition of the five bodily winds provided by the upaniṣadic sages and developed a doctrine along medical lines. The mystic's original description of the winds' locations and function relied on an āyurvedic epistemology that, among other things, involved close observation of bodily functions, and, unique to the medical school, described their function as possible agents of disease. An examination of the five breaths in four āyurvedic classics illustrates the gradual development of the classical medical doctrine of the five bodily winds. The four treatises that form the basis of classical āyurvedic medicine are: *Caraka Saṃhitā* and *Suśruta Saṃhitā*, from the early classical period; and Vāgbhaṭa's *Aṣṭāṅgahṛdaya Saṃhitā* and Vṛddhavāgbhaṭa's *Aṣṭāṅgasaṃgraha*, from the late classical period.[6]

Caraka Saṃhitā (c. 200 BCE-200 CE)

The principal teaching about wind (*vāyu*) came from a certain sage, Vāryovida, who explained that wind in the body, when it was undisturbed, had five forms, *prāṇa*, *udāna*, *samāna*, *vyāna*, and *apāna*, which upheld all the systems and the organs. More specifically, they initiated upward and downward movements, led and controlled the mind, employed all the sense organs in their activities, transported all sense objects, caused structural formations of all the bodily tissues, promoted union in the body and in speech, originated touch and sound, were the roots of auditory and tactile senses and the sources of exhilaration and courage, stimulated the digestive fire, absorbed the bodily humours (*doṣa*), evacuated excreta, formed the large and small channels, shaped the foetus, and maintained the life-span (CaSū 12.8).

This basic doctrine of the five bodily winds, attributed to the sage Vāryovida, is significant because it establishes the breaths or winds as the central forces responsible for the life of a human being by aiding in the execution and sustaining of all the vital bodily functions. The basic tenets that make up the doctrine are found in the other medical texts, where they are expanded and developed. Vāryovida's doctrine also includes perhaps a basic yogic understanding of the five breaths because of the central role they play in controlling the mind and the senses, along with the more obvious wind-functions, such as evacuation and movement.

In his chapter on the treatment of wind-disorders (*vātavyādhi*), Caraka provides a discernible āyurvedic definition of the bodily winds, emphasizing, like the upaniṣadic doctrine, their location and function, albeit in a considerably expanded form (CaCi 28.3-12):

> *Prāṇa* is located in the head, the chest, the throat (var.: the ear), the tongue, the mouth, and the nose; and it performs such functions as spitting, sneezing, belching, respiration, and digestion.
> *Udāna* is located in the navel, the chest, and the throat; and it performs such functions as speech, forward movement, effort, bodily energy, strength, and complexion.
> *Samāna* is located in the channels that convey sweat, the bodily humours, and the bodily fluids; and, situated beside the inner fire, it provides strength to the digestive fire (by fanning it).
> *Vyāna*, being fast-moving, pervades the entire body and constantly performs such functions as going, extension, contraction, and blinking.
> *Apāna* is located in the testicles, the bladder, the penis, the navel, the buttocks, the groin, the anus, and the bowels; and it transports semen, urine, faeces, blood, menstrual discharge, and the foetus.

Not aggravated and situated in their respective locations, the breaths perform their own functions; and by them the body is maintained free of disease. If they are situated in the wrong paths or become aggravated, they afflict the body with diseases derived from their particular locations and functions and quickly destroy life.

The description of the five bodily winds given here by Caraka clearly reflects early āyurvedic medical thinking. In comparison with the description of the five bodily winds in the two passages from the *Upaniṣads*, Caraka's definition, while following in form the earlier works, provides considerably more anatomical and physiological information, and mentions their role in promoting health and causing disease. The basic formulations of the doctrine of the bodily winds found in the *Caraka Saṃhitā* serve as a point of comparison for the discussions of the doctrine in the other classical medical treatises, beginning with the *Suśruta Saṃhitā*.

Suśruta Saṃhitā (c. 100-400 CE)

The first chapter of Suśruta's book of diagnosis (*nidānasthāna*) is devoted to wind-disorders (*vātavyādhi*), in which the locations, the functions, and the aetiology of the five bodily winds are found. The description of the five breaths is similar to that offered by Caraka. However, where Caraka details each wind's location and function, and provides only a general explanation for the abnormalities arising from the aggravation of the winds, Suśruta specifies the kinds of disorders that occur from the aggravation of each wind and provides only a brief description of each breath's location and function (SuNi 1.12-21b):

Prāṇa is located in the mouth, maintains the body, transports food inwards, and sustains the (twelve) elements of life.[7] When aggravated, it usually causes disorders such as hiccough and difficult breathing.

Udāna is an excellent wind, which moves upwards and performs such functions as speech and singing. [When aggravated,] it specifically causes disorders above the collar-bone.

Samāna, being connected to the digestive fire, travels in the place where raw food is being digested, assists in the digestion of food (by fanning the digestive fire[8]), and divides digested food into its different parts. [When aggravated,] it causes disorders such as abdominal tumours, defective digestion, and diarrhoea.

Vyāna, travelling all over the body, is active in the circulation of chyle (*rasa*) and sets in motion sweating, blood-flow, and the five kinds of movement (i.e. extension, contraction, raising, lowering, and oblique movement). When aggravated, it causes disease to spread throughout the body.

Apāna is located in the intestines; and, at the appropriate time, this wind draws down faeces, urine, semen, the foetus, and menstrual discharge. When aggravated, it causes vehement diseases that are situated in the bladder and anal-rectal region.

Disorders of semen and the urinary tract come from the aggravation of *vyāna* and *apāna*. There is no doubt that when (all the winds are) aggravated at the same time, they would rend the body asunder.

After this description of the five bodily winds, Suśruta explains the different diseases caused by aggravated wind in various locations of the body and discusses ailments that result from the combination of the bodily winds with the two remaining bodily humours (*doṣas*), bile (*pitta*) and phlegm (*kapha*) (SuNi 1.34-9). In this way, he provides a detailed description of the diseases, afflictions, and disorders connected with each of the five bodily winds. Suśruta's approach to the doctrine of the bodily winds, therefore, is different from that found in the *Caraka Saṃhitā*, for it specifies rather than generalizes the types of the problems associated with the improper functioning of the winds in the body. This marks the first significant advancement in the medical doctrine, reflective of āyurvedic epistemology. Moreover, a connection between the winds and mental functions seems to be almost absent from Suśruta's formulation of the doctrine, indicating a complete break with the Yoga-ascetic doctrine, which emphasizes the association between breath and the mind.

An examination of the bodily winds in the two late classical medical texts by Vāgbhaṭa and Vṛddhavāgbhaṭa provides the final step in the development of the classical āyurvedic doctrine of the five bodily breaths.

Aṣṭāṅgahṛdaya Saṃhitā and *Aṣṭāṅgasaṃgraha* (*c.* Seventh-Eighth Centuries CE)

Both of these late classical medical treatises were composed by authors with the name Vāgbhaṭa. The first is by Vāgbhaṭa and the second by Vṛddhavāgbhaṭa, 'The Elder Vāgbhaṭa'. It is unknown if these two Vāgbhaṭas refer to the same person; however, both medical works are very similar to each other and combine the previous two medical treatises' doctrines and provide an expanded medical definition of the five breaths. As in Caraka, the winds' locations and functions are found in each work's Sūtrasthāna (section of general medical principles); and as in Suśruta, the abnormalities arising from their aggravation occur in each work's chapter on the diagnosis of arthritic diseases (*vātaśoṇita*, lit. 'wind-blood') in the Nidānasthāna (section of diseases and their causes). The greatest variations between the two treatises of Vāgbhaṭa occur in the Sūtrasthāna,[9] while passages from the two Nidānasthānas in each treatise are nearly identical. The following description of the five breaths contains the latest information and formulations of the doctrine. Information already found provided by Caraka and Suśruta has for the most part been excluded.

Prāṇa is located in the head; moves in the chest and the throat; and supports the intellect, the mind, the sense faculties, and the thought process (AhSū 12.4b-5b; AsSū 20.2). It becomes aggravated by dryness, excessive exercise, fasting, over-eating, trauma, long walks, and premature initiation or suppression of the bodily urges; and it causes malfunction of (the sense organs) beginning with eyes, and many other abnormalities such as runny nose, facial palsy, thirst, cough, and difficult breathing (AhNi 16.19-20; AsNi 16.20-1).

Udāna is located in the chest; moves in the nose, the navel region, and the throat; and performs the additional functions of memory (Ah, As), nourishment of the channels, mental discrimination, courage, and mental awakening (As) (AhSū 12.5c-6b; AsSū 20.2). It becomes aggravated by suppressing sneezing, belching, and sleeping; by carrying heavy loads; by excessive crying and laughing, etc.; and it causes obstruction of the throat, mental disorders, vomiting, loss of appetite, runny nose, enlargement of the glands of the neck, etc., and other diseases above the collar-bone (AhNi 16.21-2; AsNi 16.22-3).

Vyāna is located in the region of the heart; moves quickly over the entire body; and performs the additional functions of upward and downward movement (Ah, As), yawning, tasting food, clearing the channels, causing the flow of sweat and blood, placing semen in the uterus; and, after separating the food's nutrients from its waste products (during digestion), it gradually satiates the bodily tissues with the nutrients (As)(AhSū 12.6c-7; AsSū 20.2). It becomes aggravated by excessive walking, standing (As) or contemplation (Ah), love-making, and difficult body movements; by ingesting incompatible and dry food; by fear, joy, and sorrow, etc.; and it causes decrease of manliness, of enthusiasm, and of strength; swellings; agitated mind; fever; paralysis of the entire body; intermittent pain; horripilation; lack of tactile sensation; skin disease; herpes; and other disorders affecting the whole body (AhNi 16.23-5b; AsNi 16.24-6b).[10]

Samāna is located near the digestive fire (Ah, As) and kindles it (As); moves in the stomach and bowels; in the channels that transport the humours, impurities, semen, menstrual discharge, and bodily fluids (As); and performs additional functions such as retaining the food until it is properly digested (As) (AhSū 12.8; AsSū 20.2). It becomes aggravated by unsuitable, raw, cold, and mixed foods; and by such things as sleeping and staying awake at the wrong times; and it causes afflictions affecting the stomach and bowels such as pain in the abdomen, abdominal tumours, and disorders of the duodenum (*grahaṇī*) (AhNi 16.25c-6; AsNi 16.26c-7).

Apāna is located in the large intestines or rectum (*apāna*); moves in the bladder, pelvis, penis, testicles (As), and groin; and performs functions such as evacuation of faeces, urine, etc. (as in Ca and Su) (AhSū 12.9; AsSū 20.2). It becomes aggravated by the ingestion of dry and heavy foods; by suppression of the bodily urges; by excessive straining during bowel movements; by excessive riding, sitting, and standing; and it causes many disorders of the stomach and bowels difficult to cure, such as disorders of urine and semen, haemorrhoids, and prolapsed rectum (AhNi 16.26-7; AsNi 16.28-9).

Like Suśruta, both of these treatises in the same chapter of the Nidānasthāna explain the disorders arising when each of the bodily winds is connected with the bile (*pitta*) and the phlegm (*kapha*) (AhNi 16.42c-52a; AsNi 16.44-54a).

Both the *Aṣṭāṅgahṛdaya Saṃhitā* and *Aṣṭāṅgasaṃgraha* combine the information provided in the *Caraka* and *Suśruta Saṃhitās*; and in so doing, the doctrine of the bodily winds becomes slightly expanded through the addition of new material and by reformulation. The most noticeable changes occur in the descriptions of the causes for the particular wind's aggravation and in the expanded number of maladies associated with each wind. Moreover, both Vāgbhaṭa-texts indicate more clearly and concisely than either Caraka or Suśruta the connection between the specific wind and its corresponding mental and sensory activities. This may again point to certain Yoga-ascetic influences in the formulation of the doctrine of the bodily winds in the late classical period.

Since this paper has addressed the topic of the development of the bodily winds in the medical tradition with reference to possible connections to the Yoga-ascetic tradition, it would seem both interesting and appropriate to examine the notion of *prāṇa* in a treatise that has combined both yogic and āyurvedic doctrines into one work, namely the *Āyurvedasūtra*.

Āyurvedasūtra (*c*. Sixteenth Century CE)

Although considerably later than the previous works of classical and late classical Āyurveda, the *Āyurvedasūtra* is the first Sanskrit medical treatise said to combine the basic doctrines of both Āyurveda and Yoga into one text.[11] It might, therefore, be expected that it would contain a considerable discussion of the bodily winds. However, the breaths are mentioned only in two brief prose passages (*sūtras*), which broach the topic of what happens when the flow of bodily winds is stopped, as in the advanced practice of yogic breath-control or *prāṇāyāma*, and how to avoid its negative effects:

> When the bodily winds, *prāṇa*, *apāna*, *vyāna*, *udāna*, and *samāna*, cease to move in the different bodily channels and tissues, there arise doubt and confusion (62).
>
> By means of the yogic discipline of fixing the mind on the inner self (*antarātman*), which is the cause of the discrimination of objects that stand nearby, a man is not afflicted, but rather becomes long-lived by (the practice of) arresting the bodily winds (63).[12]

These two passages address the concerns of a practitioner of Yoga, when perhaps in the course of practising breath-control, as already explained by Patañjali in his *Yogasūtra*, the bodily winds become arrested, resulting in mental confusion and doubt. The remedy for this unhealthy state has nothing to do with medicine, as described in the classical āyurvedic treatises, but rather involves a yogic technique of focusing on something within the body, which, according to Patañjali, is call *dhāraṇā*. In the *Āyurvedasūtra*, an āyurvedic understanding of the bodily winds is wanting. In its place is found a conception of the bodily winds that relies wholly on a yogic doctrine of the *prāṇa* and the bodily winds.

Conclusions

Focusing on the early Indian notion of wind and breath, this paper has traced the historical development of bodily wind from the earliest period represented by the Vedic texts. Based on the fundamental idea that knowledge gave order, which led to control, the ancient Indians sought an understanding of the cosmic winds in the human body. They acquired their knowledge through asceticism rather than through rationality; and it gave them the means to harness the breath and to control life and death. At the same time, this ascetic-based knowledge provided the basis for a rational medical doctrine of the bodily winds, which aimed at the maintenance of health and the prolongation of life. In this way, both the yogic-ascetic and the āyurvedic doctrines of the bodily winds have the same purpose of prolonging life, but approached it from two entirely different premises.

In the beginning, the idea was simple, centring on a verification of life through observing respiration. By means of yogic and ascetic practices, which included a technique for controlling and withholding the breath and thus sustaining life, a standardized formulation of five principal bodily breaths or winds developed, based largely on the meditative explorations and intuitions of yogic practitioners. This led to a rudimentary formulation of the doctrine that focused on the locations and functions of the five basic bodily winds, *prāṇa*, *apāna*, *vyāna*, *udāna*, and *samāna*. It was adopted and adapted by the thinkers of the medical tradition and found its earliest formulation in the *Caraka Saṃhitā*. A significant development in the doctrine came with the *Suśruta Saṃhitā*, which emphasized the morbidities attributed to each of the winds rather than their locations and functions. The doctrine reached its high-water mark in the medical literature of the late classical period, when the works of the two Vāgbhaṭas combined the formulations of Caraka and Suśruta with additional information which included an explanation of the winds' locations and functions, a description of their aetiologies, and an elaborate list of the morbidities ascribed to them. Moreover, perhaps in an effort to be complete, the works of the two Vāgbhaṭas reflect certain influences from the yogic doctrine of the bodily winds, which emphasizes their role in mental processes. At a considerably later period, a yogic understanding of the five basic bodily winds was advanced in the *Āyurvedasūtra*, which is purported to have been the first treatise to unite the teachings of Yoga and Āyurveda.

Although the same set of five bodily winds occurs in the two Indian systems, Yoga and Āyurveda, the one dealing with ascetic meditation and the other with medicine, each has maintained its own doctrine of bodily winds. Developments in the doctrine tended to remain largely independent of each other, with one possible exception. The medical doctrine began from a yogic formulation, from which it deviated by the application of an āyurvedic medical epistemology to the five bodily winds. Then in the late classical period, the Vāgbhaṭas included the winds' role in the mental processes, reflective of yogic doctrines, perhaps as an effort to provide a complete understanding of the doctrine of breath. Finally in the sixteenth century, when Yoga and Āyurveda were united for the first time, the yogic ideas prevailed. Today, as Āyurveda becomes ever more commercialized through contact with Western practitioners of alternative and complementary healing modalities, Yoga and Āyurveda again join hands to produce what I have elsewhere called New Age Āyurveda (Zysk 2001; 2002).

NOTES

[1] This paper serves as the point of departure for our current discussion; and the reader should refer to it for a more detailed study of the early Indian ideas about wind and breath.

[2] Ṛv 10.129.1-2. Translation by Basham (1959: 247).

[3] Ṛv 10.90.13. See Basham (1959: 241).

[4] It is sometimes also called *māruta*, from *marut*, the name of the Vedic storm-gods.

[5] The editions and translations of Sanskrit texts used in this paper are found in the list of references. The list of abbreviations immediately preceding the list of references guides the reader to the exact reference. For example, Ys 2.49-50 = *Yogasūtra*, chapter 2, sūtras 49-50, and CaSū 12.8 (p. S109) = *Caraka Saṃhitā*, Sūtrasthāna, chapter 12, verse, 8, and so on.

[6] A discussion of the five bodily breaths in the *Bhela Saṃhitā* is rather incomplete due to the fragmentary nature of the transmitted text. It contains no mention of the standard five breaths or winds, although the general notion of *prāṇa* as the principal indicator of life in living beings does occur (see BhSū 15.1, 2, 7; In 4.4-6, 9, 10; 9.4; Ci 1.42; and Si 6.12-13). For a detailed discussion of the authors, dates, and contents of these four works, the reader should consult Meulenbeld (1999-2002: Vol. 1A and B).

[7] Following the commentator, Ḍalhaṇa. At SuŚā 4.3, the twelve elements of life (*prāṇas*) are fire (*agni* = *pitta*); water (*soma* = *kapha*); wind (*vāyu*); the three qualities: *sattva*, *rajas*, and *tamas*; the five sense organs; and the soul (*bhūtātman*).

[8] Following the commentator, Ḍalhaṇa.

[9] It should be noted that the As is in prose, while the Ah is in verse.

[10] Here the sequence of the five winds is different from that found in the earlier works, where *vyāna* and *samāna* are reversed.

[11] See Meulenbeld (1999-2002: Vol. 2A, 499-501 and 2B 504-5). Cf. Shamasastry (1922: xv).

[12] Ās 3.62-3: yāvad dhātusirādisañcaratprāṇāpānavyānodānasamānānilanirodhanaṃ bhramahetukem// 62// āsannaviṣayakajñānahetukāntarātmāntaḥkaraṇayogābhyāsavaśāt pavananirodhanād arogī sa cirāyur bhavati//63//.

ABBREVIATIONS

Ah Aṣṭāṅgahṛdaya Saṃhitā
As Aṣṭāṅgasaṃgraha
Ās Āyurvedasūtra
Bh Bhela Saṃhitā
Ca Caraka Saṃhitā
Ci Cikitsāsthāna
Ṛv Ṛgveda
In Indriyasthāna
Ni Nidānasthāna
Śā Śārīrasthāna
Si Siddhisthāna
Su Suśruta Saṃhitā
Sū Sūtrasthāna
Ys Yogasūtra

REFERENCES

[Ānandāśramasthapaṇḍitāḥ (ed.) 1984] Vācaspatimiśraviracitaṭīkāsametaśrībyāsabhāṣyasametāni. *Pātañjalayogasūtrāni* | etat pustakam ānandāśramasthapaṇḍitaiḥ saṃśodhitam, tac ca puṇyapattane ānandāśramamudraṇālaye mudrayitvā prakāśitam | caturthīyamaṅkanāvṛttiḥ śakābdāḥ 1906 khristābdāḥ 1984 (Ānandāśramasaṃskṛtagranthāvaliḥ granthāṇkaḥ 47).

[Āṭhavale, Ananta Dāmodara (ed.) 1980] Śrīmadvṛddhavāgbhaṭaviracitaḥ *Aṣṭāṅgasaṅgrahaḥ* induvyākhyāsahitaḥ sampādakaḥ vaidya anaṃta dāmodara āṭhavale ... śrīkṛṣṇāṣṭamī, śake 1902, 1 September 1980 ... maheśa anaṃta āṭhavale ... pune 4.

Basham, A.L. 1959. *The wonder that was India.* New York: Grove Press.

[Bhiṣagācārya Harīśāstrī Parāḍaka (ed.) 1939/1982] Śrīmadvāgbhaṭaviracitam *Aṣṭāṅgahṛdayam* śrīmadaruṇadattaviracitayā sarvāṅgasundarākhyayā vyākhyayā, hemādripraṇītayā āyurvedarasāyanāhvayā ṭīkayā ca samullasitam ... aṇṇā moreśvara kuṃṭe ... , kṛṣṇaśāstrī navare ity etaiś ca pūrvaṃ saṃskṛtam parāḍakaropāhvane sadāśivasūnunā hariśāstriṇā bhiṣagācāryeṇa saṃśodhitam. ... Caukhambhā Orientalia ... Vārāṇasī, Dillī, 1982 (Jayakṛṣṇadāsa Āyurveda Granthamālā 52). (Originally published in 1939 by N.S. Press, Bombay.)

Hariharānanda Āraṇya, Swāmi 1981/1983. *Yoga philosophy of Patañjali.* Containing his Yoga aphorisms with Vyāsa's commentary in Sanskrit and a translation with annotations including many suggestions for the practice of Yoga. Rendered into English by P.N. Mukerji; rpt Albany: State University of New York Press.

Meulenbeld, G.J. 1999-2002. *A history of Indian medical literature.* 5 parts in 3 vols. Groningen: Egbert Forsten.

Shamasastry, R. (ed.) 1922. *Āyurvedasūtram yogānandanāthabhāṣyasametam.* (University of Mysore Oriental Publications, Sanskrit Series 61). Mysore: Printed at the Government Branch Press.

Sharma, Priyavrat (ed. & trans.) 1981-94. *Caraka-Saṃhitā.* Agniveśa's treatise refined and annotated by Caraka and redacted by Dṛḍhabala. (Text with English translation). (Jaikrishnadas Ayurveda Series 36). 4 vols. Varanasi and Delhi: Chaukhambha Orientalia.

——— (ed. & trans.) 1999-2001. *Suśruta-Saṃhitā*, with English translation of text and Ḍalhaṇa's commentary along with critical notes. (Haridas Ayurveda Series 9). 3 vols. Varanasi: Chaukhambha Visvabharati.

Srikantha Murthy, K.R. (trans.) 1991-5. *Vāgbhaṭa's Aṣṭaṅga Hṛdayam* (text, English translation, notes, appendices, indices). (Krishnadas Ayurveda Series 27). 3 vols. Varanasi: Krishnadas Academy.

——— (trans.) 1995-7. *Aṣṭaṅga Saṃgraha of Vāgbhaṭa* (text, English translation, notes, index). (Krishnadas Ayurveda Series 79). 3 vols. Varanasi: Chaukhambha Orientalia.

[Trivikramātmaja Yādava Śarman, ed. 1941/1981] Maharṣiṇā punarvasunopadiṣṭā tacchiṣyeṇāgniveśena praṇītā carakadṛḍhabalābhyāṃ pratisaṃskṛtā *Carakasaṃhitā* | śrīcakrapāṇidattaviracitayā āyurvedadīpikāvyākhyayā saṃvalitā | ācāryopāhvena trivikramātmajena yādavaśarmaṇā saṃśodhitā | (tṛtīyāvṛttiḥ) | mumbayyāṃ satyabhāmābāī pāṇḍuraṅga ityetābhiḥ nirṇayasāgaramundraṇālayasya kṛte tatraiva mudrāpayitvā prasiddhiṃ nītā | śakābdaḥ 1863, kristābdaḥ 1941. (Reprinted as a fourth edition, New Delhi: Munśīrām Manoharlāl Publishers Pvt Ltd, 1981.)

[——— & Nārāyaṇa Rāma Ācārya 'Kāvyatīrtha' (eds) 1938/1980] Maharṣiṇā suśrutena viracitā *Suśrutasaṃhitā* | śrīḍalhaṇācāryaviracitayā nibandhasaṃgrahākhyavyākhyayā nidānasthānasya śrīgayadāsācāryaviracitayā nyāyacandrikākhyapañjikāvyākhyayā ca samullasitā ārambhastaś cikitsāsthānasya navamādhyāyaparyantā ācāryopāhvena trivikramātmajena yādavaśarmaṇā śeṣā ca nārāyaṇa rāma ācārya 'kāvyatīrtha' ity anena saṃśodhitā. ... caukhambhā oriyanṭāliyā ... vārāṇasī/dillī, 1980 (reprint of 1938 edition). (Jayakṛṣṇādāsa Āyurveda Granthamālā **34**).

ZYSK, K.G. 1993. The science of respiration and the doctrine of the bodily winds in ancient India. *Journal of the American Oriental Society* **113**, 198-213.

——— 2001. New Age Āyurveda or what happens to Indian medicine when it comes to America. *Traditional South Asian Medicine* **6**, 10-26.

——— 2002. Classical Ayurveda and its modern practice: study and fieldwork of Ayurveda in India and in America. In *Ayurveda at the crossroads of care and cure.* Proceedings of the Indo-European seminar on Ayurveda held at Arrábida, Portugal, in November 2001 (ed.) A. Salema, 218-28. Lisbon and Pune: Centro de História de Além-Mar Universidade Nova de Lisboa.

8
The experience of wind in early and medieval Chinese medicine

ELISABETH HSU *University of Oxford*

Qi and *feng*, and the Chinese articulation of the dialectic of nature and culture

Qi 氣 (breath, vapour, air), which was only occasionally mentioned in pre-dynastic texts, became a concept central to elite medical writings of the Han dynasty (206 BCE–220 CE) and later.[1] It has been defined as 'stuff that makes things happen' or 'stuff in which things happen' (Sivin 1987: 47). As elusive, transformative, and dynamic matter, like breath, fog, airs, cloud, and vapour, *qi* had agency; it moved and caused movement, transformed, was transformed, could accumulate and dissipate. An early Han text notes that, in following warmth, it had a tendency to rise (see p. S129 below). Its graph 氣 encloses the radical for 'rice' (*mi* 米), which suggests that Han lexicographers thought that Chinese 'ethnophysiology' drew on the food technology of vaporization. Vaporisation technology developed as early as in the Neolithicum and the Zhou dynasty (eleventh century–221 BCE), as is evident from archaeological finds of clay pots with holes in the bottom and so-called '*yan*' bronze vessels (Rawson 1990: vol. 2, 335-44),[2] and it has remained a pivot of Chinese cooking ever since. A rubbing from a relief of a Han dynasty kitchen depicts vapour as 'real' as furnaces and pans, meat and poultice, in that it has form and colour as they do, and a pattern that indicates presumably upwards movement (An Jinhuai & Wang Jugang 1972: 61).

Qi became a 'key term in the Chinese articulation of the dialectic of nature and culture' (Lewis 1990: 218), when human action started to be explained in terms of an 'all-embracing interdependence'. Lewis (1990: 213) speaks of *qi* as 'shared substrate' within which humans and the physical world not only followed common principles but also acted upon each other through a common medium, much like Ingold (this volume) suggests that the kite needs wind to fly and the painter air to paint a tree. Lewis links the rising importance of *qi* during the last three centuries BCE to a change in the political order: 'The aristocratic pattern of sanctioned violence in the Zhou city-states [changed] to the universal authoritarian pattern that characterized the territorial states' (1990: 234). After the unification of these city-states and the installation of the imperial 'feudal bureaucracy' of the Qin (221-206 BCE) and Han, as state authority aimed at reaching out to the most remote regions of the empire, *qi* became prominent as universal medium in medicine, the sciences, and philosophy.

Qi was all-pervasive, permeating the macrocosm and the microcosm. However, even as a unifying concept, it lent itself to the expression of diversity (Hsu 1999: 81-2). What mattered was not one *qi* but a whole chorus of them, as it/they resonated in mutual interdependence with locality. We observe here a very different understanding of how humankind related to the universe from that of the detached, interiorized Cartesian subject that engages in a gendered relation with nature, outlined by Bordo and Moussa (1999) as the abstract, universal 'Man' of modern Europe, who has risen above the limitations of any locality-specific perspective, and strives to tame 'Nature'.

Despite these differences between the ancient Chinese and the modern European 'body ecologic', their body politic has strikingly similar features. China's dynastic bureaucracy fostered regulated bodies, not entirely unlike the way in which the modern nation-state inscribed itself in 'docile bodies' (Foucault 1979 [1975]; 1989 [1963]).[3] The canonical Chinese medical texts were composed and compiled within a society where the power of governance was to a significant extent absorbed by administrative institutions, and thereby was made invisible and diffuse, although the political order rested on an ideology of the emperor's sovereignty, and although in practice the kin relations and family factions among the nobility who challenged it remained a constant concern for the imperial household (Lewis 1990; Twitchett & Loewe 1986). Canonical Chinese medicine was a medicine of moderation that preached against the life style marked by periodic feasting and exuberance, indulgences, and excess that was intrinsic to the ritual life of the Zhou. It appealed to the responsibility of the self for the self and advocated regularity in food intake and drinking, sleep and waking, feelings and emotions. It was within this medicine of moderation that *qi* figured as universal medium and principle of agency.

The term *feng* 風 (wind) is older than that of *qi* and was already known from oracle bone inscriptions of the second millenium BCE (Kuriyama 1994: 34 cites Hiraoka 1968: 48 and Akatsuka 1977: 442; see also Unschuld 1980: 26). In medical writings, the notion of *qi* never entirely replaced *feng*. When Wang Chong 王充 of the first century CE interpreted the graph 風 as a composite of *fan* 凡 (ordinary) and *chong* 虫 (insect), he associated wind with a life-engendering principle rather than with contagion through harmful microbes (see p. S128 below). However, Kuriyama takes a different stance when he points out the distinctive semantic fields of wind and *qi*: 'Although the timely, "proper" winds ordering the four seasons were gradually subsumed into the notion of *qi*, the notion of wind survived and flourished in classical medicine especially in the form of disorderly, "empty" winds' (1994: 35). The concept of *qi* was used for referring to the regular occurrences of wind events, while *feng*-winds 'embodied contingency and chance ... whence the association of winds with the most dramatic illnesses – stroke, epilepsy, madness' (1994: 36). Kuriyama is careful, however, to speak of trends and not clearly demarcated dichotomies. While insistent that 'despite their genetic connection and semantic overlap, wind and *qi* never became identical' (1994: 35), he indicates that winds were sometimes thought to refer to regular (seasonal) change without bearing any harm, and *qi* to noxious or sudden transformations.

Although Kuriyama noted that 'the imagination of winds is virtually invisible in the historiography of medicine' (1999*a*: 234) when he spoke of the secondary literature on Greek medicine from the early twentieth century, this does not apply to the history of Chinese medicine. Japanese scholarship discussed the centrality of wind in shamanic practice and medical rationale (e.g. Ishida 1991; Yamada 1980), as has Unschuld (1980; 1982), while Kuriyama's (1994; 1999*a*; 2000) imaginative writings on the Greek and Chinese winds have been seminal in bringing the history of the body into focus.

This paper discusses mostly winds of the late Warring States (475-221 BCE) and early Han, but sometimes also ventures into the medieval Tang (618-907 CE). It demonstrates that in contrast to canonical medical writings, early Chinese texts on self-cultivation and medicine distinguished between *qi* and *feng* as inner and outer winds. Given that early texts emphasized the regulation of *qi*-breath and referred to *feng* as environmental forces, winds, gales, and also daemons, all of which were capricious, the contrast Kuriyama makes between the regular *qi* and the unruly *feng* finds in them a faint echo. However, since his writings have a tendency to underestimate historical change, the contrast he makes reflects perhaps more an understanding of late imperial than early China.

In the late Warring States and early Han, the internal regulation of breaths and emotions tended to be related in the language of *qi* (e.g. *Guanzi* 49: 78), and although *qi* was sometimes mentioned as an aspect of heaven or cloud, seasonal, climatic, and weather conditions were given primarily in terms of *feng* (e.g. *Zuo zhuan* 41, 'Zhao' I; see also *Ling shu* 77: 468-9 and 79: 475-6). This finding can be reconciled with one of Kuriyama's more recent statements that 'people fell ill for many reasons, but two factors mattered most: the emotions and the weather' (2000: 4). The emotions tended to be communicated in the language of *qi* and the weather in terms of *feng*; both arose from the attention physicians gave subtle atmospheric change.

Internal qi *in early China, and the winds of the environment*

Every student of Chinese medicine will tell you that 'wind is the origin of the hundred disorders' (*feng bai bing zhi shi* 風百病之始) (*Ling shu* 49: 400, and a variant in *Su wen* 19: 61), but as Kuriyama (1994: 38) points out, this is a hyperbolic claim because medical texts mention many more aetiologies. Furthermore, medical reasoning in terms of wind may not have been as prominent in pre- and early imperial China as is generally assumed. As this paper will show, it is most unlikely that the above claim applies to medical practice of the third and early second century BCE, when excess in *yang*-heat or *yin*-coldness/numbness, in particular, were experienced as illness-inducing.

Based on the above statement, Unschuld (1982) and Kuriyama (1994: 23) have emphasized the aspects of wind as harbinger of disorder. With regard to pre-imperial China, Unschuld emphasized wind's association with daemonic illness causation. To this close connection between *feng*-winds and *gui* 鬼 ghosts I add that there was also one between *qi* and *shen* 神 (spirits). In other words, *feng* and *qi* both connoted the spirit world. To be sure, *gui* and *shen* were closely related beings, and in some contemporary contexts *gui* of recently deceased persons, which generally are feared as evil, eventually turn into *shen*, as they lose their human qualities and take on more ancestral ones. *Shen*-spirits and ancestors tend to be associated with benevolent powers, but they also can be punitive and need to be ritually appeased (e.g. Poo 1993; Shahar & Weller 1996; Wolf 1974; see also Hsu 2000).

In texts of the third and second century BCE, *gui*-daemons and *feng*-winds usually attack from the outside, and treatment aims at expelling them (e.g. Harper 1996). *Shen*, by contrast, whose inhabitance of specific localities of the landscape made those numinous, eventually took the heart as their abode, particularly in Han medical texts, which thus became the seat of cognition, morality, and emotion (e.g. *Su wen* 23: 76 and 62: 167). This associates wind and *gui* with environmental forces that threaten to invade the person, and against which one has to protect oneself, and *qi* and *shen* with internal ones, strengthened through breath regulation and moderation of emotion.[4] In a similar vein, the *Zuo zhuan* mentions wind among six ecological variables when it states that an excess of *yin* 陰 and *yang* 陽, wind (*feng*) and rain (*yu* 雨), the dark (*an* 暗) and bright (*ming* 明) gives rise to disorder (Legge 1991 [1872]: 573, 580-1), and an early Han manuscript text (Zhangjiashan 2001: 243) lists *qi* among six internal body constituents, together with bone (*gu* 骨), muscle/sinew (*jin* 筋), blood (*xue* 血), vessels (*mai* 脈), and flesh (*rou* 肉). These early texts allude to body-external *feng*-wind pregnant with rain and body-internal *qi*-breath and blood.

From a phenomenological viewpoint, one may point to the perceived distinction between the indoor 'draft' and stormy 'winds' in Victorian England (Jancovic, this volume) and the contemporary Swiss alps (Strauss, this volume). However, the distinction the Chinese lexicon invokes here refers not to the indoor-outdoor boundary of the self inhabiting a house. Rather, the distinction between body-internal *qi* and body-external *feng* parallels that between *vata* and *vayu* in the environment and *prana* in a living organism, as given in the *Egveda*. Although Zysk (this volume) and Lewis (2006) emphasize that philosophers of Vedic India and early China posited a continuum between body internal and environmental winds, the lexicon points out a semantic distinction, which is reinforced by the above passages from the third and second century BCE. This distinction between one's bodily interior and the environment, which may well have implied a phenomenology of experiencing oneself as the centre of one's environment (Lewis 2006: 22-3),[5] is grounded in a life experience found cross-culturally.

The experience of the self and conceptions of the body

Ways in which the self is experienced are closely related to conceptions of the body, and moral tensions within the self are often located in different body parts (Lambek 1998). Among the Baga in West Africa, for instance, selfish greed is located in the belly (Sarro 2000), while awareness of social relatedness is expressed through one's throat, which has the faculty to make moving moral speeches. In Homer a protagonist may, in self-reflexive ruminations, speak to his *thumos* (diaphragm), and in Renaissance and Enlightenment Europe, the emergent forms of 'civilized' society at court that demanded self-restraint had people recognize and cultivate the interiority of the self (Elias 1978-82 [1939]). Out of such particular socio-cultural conditions in seventeenth-century France grew the conception of the Cartesian subject that knows itself primarily through introspection and experiences itself as an autonomous thinking subject. This dividing line between the inner and outer, private and public, shapes and expresses power relations within society for both Norbert Elias and Michel Foucault, and those relations clearly are forged and contained with and in language (Bordo & Moussa 1999).

Texts from retainers kept at the courts of the Warring States nobility suggest that the self was apprehended in a way that appreciated its interiority. When these authors related to the self, they spoke of an outwardly perceived 'form' (*xing* 形) that provided an abode for the invisible *qi* in the body's interior. In early medical manuscript texts of the mid-second century BCE and excerpts from the *Inner canon* that have been interpreted to record body concepts dating to the Warring States, this 'form' had outwardly visible 'colour' (*se* 色), which could be 'freshly white' or 'moldy black' or 'jade'-like, and 'vessels' (*mai* 脈), which visibly 'had exuberance' or were 'insufficient', were 'full/replete' or 'empty/depleted'.[6] The *Guanzi*, a collection of texts of the Warring States, advocates firming up the outward 'form' by means of breathing techniques:

> Stabilize the heart in the interior/centre of the body, make ears and eyes sharp and clear, the four limbs hard and firm, then it can become the abode for the seminal essences. The seminal essences are the seminal essences of *qi*.
> 定心在中 耳目聰明 四肢堅固 可以爲精舍 精也者 氣之精者也 (*Guanzi* 49, 'Nei ye', p. 78, based on translation by Rickett 1998: 43).

The breathing techniques recommended in the *Guanzi* advocate a firming up of muscle and sinew to provide a shelter for the 'seminal essences of *qi*' inside the body. They are reminiscent of those described in Sanskrit medical texts, where the aim of breath control was the mind's stabilization (Zysk, this volume).[7] In early Chinese texts the mind and emotions were related to body-internal processes comprehended in terms of *qi*.

In Kuriyama's (1994: 27-8, *passim*) view, thinking with and of winds led to the discovery of the body. This makes sense in the light of the above-mentioned texts on spell-binding, where the affliction from daemons causes trouble and their ritual propitiation often takes one's house and homestead as the unit of the self (Harper 1996). However it contradicts Lewis (2006: 14), who situates the discovery of the body in the fourth century BCE, on the basis that ritual as a basic Confucian category gave the body a central position.[8] Moreover, the pre-Han *Guanzi* also refers to a body, namely one delimited by an outward 'form'. What is special about the body susceptible to wind is that it had a pore pattern (*cou li* 腠理).

> Straightforward noxiousness – in cases where the body form, after exerting oneself, sweat coming out, the skin's pore pattern opening, meets with depleting winds – it strikes the centre/interior of the person, subtly, hence no one recognizes its state and no one has seen its form.
> 正邪者 身形 若用力 汗出 腠理開 逢虛風 其中人也 微 故莫知其情 莫見其形 (*Su wen* 26: 82).

In *Su wen* 26, the bodily 'form' is endowed with a pore pattern, which can open and close, let internal waters out and external winds come in. It is noteworthy that all texts that Kuriyama (1994: 37) mentions emphasize that wind can attack a body only if it has become weak and depleted (*Su wen* 3, 26, 35; *Ling shu* 46, 50, 79; see also Unschuld 1982). Evidently, wind was thought to attack only certain bodies, those whose physiology was framed in terms of 'depletion' and 'repletion' (*xu shi* 虛實), and, among those, only the depleted ones. Repletion and depletion were visible qualities that could be seen on the surface of the Warring States body 'form', while the canonical *Su wen* 26 assesses them in terms of ecological variables: the winds and waters. The loss of essential waters through sweating, which resulted in states of depletion, allowed wind to gain entry.

Protection against winds consisted of keeping the pore pattern 'tight' (*mi* 密). This is in line with early texts on breathing techniques and gymnastics of 'pulling and guiding' (*dao yin* 導引), which spoke of making the outwardly visible body 'hard' (*jian* 堅) and 'solid' (*gu* 固), like a shiny jade stone, in order to provide a shelter for the mind inside.[9] It is also in line with the *Inner canon*, which has little to say on breath regulation but is eloquent on self regulation: through avoidance of excessive food intake and drinking, which would render flesh and skin flaccid and flabby (e.g. *Ling shu* 46: 388); avoidance of strong emotions, like 'anger' (*nu* 怒), which were 'hard' (*gang* 剛), and would heat up the body and thereby soften flesh that should be firm (e.g. *Ling shu* 46: 388); and avoidance of excessive physical toil, which would make the body surface porous (see above-quoted *Su wen* 26).

My research on the medical case histories in *Shi ji* 105 suggests that among the Han nobility the sort of physical exertion that posed a threat to health was not the tilling of fields but sexual licentiousness (and games of leisure, like the ballgame *cu ju* 蹴踘 in case 25): among the twenty-five medical cases recorded, about half were contracted from an indulgence in wine, sex, and/or sex-induced sweating.[10] Perspiration was not primarily associated with odours, as among the Ongee on the Andaman islands (Pandya, this volume), but brought in association with waters, namely the life-giving waters stored in the womb/bladder and kidneys, and their loss through perspiration (Hsu in press *a*; see cases 4 and 5). Excessive sweating was given as a cause for wind-induced disorders (cases 5 and 9), and, following the rationale of *Su wen* 26, one could argue in a rather mechanistic manner that the loss of these essential waters through an open pore pattern weakened the body, and enabled wind's entry. However, another explanation, grounded in a different connotation of *feng*-winds, is also possible (see pp. S127-9 below).

What causes madness, yang*-heat or wind?*

While the wind-induced disorders in cases 5 and 9 in *Shi ji* 105 highlight a close affinity between sex and wind, contemporary Chinese doctors speak of one between wind and madness. The idiom *fengle* 瘋了 's/he has become windy' means in colloquial language 's/he is mad', and the term *fengbing* 風病 'wind-induced disorder' is synonymous with 'mental illness'. However, in early Han China 'madness' (*kuang* 狂) was caused by rising *yang*-heat, rather than by wind, as evident from case 6 in *Shi ji* 105, early manuscripts, and canonical medical texts.

According to Messner (2000), it was only in the Ming dynasty (1368-1644) that the category *feng bing* became firmly established for disorders of madness, and Chen (2002) provides convincing evidence that the first texts that consistently associate wind and madness date to medieval times. She discusses the *Zhu bing yuan hou lun* of 610 CE and a Dunhuang manuscript (seventh-eleventh century CE) on wind maladies, which with few exceptions manifested in madness. However, neither Messer nor Chen attempts to explain why wind became the main cause of madness by medieval times and later.

Chen does remark that early medical texts associated madness with an affection of the *yang ming* 陽明 (*yang* brightness), and, as will become apparent below, heat was *yang*, and *yang* at its most intense was *yang ming*. Heat affected the *yang* parts of the body, and the *yang ming* comprised the region of heart and stomach in particular. So, in early China, it was not hot-headedness, but rather an over-heated heart that resulted in madness.

Wind, like heat, could have *yang* qualities and affect the body parts above the diaphragm, particularly when contrasted with *yin* coldness that congealed the ones below (e.g. *Su wen* 7: 26). Now, if *yang*-heat and *yang*-winds both could affect the *yang* region of the heart,[11] why would wind rather than heat start to cause madness from medieval China onwards, and why not already in Han times? To gain a fuller understanding for answering this question, let us further explore how winds were experienced in early and medieval China.

Winds, songs and music, local mores and moods

In early China wind was not always associated with the pathological and daemonic. *Feng* meaning airs and winds related also to song and music, local mores and moods. Lewis (1990), in particular, emphasized the close relatedness between wind, mores, and local custom, *feng su* 風俗, and Kuriyama (1994: 32) also noted that *feng*-wind meant *feng*-song in Zhou dynasty China. Both authors point to the constituent *feng* in the title 'Guo feng' 國風 (The Airs of the States) for a collection of poems in the *Shi jing* (Book of Odes), which dates to the first half of the first millennium BCE.

The relation between song and mood is important here, for music was thought to modulate human emotion and morality; therefore, Confucius emphasized the rites, ritual, and music (Nylan 2001). *Feng* in the sense of song and music invokes tunes that communicate rhythms of sociality and modulate emotion, and in the sense of the song-line comes close to the notion of *dao* 道 , the morally right 'way'. *Feng* as 'song' and *dao* as 'morally guiding song-line' have a strikingly close affinity with concepts described in ethnographies of contemporary Southeast Asia, where Roseman (1991: 66), for instance, speaks of the song-line as a 'way' or 'path'. It appears as though ancient China and contemporary Southeast Asia belonged to a larger cultural region, within which the directionality of the wind's blowing or the shaman's singing, the song-line and moral guide-line, were heard and felt in similar ways, even though their medical theories and practices each reflect historically contingent cultural specificity.

Wind as the breath of life

The trigram *xun* 巽 of the *Yi jing* (*Book of changes*, e.g. *Zhou yi*: 69) has been glossed as life-enhancing breath. The 'Great commentary' (Da zhuan 大傳) to the *Yi jing* associates *xun* with spring-time: the worldly cycle of the eight trigrams, which differs from the heavenly cycle in that it orders the trigrams according to seasonal change, begins in the east with the life-engendering 'thunder' (*zhen* 震) and continues in the southeast with this 'wind', *xun*. As a contemporary senior Chinese doctor put it, thunder initiates the sprouting of the seedlings, while this mild wind enhances their growth by gently stroking them (Hsu 1999: 114-16). Here *xun* referred to gentle life-enhancing breezes and this aspect of wind, tender and tactile, was in Han China associated with the season of the emergence of life.

Xun as 'breath of life' is generally not mentioned in medical texts and has not been discussed in the above-quoted secondary literature on wind. The connotations of gently effecting change are an attribute not merely of *xun*, as the changes induced by the external wind *feng* and internal breath *qi* were also called 'subtle' (*wei* 微; e.g. above-quoted *Su wen* 26). Perhaps it was precisely the subtlety of wind physiology and pathology, and its affinities with songs and music, the emotions and morality, rhythm and seasonality, that made it a central concept of Han elite medicine. It allowed for reasoning in terms of possibilities and potentialities in the subjunctive mood (Hsu 1999: 210-12). *Qi*, in particular, became the term *par excellence* for referring to potential and subtle processes of change within the universe at large.

Feng *and* qi *in five agents doctrine*

Canonical medical texts mention neither *qi* nor *feng* as one of the 'five agents' (*wu xing* 五行) 'wood', 'fire', 'earth', 'metal', and 'water'. By contrast, 'air' (*aer*) is one of four constituents that make up the universe in Greek correlative thinking, where already the Hippocratic corpus differentiated between the elements 'water', 'fire', 'earth', and 'air'

(Lloyd, this volume). In full appreciation of the culture-specific connotations of the Greek and Chinese terms for 'fire', 'water', and 'earth', one nevertheless ponders over the absence of 'air' as one of the Chinese five agents. Here considerations of dating may come into play. The Greek system dates to the fifth and fourth century BCE, the Chinese one, due to difficulties in dating the different textual layers of the medical canons, from between the first three centuries BCE and the eleventh century CE. It is likely that when five agents doctrine became prominent in Han China, the terms *feng* and *qi* were already used in a generic sense.[12]

Five agents doctrine drew out a body ecologic sensitive to seasonal change, but the two main texts that outline this doctrine, *Su wen* 4: 17 and 5: 21, did not mention words designating the seasons. Instead, they spoke of the four cardinal directions and the centre (Hsu in press *b*). There is little doubt that changes in wind direction were thought to trigger seasonal change (as noted in almost all papers of this volume). It is unlikely that changes in weather and seasons were experienced with regard to every one of the above five winds, but certainly the cosmological scheme elaborated on the experiential reality that the weather changes with the wind direction.

The spring winds of the medieval body ecologic

Su wen 66: 182, which belongs among the chapters thought to have been interpolated by its medieval editor Wang Bing (fl. 762), is unusual for it includes wind among the five different disorder-inducing ecological variables. Notably, these environmental influences differ from the ancient six mentioned in the *Zuo zhuan* (on p. S120 above). They are mentioned as manifestations in heaven, namely 'wind' (*feng*), 'summer heat' (*shu* 暑), 'humidity' (*shi* 濕), 'dryness' (*gan* 干), and 'coldness' (*han* 寒), and contrasted with the five agents that are given as manifestations on earth. Lived experience of seasonal change in northern China makes plausible the correlation of the hot with summer and the cold with winter, the dry with autumn and the humid with the long summer, which is the rainy season. Interestingly, these four ecological variables are the same as those in Galenic and Islamic medicine, namely the hot and cold, dry and humid. We are reminded that chapter 66 belongs among the seven that became a constitutive part of the *Su wen* presumably in the Tang, when China vividly entertained commercial and cultural exchanges with Central Asia, India, and Europe.

The fifth ecological variable, wind, is particular to Chinese medical reasoning. It correlates with the season spring (as it does in the partly medieval *Su wen* 5 but not in *Su wen* 4). It thus shows continuity with the Han understanding of *xun* that the winds that unfold life arise in the beginning of the yearly cycle, and it also appears to relate a lived experience of seasonal change, much like the above four ecological variables in *Su wen* 66. As anyone knows who has lived in Beijing, and much of northern China, spring winds can be enormously strong and violent. However, the direction whence the spring winds come is not the east, as five agents doctrine has it, which associates spring with the east, summer with the south, autumn with the west, winter with the north, and the long summer with the centre. Today, as in the past, spring winds come from the northwest, from the Gobi desert, whence they have blown for many thousands of years as they brought with them the fine dust particles that form the contemporary fertile loess of Shaanxi province.

So, why were the spring winds associated with the east? Instead of postulating that in antiquity spring winds blew from the east, it is more probable that a complex interweaving of different domains of experience with culture-specific meanings led to the correlation between spring, wind, and the east in five agents doctrine. Whilst the association of wind with the season of spring may well have arisen from lived experience, the association of spring with the east may have been derived from an analogy, or, in structuralist terms, a homology. In the yearly cycle, spring is the season of life's emergence, unfolding, and 'expansion' (*zhang* 張), just as in the daily cycle the east indicates the beginning of a day, for that is where the sun rises. These varied considerations, which all centre on the emergence of life (and the Han interpretation of the age-old *xun*), bring spring, the east, and the *feng*-winds in association with each other.

The above suggests that violent spring winds as harbingers of disorder became an aspect of the 'body ecologic' most evidently by medieval times. At latest by the Song (960-1127) a sixth ecological variable had been added to the above five, 'fire' (*huo* 火), which made out of them a separate diagnostic scheme, today known as that of the 'six excesses' (*liu yin* 六淫) (Sivin 1987: 275-86). *Su wen* 66, which mentions *feng* as a threatening environmental agent within five agents doctrine, implicitly still alludes to the early Chinese experience of wind as pregnant with life-engendering qualities. Yet from the Tang dynasty onwards, *feng*-winds increasingly became associated with the erratic, unpredictable, violent, and disruptive, and for this reason probably became known as such in Western scholarship.

Early medical case records of wind and heat-induced disorders in *Shi ji* 105

The Han medical literature comprises texts of the received tradition, such as the *Inner canon* (which was repeatedly edited in the Tang and Song), and manuscript texts from Mawangdui and other localities (which have been heavily interpreted in contemporary transcription projects). Furthermore, the main dynastic history of the Han, the *Records of the historian* (*Shi ji*) by Sima Qian 司馬遷 (*c*.145-*c*.86 BCE), contains twenty-five medical case histories in the Memoir of the physician Chunyu Yi 淳于意, which constitutes the second part of the 105th chapter (*Shi ji* 105, 2794-817). This case material attends to the individual in that it reports on each patient's gender, social status, and place of residence and has a totalizing aspect in that it systematically records prognostic, diagnostic, and therapeutic practices.[13] It appears to reflect on a period of transition in medical reasoning insofar as in the late Warring States and early Han, the body tended to be discussed in terms of *yin* and *yang* primarily, and physicians paid attention, in particular, to ascending and descending movements, while by the later Han and Tang, bodily processes were primarily framed in terms of wind physiologies and pathologies, regulated by the seasonal cycle (Hsu in press *a*).

Yi had been an official at the kingdom of Qi until 180 BCE, the year in which the king of Qi 齊, after the death of Empress Lü 呂, made a futile attempt to usurp the throne. In this very year, Yi (perhaps a Lü loyalist?) relinquished his post and devoted himself fully to the study of medicine. He had studied for three years when, in 178 BCE,[14] as he practised medicine by wandering 'to the left and right among the feudal lords', he was accused of refusing to treat a patient who had called for him. He was sent to Chang'an 長安, the capital of the Han empire, to be punished by mutilation. Yet as the story goes, his fifth daughter Ti-ying 緹縈, a woman who later was praised for her superb faculty of argument, persuaded the emperor in that very year to rescind all punishment. Yi was sent home and put under house arrest, and also summoned by imperial edict to outline his medical practice.

Inspired by textual research on non-medical, pre-dynastic, and early dynastic texts (e.g. Keegan 1988; Kern 2002), I have gone so far as to suggest that Yi's Memoir is a heavily edited compilation of texts assembled from multiple second-century sources and that the primary source material for the first ten cases may have been composed as early as in the early second century, say around 178 BCE, the year Yi was in Chang'an. I suggest that this medical document contained ten terse case records, which were embellished if not entirely rewritten, in free style prose, by Sima Qian and his team before his death in *c.*86 BCE. If this hypothesis is correct, a single case history (among cases 1-10) can frame bodily processes in terms of *yin* and *yang* in some passages, which appears to have been usual in the third and early second century BCE, and in terms of wind physiologies and pathologies in others, which became fashionable by the first century BCE and later.

Wind as cause of disorder

The case histories are formulaic, and systematically provide information on twenty-five different 'names' of the disorders, their 'causes', and what I have called their corresponding 'qualities' (e.g. the tactile quality of the pulse that is taken as a sign of the disorder). In this reading, *feng*-wind is mentioned as a cause of the disorder in cases 13, 15, and 24. Interestingly, not one single case gives wind as sole cause of the disorder; it is always mentioned in combination. In case 13, 'Wind and sleeping with an open mouth; eating and not rinsing the mouth' (*feng ji wo kai kou, shi er by sou* 風 及臥開口 食而不嗽) is given as cause for tooth caries, and in case 15, 'sweating and frequently going outside; after roasting by the fire, being exposed to great winds' (*liu han shuo chu, jiu yu huo er yi chu jian da feng ye* 流汗數出 灸於火而以出見大風也) is the cause for a damaged spleen. In case 24, wind figures in both the cause and the name of the disorder. The cause is 'frequent wine consumption [probably millet beer] and exposure to strong wind *qi*' (*shu yin jiu yi jian da feng qi* 數飲酒以見大風氣) and the patient is said to suffer from a 'talkative wind' (or 'wind of sluggishness' *ta feng* 沓風, depending how one translates *ta*). Since wind is never given as sole cause of the disorder, it is possible that the source material for the above cases 13, 15, and 24 initially mentioned only 'sleeping with an open mouth', 'sweating and frequently going outside', and 'frequently getting drunk', and that the wind aetiology was added later.

In cases 1-10, wind is not given as a cause of the disorder, but other doctors whom the patient had previously consulted mention it. In Yi's view, these doctors were always wrong: in case 3, they gave the misdiagnosis of a 'numbness entering the interior' (*jue ru zhong* 蹶入中), in case 8, of a 'coldness in the interior' (*han zhong* 寒中), and in case 10, of 'wind entering the interior' (*feng ru zhong* 風入中). In case 10, Yi gives as correct diagnosis a '*qi* in the abdomen/bladder'. Thus, in cases 1-10, neither Yi's notion of *qi* nor the common doctors' of *feng* designates the generic *qi* and *feng* of five agents doctrine. Rather, as in other early texts, *feng*-wind from the environment threatens to intrude into the body, while the body-internal amassment is one of *qi*.

Wind as a diagnostic quality

The pulse quality *feng qi* occurs in cases 5, 8, and 9, and in a first instance appears to correlate with the constituent *feng* in the name of the disorder, namely a 'wind-induced state of utter exhaustion lodged in the bladder' (*feng dan ke pao* 風癉客脬) in case 5, a 'wind-induced numbness' (*feng jue* 風蹶) in case 9, and a 'wind of the void' (*dong feng* 迵風) in case 8 (see also case 20). However, in case 8, the pulse which is 'slippery' (*hua* 滑) has been shown to correlate with the constituent 'wind' in the name, as it does in *Su wen* (18: 55), and it is very likely that '*qi* coming from within' (*nei qi* 內氣) correlated with 'the void' (*dong* 洞). The *dong*-void is an early cosmological concept (e.g. Mawangdui *Huangdi si jing*, 'Dao yuan'; see Yu Mingguang 1993: 203 and 322), cognate with the *dong* 洞-cave. Even to a modern non-Chinese reader its use here makes sense as it so aptly describes the pan-human experience of diarrhoea. In other words, it is only in cases 5 and 9 that the pulse quality 'wind' correlates with 'wind' in the name.[15]

It has been possible to demonstrate that in cases 1-10 every pulse quality mentioned in a case history correlates with a constituent in the name of the disorder (Hsu, in press a). These correlations are not always straightforward, but become intelligible once one understands the medical rationale in which they are grounded. Cases 5 and 9, where 'wind *qi*' as pulse quality correlates with 'wind' in the name, and case 7, where *jia qi* 瘕氣 as pulse quality correlates with *jia* in the name *yi ji jia* 遺積瘕, a 'conglomeration disorder of remnant accumulations', are anomalies insofar as the correlations are facile. No medical training is required to set them up.

Anyone familiar with early medical texts knows that the term *jia* was fashionable and referred to any kind of lump in the bowels (see, e.g., 'Maishu', in Zhangjiashan 2001),[16] and the pervasive use of *feng* and *qi*, once ever-present in medical language, must have been noted also by those who were not practising physicians. A mischievous editor of the early first century may have interpolated here and there modish terms like *feng* (wind) and *jia* (conglomeration). Accordingly, the patient died in case 7 of constipation and in case 8 of diarrhoea, while cases 5 and 9 may well report on editorially wind-induced conditions.

The wind-induced conditions suffered by royalty

If the above considerations are correct, the early first-century editor may have made out of the disorders *dan* (condition of utter exhaustion) and *jue* (numbness), which are widely attested in early texts, the wind-induced conditions *feng dan* and *feng jue*, terms that do occur in other medical texts, but in a different sense. Cases 5 and 9 both concern royalty: the queen dowager of Qi and the king of Jibei 濟北. In both cases, profuse sweating is given as one of the causes of the disorder, which, no doubt, euphemistically hinted at sexual indulgences (see below). From a canonical medical viewpoint (e.g. above-quoted *Su wen* 26), one could argue that profuse sweating happens when the pore pattern is open and that this gives rise to wind-induced conditions. However, as we will see below, the source material for cases 5 and 9, which probably reflects medical reasoning of the early second century, assesses bodily processes within a framework not of wind, but of *yin* and *yang*; *yin* being associated with the cool and cold, and *yang* with the sun's light and heat.

In case 9, the cause of the disorder is said to arise from the king's profuse sweating while 'lying prostrate on the ground'. This ground certainly was earthy and cool and the monosyllabic disorder *jue* meaning 'numbness', as which it was presumably given in the early second century document, is best assessed by a terse passage at the very end, which states that an excess of cool *yin* from the ground had entered the body. However, in its edited form, case 9 concerns a 'wind-induced numbness'. It appears as though the editor of the early first century transformed the *yin*-induced 'numbness' (*jue*) of the early second-century document into a 'wind-induced numbness' (*feng jue*).

In case 5, the cause of the disorder of the queen dowager of Qi is that 'dripping with sweat, she went outside to *xun*' (流汗出循). The term *xun* is opaque to all commentators, but after extensive research appears to designate 'sunbathing', particularly if one takes Yi's subsequent explanation at face value: 'In the case of *xun*, after one takes off one's clothes, the sweat dries in open sunlight' (*xun zhe qu yi er han xi ye* 循者去衣而汗晞也). This sentence makes clear that the queen dowager exposed herself to the excessive *yang* heat of the sun, whereas the quality 'wind-*qi*' and the name of the disorder, 'wind-induced condition of utter exhaustion', suggest that she exposed herself to outdoor winds.

If the king of Jibei's numbness was induced by *yin*-coldness entering from the ground on which he lay after, as Yi puts it in a rather suggestive phrase, 'excessively having made his *yang* enter [a woman's lower orifice]' (*guo ru qi yang* 過入氣陽), and if the queen dowager's exhaustion came from sunbathing and excessive exposure to *yang* sunlight, the bodily processes described in cases 5 and 9 were framed in *yin-yang* reasoning. However, in both cases the bisyllabic name of the disorder suggests that the conditions were wind-induced.

Why would an editor make out of these two cases wind-induced ones? Here a passage from the *Zuo zhuan* (Duke Xi, year 4) comes to mind: 'Windy horses and cattle cannot reach each other' (*feng ma niu bu xiang ji ye* 風馬牛不相及也). Nowadays, this expression is used to signify that people have no dealings with each other, but its early meanings refer to mutual sexual attraction, as indicated, not in any contemporary dictionary, but in the defamed *Matthews*': *feng ma* 風馬 means 'horse on heat'. Indeed, wind was a generative principle (Sterckx 2002: 169-71), and some texts associated it with 'germination' (*meng* 萌) and the generative principle of 'insects' (*chong* 蟲). So, if the *Shi ji* editor indicated that the king of Jibei's numbness and the Qi queen dowager's state of utter exhaustion were wind-induced, he implicitly likened the sexual pleasures of royalty to the generative principle of insects.

Yi, who may have been the medical author who wrote the document of *c.*178 BCE, and the Grand Historian-Astrologer Sima Qian, who may have edited it, have in common that they both were wronged, the former by Qi nobility, the latter by Emperor Wu 武帝. It is widely accepted that Sima Qian had a politico-moral agenda, but his critique could only be expressed in a coded language, which medical jargon is. Since the twenty-five medical case histories form part of a dynastic history, they cannot be read as medical documents only.

Heat-induced madness

Case 6 reports on a patient who eventually went into a state that matches madness (*kuang*), ran about in a delirium, and died three days later. Medical reasoning is complex and protracted, and cannot be reproduced here. In the Mawangdui 'Yinyang vessel text' (1980-5: vol. 4, 10) and corresponding text in *Ling shu* 10: 301, and the so-called 'Yang ming' chapter (*Su wen* 30: 91), madness presents in a similar state of the patient running about manically. In all those texts, the *yang ming* vessel is affected; in case 6, as Yi explains, this is due to rising *yang*-heat. This suggests that in early Han China heat rather than wind was thought to cause madness. One wonders why.

Here the above parallels to contemporary Southeast Asia become important again. They concern not only the notions of *feng* as 'song-line', and *dao* as 'way', but also valuations of hot and cold. The idea that it is good to keep the head cool (and the feet warm) belongs among early Chinese medical rationales (Zhangjiashan 2001: 244), and among basic wisdom in contemporary South and Southeast Asia. In her discussion of ritual surrounding birthing and post-natal care, Laderman (1987) points to the Southeast Asian hot-cold beliefs, which are in certain aspects directly opposed to the

Galenic-Islamic ones. This concerns, in particular, the valuation of the cool. In Southeast Asia, the cool is held in high esteem, while Galen's idea of vital pneuma in the arterial system, which was closely connected to fire in the heart, built on Aristotle's of vital heat as life-engendering (Lloyd, this volume).

However, in the tropical forests of the Orang Asli, *kahyek*, 'a cool, spiritual liquid', continues to be infused into the head souls and heart souls of the ill in ritual (Roseman 1991: 30-2). An Ayurvedic doctor is also recorded to have commented: 'The head must always be cool. Judgment (*putti*) must always be cool. The feet must always be hot. If the feet become cool it is very bad for the body' (Trawick 1992: 141). These examples highlight how highly esteemed coolness is in certain religio-medical contexts of South and Southeast Asia.

In China, the qualities attributed to *yin* and *yang*, the hot and cold, changed over the centuries, and by medieval times their attributes had become inverted (e.g. *Su wen* 5, discussed in Hsu in press *a*). In texts of early China, *qing* 清, which is the desired quality of water, means both 'cool' and 'clear'; it is *yin*. In accord with contemporary Southeast Asian ritual settings, these early Chinese texts esteem the cool and, one surmises, also coolness and clarity of mind.

Yi's case 1, like case 6, is very long and also mentions in the second half rising *yang*-heat that eventually leads to death. Although the text does not explicitly state it, there are sufficient indirect indices to suggest that this rising *yang*-heat was a manifestation of rising hot blood. Thus, the pulse quality of '*qi* coming from the liver', which was the storage place for blood in canonical medicine, was 'murky yet still' (*zhuo er jing* 濁而靜). The murky must have been *yang*, as was the '*yang* murky' (*yang zhuo* 陽濁) in two texts from Mawangdui (1980-5: vol. 4, 85 and 147). So, rising blood perceived as murky and red, thick and hot, implicitly contrasted with clear and cool water, which typically flows downwards. There is an experiential dimension to this, which makes it easy to appreciate that in early China rising heat and hot blood caused madness.

However, in texts of medieval times and later, for instance in *Su wen* 5, the qualities of *yin* and *yang* are inverted: now *yin* is murky (*yin zhuo* 陰濁) and descends due to its heaviness, while *yang* is clear (*yang qing* 陽清). With 'lightness' (*qing* 輕), *yang* rises, which is now highly valued. These changes in the experience of *yin* and *yang* happened presumably in medieval times for reasons the above can only hint at but impossibly prove. Regardless of the reasons for the observed changes, it is obvious that once rising *yang* was positively valued, it became unacceptable that rising *yang*-heat should result in madness. From medieval times onwards, when the violent spring winds had become one of five harmful ecological correlates within five agents doctrine (see *Su wen* 5 and 66; see p. S124), wind rather than rising heat caused madness.

Discussion

Feeling the airs and winds is a pervasive experience, breathing a *sine qua non* of life. We feel it inside out, tactually as it strokes our skin, warms us up, cools us down, rhythmically relaxes and lulls; panting, we hear it; pounding, wheezing, it squeezes us. Violent, it hits, whips, whistles; hard, dry, soft, gentle, subtle, barely perceptible, elusive, it disintegrates, shudders, vanishes.

There are many words for wind, airs, songs, mores, moods, vapours, gases, breezes, and breathing in Chinese, and this article has only explored three, *qi*, *xun*, and *feng*. During Zhou feudal rule *qi* was a term that referred to internal breaths, feelings and emotions, mind and moods, sheltered within a firmed-up bodily form, but as political authority changed, it was projected out from the centre, relinquished the shell which assured its interiority; *hao ran* 浩然, overwhelming and all-encompassing, it rose and spread like vapour, as imperial powers reached out to the periphery. As medium of mutual interdependence, it resonated with locality, and in chorus allowed for dynamics of diversity in the body ecologic. It became central to the medicine of moderation that canonical Chinese medicine is, and within the body politic it imposed regularities of respiration, even if rephrased as life-ensuring rhythms.

The mild and life-engendering airs, the gentle and tenderly stroking breeze, the emergence of life in spring-time, were attributes of the trigram *xun* in the worldly cycle of the trigrams of the *Yi jing*. Such subtle life-engendering feelings that *xun* inspired were not emphasized by medical texts but covertly contained in the connotations of both *qi* and *feng*, which were conceived as agents of 'subtle' change.

Winds, songs, mores; *feng* blew moral tunes already in Zhou times, and as the imperial order asserted itself the winds became a regulatory force within five agents doctrine insofar as those from the four cardinal directions and the centre brought on seasonal change. In early China, *feng*-winds were also a generative principle, as the above discussion of wind-borne insects, the 'windy' horses and cattle (that were on heat), and the sexually indulgent royalty would suggest. They retained their capriciousness, their unpredictable ways, their daemonic and violent characteristics, and became madness-inducing, particularly from medieval times onwards. Thus, the experience of wind as found in early and medieval Chinese medical texts brought into play the senses, emotions, morality, politics and governance, layers of cultural connectedness and historical contingency.

NOTES

This paper presents material derived from longstanding research for a translation and anthropologically informed interpretation of the Memoir of two medical doctors in *Shi ji* 105, and their medical case records. It also includes on observations that colleagues who work on early Chinese texts communicated to me in conversation, most notably Hans van Ess, Brandon Miller, Jörg Schuhmacher, and Roel Sterckx. The research on *Shi ji* 105 was funded by the National Science Foundation of the United States, the Swiss National Foundation, and the Chiang Chingkuo Foundation. The paper benefited from editorial advice by two anonymous reviewers and Chris Low.

[1] 'Chinese medicine' is shorthand in this volume for referring to a wide range of literate traditions of elite medical learning in imperial China. Their learning elaborates on knowledge and practice recorded in so-called 'canonical medical texts', first compiled in the Han dynasty, which comprise, most importantly, the *Huangdi nei jing* (Yellow Emperor's inner canon), short: *Nei jing*, which consisted of the two books *Su wen* (Basic questions) and *Ling shu* (Divine pivot), the *Zhen jiu jia yi jing* (A-B canon of acupuncture and moxibustion), *Shang han za bing lun* (Discourse on cold damage and miscellaneous disorders), and the *Shennong ben cao jing* (Divine husbandsman's canon of the materia medica). Each of these texts has a complicated textual history, and in its extant version may not only reflect ideas specific to the Han dynasty. On their dating, see Keegan (1988), Ma Jixing (1990), Sivin (1993), Unschuld (2003: 3-7); on the dating of pre-Han and other Han texts, see Loewe (1993).

[2] See also Harper: '[T]he graph *qi* 氣 ... may have had earlier associations with food and breath' (1999: 862).

[3] This is said in awareness that in his essay 'The subject and power', Foucault said:

> Since the sixteenth century, a new political form of power has been continuously developing. This political structure, as everyone knows, is the state ... the state power ... is both an individualizing and a totalizing form of power. Never, I think, in the history of human society – has there been such a tricky combination in the same political structures of individualization techniques, and of totalization procedures (1982: 213).

This statement, to date, does not appear to have been substantiated in a comparative, cross-cultural case study.

[4] Again, it is important to note that there is no one standard and that some texts, particularly later ones, claim the contrary. In the medieval *Su wen* 66: 182, *shen*, much like *qi*, is said to permeate the universe (translated by Hsu 1999: 116-18) and in the *Canon of categories* of 1624, *gui* can arise in the heart if there is emotional imbalance (Messner 2000: 105 quotes *Zhangshi lei jing* 20: 246a).

[5] *Zhong* 中 designates mostly an undefined 'interior' in early Chinese medical texts, and only later takes on meanings of the 'centre' or 'striking the centre' (Hsu in press *a*).

[6] Detailed textual references and translations are given in Hsu (in press *a*).

[7] They appear to differ from Sanskrit texts, however, as Zysk speaks of a 'binding' of the cosmic winds through these breathing techniques, which is reminiscent of the contemporary 'binding' of the souls among the Orang Asli (Roseman, this volume), but all the early texts that Lewis (2006: 22 fn. 38) cites, which are relevant in this context, do not refer to winds, even when they invoke a menacing external world.

[8] Lewis also points out the phonetic and graphic link between 'ritual' (*li* 禮) and 'body' (*ti* 體), a similarity which however primarily reflects Han lexicography.

[9] If this outward form was also to preserve 'face' (*mian zi* 面子), even in cases of internal turmoil, it may have laid early foundations for ways in which emotionality is dealt with in contemporary China, where a 'loss of face' (*diu lian* 丢臉), although considered a remnant of 'feudal China', is equivalent to loss of one's social persona.

[10] To be precise, the cause was sex in five cases, and sex-induced sweating in three cases, wine in three cases, and wine and women in two cases, making thirteen cases in total. In cases 1-10, eight out of ten were caused by an indulgence in wine and/or women.

[11] Not all harm that heat and wind caused in the upper body parts resulted in madness. Rising heat could also lead to a headache (*Shi ji* 105, case 1), and wind to pain in the head and eyes (*Su wen* 42: 119-20; Chen 2002: 129-30).

[12] This is said in awareness that occasionally they did take on specific meanings. For instance, *qi* meaning belching and flatulence, as known from the second-century Mawangdui and Zhangjiashan manuscripts, occasionally occurs in this sense also in later texts. On *feng*-wind, see below.

[13] The Memoir of the legendary physician Bian Que 扁鵲, recorded in the first part of the chapter, also concerns medicine and *qi* but does not discuss *feng*-wind.

[14] I take the date that is given in the text at face value. Loewe (1997) makes use of the dates given in parallel passages of other chapters and of the names and titles of Yi's clientele, and dates the composition of the Memoir to 164–153 BCE. I question the latter method of dating because some names of the patients have a literary quality in that they sometimes rhyme or are nicknames. Even if one takes the titles of Yi's clientele as indices for dating, the titles mentioned in cases 1-10 existed already in 178 BCE (Hsu in press *a*).

[15] *Feng* is a constituent in the name of the wind-induced disorders of cases 5 and 9, the 'wind of the void' in cases 8 and 20, and the above-discussed case 24.

[16] The pervasive *jia* disorders in early Han China are curiously similar to *katakori*, which became a fashionable disorder in Edo Japan (Kuriyama 1999*b*).

REFERENCES

A. Modern works

AKATSUKA, K. 赤塚忠 1977. Kaze to miko 風と巫女 (Wind and spirit medium). In *Chûgoku kodai no shûkyô to bunka: Yin ocho no saishi* 中國古代の宗教と文化: 殷王朝の祭祀 (Religion and culture in ancient China: a study of the rituals of the Yin dynasty), K. Akatsuka, 415-42. Tokyo: Kadokawa Shoten.

AN JINHUAI 安金槐 & WANG YUGANG 王与剛 1972. Mixian Dahuting Handai huaxiang shimu he bihua mu 密縣打虎亭 漢代畫象石墓 和 壁畫墓 (The Han tombs with stone reliefs and wall paintings from Dahuting in Mi prefecture). *Wenwu* **10**: 49-63.

BORDO, S. & M. MOUSSA 1999. Rehabilitating the 'I'. In *Feminist interpretations of René Descartes* (ed.) S. Bordo, 280-304. Pennsylvania: Pennsylvania State University Press.

CHEN, C. 2002. Medicine, society, and the making of madness in imperial China. Ph.D. thesis in history, University of London.

ELIAS, N. 1978-82 [1939]. *The civilising process* (trans. E. Jephcott). Oxford: Blackwell.

FOUCAULT, M. 1979 [1975]. *Discipline and punish: the birth of the prison* (trans. A.M. Sheridan). London: Penguin.

——— 1982. The subject and power. In *Michel Foucault: beyond structuralism and hermeneutics* (eds) H. Dreyfus & P. Rabinow, 208-26. Chicago: University Press.

——— 1989 [1963]. *The birth of the clinic: an archaeology of medical perception* (trans. A.M. Sheridan). London: Routledge.

Harper, D. 1996. Spellbinding. In *Religions of China in practice* (ed.) D.S. Lopez, 241-50. Princeton: University Press.

——— 1999. Warring States natural philosophy and occult thought. In *The Cambridge history of ancient China: from the origins of civilization to 221 B.C.* (eds) M. Loewe & E. Shaughnessy, 813-84. Cambridge: University Press.

Hiraoka, T. 平岡禎吉 1968. *Enanji ni arawareta ki no kenkyû* 淮南子に現われた気の研究 (A study on *qi* in the *Huainanzi*). Tokyo: Risôsha.

Hsu, E. 1999. *The transmission of Chinese medicine.* Cambridge: University Press.

——— 2000. Spirit (*shen*), styles of knowing, and authority in contemporary Chinese medicine. *Culture, Medicine and Psychiatry* **24**, 197-229.

——— in press *a*. *The telling touch: pulse diagnosis in early Chinese medicine. With translation and interpretation of twenty-five medical case histories and the entire Memoir of Chunyu Yi in the Shi ji, chapter 105 (ca 86 BCE).* Cambridge: University Press.

——— in press *b*. The cultural in the biological: the five agents and the body ecologic in Chinese medicine. In *Holistic anthropology: emergences and divergences* (eds) D. Parkin & S. Ulijaszek. Oxford: Berghahn.

Ishida, H. 石田博 1991. Kaze no kami no hakken 風の神の発見 (The discovery of the god of wind). In *Chûgoku no shinwa* 中国の神話 (Chinese myths), H. Ishida, 76-109. Tokyo: Chikuma shobô.

Keegan, D.J. 1988. The 'Huang-ti Nei-Ching': the structure of the compilation; the significance of the structure. Ph.D. thesis in history, University of California at Berkeley.

Kern, M. 2002. Methodological reflections on the analysis of textual variants and the modes of manuscript production in early China. *Journal of East Asian Archaeology* **4**, 143-81.

Kuriyama, S. 1994. The imagination of winds and the development of the Chinese conception of the body. In *Body, subject, and power in China* (eds) A. Zito & T.E. Barlow, 23-41. Chicago: University Press.

——— 1999*a*. *The expressiveness of the body and the divergence of Greek and Chinese medicine.* New York: Zone Books.

——— 1999*b*. The Japanese complaint of *katakori* and the puzzle of local diseases. In *Medicine and the history of the body: proceedings of the 20th, 21st and 22nd International Symposium on the Comparative History of Medicine: East and West* (eds) Y. Otsuka, S. Sakai & S. Kuriyama, 3-21. Tokyo: Ishiyaku EuroAmerica, Inc.

——— 2000. Epidemics, weather, and contagion in traditional Chinese medicine. In *Contagion: perspectives from pre-modern societies* (eds) L.I. Conrad & D. Wujastyk, 3-22. London: Ashgate.

Laderman, C. 1987. Destructive heat and healing prayer: Malay humoralism in pregnancy, childbirth and postpartum period. *Social Science and Medicine* **25**, 357-65.

Lambek, M. 1998. Body and mind in mind, and body and mind in body: some anthropological interventions in a long conversation. In *Bodies and persons: comparative perspectives from Africa and Melanesia* (eds) M. Lambek & A. Strathern, 103-23. Cambridge: University Press.

Legge, J. 1991 [1872]. The Chinese classics, vol. 5: *The Ch'un ts'ew with the Tso chuen.* Taipei: SMC Publishing.

Lewis, M.E. 1990. *Sanctioned violence in early China.* Albany: State University of New York Press.

——— 2006. *Construction of space in early China.* Albany: State University of New York Press.

Loewe, M. (ed.) 1993. *Early Chinese texts: a bibliographical guide.* Berkeley: Society for the Study of Early China & the Institute of East Asian Studies, University of California.

——— 1997. The physician Chunyu Yi and his historical background. In *En suivant la voie royale: mélanges en hommage à Léon Vendermeersch: études thématiques* 7 (eds) J. Gernet & M. Kalinowski, 297-313. Paris: École Française d'Extrême-Orient.

Ma Jixing 馬繼興 1990. *Zhongyi wenxianxue* 中醫文獻學 (Study of the Chinese medical literature). Shanghai: Shanghai kexue jishu chubanshe.

Mawangdui Hanmu boshu zhengli xiaozu 馬王堆漢墓帛書整理小組 (eds) 1980-5. *Mawangdui Hanmu boshu* 馬王堆漢墓帛書 (Silk documents from a Han tomb at Mawangdui). 4 vols. Beijing: Wenwu chubanshe.

Messner, A.C. 2000. *Medizinische Diskurse zu Irresein in China (1600-1930).* Stuttgart: Steiner.

Nylan, M. 2001. On the politics of pleasure. *Asia Major* **14**, 73-124.

Poo, M.-C. 1993. Popular religion in pre-imperial China: observations on the almanacs of Shui-hu-ti. *T'oung Pao* **79**, 225-48.

Rawson, J. 1990. *Western Zhou ritual bronzes from the Arthur M. Sackler collections.* 2 vols. Washington, D.C.: Arthur M. Sackler Foundation.

Rickett, W.A. 1998. *Guanzi: political, economic, and philosophical essays from early China*, vol. 2. Princeton: University Press.

ROSEMAN, M. 1991. *Healing sounds from the rainforest: Temiar music and medicine*. Berkeley: University of California Press.

SARRO, R. 2000. The throat and the belly: Baga notions of morality and personhood. *Journal of the Anthropological Society of Oxford* **31**, 167-84.

SHAHAR, M. & R.P. WELLER 1996. *Unruly gods: divinity and society in China*. Honolulu: University of Hawaii Press.

SIVIN, N. 1987. *Traditional medicine in contemporary China: a partial translation of revised outline of Chinese medicine (1972) with an introductory study on change in present-day and early medicine*. Ann Arbor: Center for Chinese Studies, University of Michigan.

——— 1993. Huang ti nei ching. In *Early Chinese texts: a bibliographical guide* (ed.) M. Loewe, 196-215. Berkeley: Society for the Study of Early China & the Institute of East Asian Studies, University of California.

STERCKX, R. 2002. *The animal and the daemon in early China*. Albany: State University of New York Press.

TRAWICK, M. 1992. Death and nurturance in Indian systems of healing. In *Paths to Asian medical knowledge* (eds) C. Leslie & A. Young, 129-59. Berkeley: University of California Press.

TWITCHETT, D. & M. LOEWE (eds) 1986. The Cambridge history of China, vol. 1: *The Ch'in and Han Empires, 221 BC–AD 220*. Cambridge: University Press.

UNSCHULD, P.U. 1980. *Medizin in China: eine Ideengeschichte*. Munich: Beck.

——— 1982. Der Wind als Ursache des Krankseins. *T'oung Pao* **68**, 92-131.

——— 2003. *Huang di nei jing su wen: nature, knowledge, imagery in an ancient Chinese medical text*. Berkeley: University of California Press.

WOLF, A.P. 1974. Gods, ghosts, and ancestors. In *Religion and ritual in Chinese society* (ed.) A.P. Wolf, 131-82. Stanford: University Press.

YAMADA, K. 1980. The formation of the Huang-ti Nei-ching. *Acta Asiatica* **36**, 67-89.

YU MINGGUANG 余明光 1993. *Huangdi sijing jinzhu jinshi* 黃帝四經今注今譯 (The Yellow Emperor's four silk canons, with modern annotations and modern translation). Changsha: Yuelu shushe chubanshe.

Zhangjiashan 247 hao Hanmu zhujian zhengli xiaozu 張家山二四七號漢墓竹簡整理小組 (eds) 2001. *Zhangjiashan Hanmu zhujian* 張家山漢墓竹簡 (247 hao mu 二四七號墓) (Bamboo strips from the Han tomb Zhangjiashan [No. 247]). Beijing: Wenwu chubanshe.

B. Premodern sources

Guanzi 管子 (Master Guan). Zhou-Han, fifth century-first century 5th BCE. In *c.*26 BCE edited by Liu Xiang 劉向. *Si bu bei yao* 四部備要. Zhonghua shuju (Shanghai), 1936.

Huangdi nei jing 黃帝內經 (Yellow Emperor's inner canon). Zhou to Han, third century BCE-first century CE. Anon. References to *Huangdi neijing zhangju suoyin* 黃帝內經章句索引 (ed.) Ren Yingqiu 任應秋. Beijing: Renmin weisheng chubanshe, 1986.

Ling shu 靈樞, see *Huangdi nei jing* 黃帝內經.

Shi ji 史記 (Records of the historian). Han, *c.*86 BCE. Sima Qian 司馬遷. Beijing: Zhonghua shuju, 1959.

Su wen 素問, see *Huangdi nei jing* 黃帝內經.

Yi jing 易經 (Book of changes). Anon. Ninth-second century BCE. References to the *Zhou yi* 周易, in *Shi san jing zhu shu* 十三經注疏 (Commentary to the thirteen canons), vol. 1. Qing, 1816. Edited by Ruan Yuan 阮元 . Reprint by Zhonghua shuju (Beijing), 1980.

Zhangshi lei jing 張氏類經 *(The Zhang family's* canon of categories*)* [1624]. Zhang Jiebin 張介賓. Taipei: Wengguang tushu youxian gongsi, 1983.

Zuo zhuan 左傳 (Zuo tradition). Zhou to Han, third-first century BCE. Anon. References to Legge in bibliography A.

9
Pneuma between body and soul

GEOFFREY LLOYD *University of Cambridge*

Two superficial assumptions, one positive, the other negative, have been, and continue to be, made about the ancient Greeks. The first is that they – some of them at least – engaged in a more or less successful all-out attack on superstition (*deisidaimonia*) in a move, dubbed by some extremist commentators the Greek 'miracle', in which *logos* or rationality replaced *muthos*, myth. The second is that they invented a whole string of dichotomies that have hamstrung Western thought ever since, the polar oppositions between being and becoming, reality and appearance, subject and object, nature and culture, intelligible and perceptible, and, not least, mind and body. In both cases the assumptions represent drastic simplifications, if indeed they have any grain of truth in them at all. A brief study of *pneuma* is one way of showing how very much more complex and interesting the problems were.[1] In particular, that concept lies at the heart of several Greek attempts to bridge the gap that they themselves opened up between mind and body, attempts that met, as we shall see, with only limited success. Yet in that regard it is worth noting, at the outset, that the mind-body problem can hardly be said to have been resolved, even today, with all the advances that have been made in neurophysiology and cognitive science.

A distinctive feature of much ancient Greek thought on a wide range of problems is that there was no consensus, let alone anything approaching an orthodoxy, on the solutions. Our written sources, from Homer onwards, provide evidence of a bewildering array of views about the nature of wind and air outside the body, on the role of breath or air within it, on the relations between these two, and many other questions. Moreover, those views were expressed in a vocabulary that was far from stable and agreed. Different authors appropriate the same expressions for quite different functions in their own particular theories. If I am asked for the meaning of some of the main terms used in this area, such as *pneuma* or *aer*, I am unable to answer for the Greeks as a whole, but have to relativize my reply to particular authors.[2]

Let me justify that last point with a little basic philology, which will serve at the same time to give a first indication of some of the differences in the beliefs that were entertained. There are no less than five main terms for air, breath, wind, namely *aer*, *aither*, *pneuma*, *phusa*, and *anemos* – as well as a lot of minor ones (e.g. *aella*, *thuella*, and *anathumiasis*, where the distinction between two kinds of *anathumiasis* figures prominently in Aristotle's *Meteorology*). Let me take my five in reverse order, since the last, *anemos*, is the least problematic, even though there is no shortage of variety in the beliefs associated with it.

Anemos is a regular term for (external) wind, though it is also used of 'winds' inside the body. But there is plenty of evidence in our early texts of beliefs about the powers of winds. Let me rehearse a little of this.

In Hesiod's *Theogony* (378ff.), *anemos* is the generic term used for the 'strong-hearted' winds that Dawn (*Eos*) bore to *Astraios* ('Starry one'), 'a goddess mating in love with a god'. The three most important winds, Zephyrus (West), Boreas (North), and Notus (South), are named as their offspring. Since the whole story of the generation of things in Hesiod is mainly (though not exclusively) cast in genealogical terms, as the outcome of sexual reproduction in other words, it is natural for the winds, too, to be personified. Yet there is much more to it than that. In the *Iliad* (23.194ff.), Achilles prays to Boreas and Zephyrus to blow on the funeral pyre of Patroclus. Iris (rainbow) hears his prayer and goes to fetch them to answer his call. Cults dedicated to the winds are attested in the literary and archaeological sources, even before Homer. A 'priestess of the winds' (*anemon hiereia*) is recorded in the earliest evidence for written Greek, the Linear B tablets in this case from Cnossos. One of the most famous buildings dedicated to the winds is the so-called Tower of Winds, the Horologion of Andronikos, at Athens. In a famous passage in Plato's *Phaedrus* (229bff.), mention is made of an altar to Boreas outside the city marking the place where the god was supposed to have raped Oreithyia. By the time Plato wrote, there were theorists who were doing their best to rationalize such stories. Socrates himself offers an example: what happened was that the girl was caught by a violent gust of wind when playing on the rocks by the river and met her end that way. But Socrates himself is made to say that he has no time for such accounts.[3]

The theme of the power of the winds is worked out especially in connection with sex – though also, as we shall see later, in relation to disease. The winds were reputed to be able to impregnate mares, animals whom the Greeks thought to be particularly sex-mad. That idea is repeated many times, including in a fragment of Aristotle. It goes back to Homer, though there, in the *Iliad* (20.221ff.), Boreas is said to take the form of a stallion to impregnate the mares of Erichthonius. In the *History of animals* (573b34ff.) Aristotle says that if sheep or goats copulate when the north wind is blowing, they produce male offspring, if when the south wind does, females, and he adds that female-bearing animals may change and produce males if they face north (Boreas) when copulating. However, when he repeats those points in *On the generation of animals* (*GA*) (767a8ff.), he says that that is 'what shepherds say'.

As we shall see, quite a few doctors and natural philosophers claimed to know a lot about the effects of the winds. But then there were also those reported to be able to control them. Herodotus has a field day describing the wreck of the Persian fleet off Sepias before the engagement at Thermopylae. The Athenians, Herodotus says (VII 189), had been advised in an oracle to pray to Boreas to help them, and they were convinced that their prayers were answered, when a storm then arose that destroyed 'countless' Persian ships. But on the opposite side, the Persian Magi are said to have brought the storm to an end after three days by sacrifices and incantations – unless, Herodotus adds, the wind abated 'of his own accord'. But if Herodotus characteristically hedges his bets on the matter of whether or not humans could control the wind, the Presocratic philosopher Empedocles, for his part, has no compunction in claiming that he can 'quell the might of the winds' (*menos anemon*) in a fragment (111) in which he also says he can raise the dead to life again. This comes from a man who made important contributions to element theory, being the first Greek to propose the view that the material constituents of things are earth, water, air, and fire. But he also said he went around among his fellow-citizens at Acragas accepted by them as an immortal god. So much, one might say, for the triumph of unqualified Greek rationalism.

Phusa, the next of my five terms, belongs to a more prosaic register and needs less comment. It comes from *phusao*, to blow, to puff, and is used of blasts of different kinds: it is one term for 'bellows', and by extension for the bladders from which they were made. It is also used for the crater of a volcano.

The basic senses of *pneo*, next, are blow (of air or breath), breathe in the sense of be redolent of ('smell' in that sense), and breathe in the sense of draw breath, inhale. Homer does not have *pneuma* but uses another cognate noun, *pnoie*, for blasts or breezes. The meanings of *pneuma* include breeze and breath/respiration but stretch to spirit, inspiration, and eventually to ghost, as in what used to be called the Holy Ghost, but is now more often referred to as the Holy Spirit. It is a key term that several theorists use in their attempts to deal with the mind/body problem, and a point to which I shall return.

Finally we have *aither* and *aer*. The latter is distinguished from the former in Homer and Hesiod as mist or haze to clear, bright sky. The main Greek dictionary, Liddell-Scott-Jones, criticizes the ancient grammarians who took *aer* to be the lower, *aither* the upper air in Homer already, but that distinction was made by some ancient authors (e.g. Diogenes Laertius VIII 27, reporting Pythagoras). Both terms figure prominently in early Greek element theory. *Aer* is regularly used of elemental air either on its own, in monistic theories, or as a member of the tetrad fire, air, water, earth (though in that connection Empedocles, who, as I have just noted, introduced that element theory, used *aither* for air, e.g 71, 98, 109, 115, though *aer* in the clepsydra fragment 100).

But of course many early Greek element theories were *not* based on that tetrad. Democritus' principles were atoms and the void, and the atoms were undifferentiated substances. In Plato's version of atomism, there are four simple bodies, to be sure, namely fire, air, water, earth, but they are equated with the regular geometrical solids, tetrahedron, octahedron, icosahedron, and cube, respectively. Aristotle thought that Anaxagoras used *aither* for fire (in his fr. 2 *aer* and *aither* are distinguished as things separated off early in the world-forming process, but that does not vindicate Aristotle's interpretation); but more momentously Aristotle himself introduced that term, on his own account, for his fifth element, the stuff of the heavens, neither hot nor cold, neither wet nor dry, and possessing the property of natural eternal circular motion.

While *aither* took on that particular role in Aristotle, *pneuma* became the key term in Stoicism – and it already has some interesting uses in Aristotle himself, as we shall see (see most recently Berryman 2002). *Pneuma* for the Stoics becomes the 'sustaining principle of the world' (Long & Sedley 1987: I, 287). They distinguished different modes of unity, 'tenor' (*hexis*), 'physique' (*phusis*, nature), and 'soul' (*psuche*). The distinction between the last two corresponded to two kinds of *pneuma*, 'physical' and 'psychic'.

This preliminary run-down on vocabulary gives a foretaste of the problems of interpretation. Some basic distinctions seem reasonably secure, but the appearance often turns out to be deceptive. Plenty of Greek writers provide explicit comments on how the terms should be used, but although we find them keen to legislate on the distinctions, they are sometimes less reliable in keeping to those distinctions themselves. Nor were their recommendations always accepted by others; in fact the problems were never completely resolved.

Take the writer of the Hippocratic treatise *On breaths* (late fifth or early fourth century BCE). Admittedly he has a particular thesis to sell, namely that all diseases come from 'breath' (*phusa*), and he certainly has his work cut out to make that idea stick. But he starts off in chapter 3 with what looks like a useful distinction. The *pneuma* that is in the body, he says, is called *phusa*; that outside the body is called *aer*. That would make *pneuma* the genus, and *phusa* (breath) and *aer* (air) its species. In the subsequent discussion, however, he is perfectly happy to use *aer* of what is enclosed in bodies (where we might have expected *phusa*) (chaps 5, 6, 7, 10): in chapter 12 *phusa* and *aer* are apparently used interchangeably, and in the account of dropsy in that same chapter it seems that all three (*pneuma* included) are intersubstitutable.

On breaths makes exceptional play with this group of terms in its explanations of diseases. But other treatises also do so to a lesser extent. The idea in *On breaths*, chapters 6 and 7 is that there are two kinds of fevers (*puretoi*), namely common and particular. The common kind, called plague, comes from the *pneuma* that everyone equally inhales. But there are other fevers that come from diet. The diets of different individuals differ and so, too, do their fevers in such cases, though the writer still manages to ascribe these, too, according to his overarching thesis, to the greater or lesser quantity of *pneuma* that is ingested with food and drink: witness belching. But a similar idea, without the overall thesis, occurs in *On the nature of man*, chapter 9 (not an integral part of the main treatise, chaps 1-8). When all humans are attacked by the same disease at the same time, we have to put that down to the air we all breathe, for it cannot be diet/regimen that is to blame in such cases, since that differs, as between young and old, men and women, wine-bibbers and the abstemious. But when diseases of all sorts and kinds occur at one and the same time, then it is diet/regimen that is responsible and so that should be changed.

Meanwhile the importance of considering the 'airs' or winds of each place forms one of the three great lessons developed in the Hippocratic *On airs, waters, places* (cf. also *On regimen* II, chap. 38) instructing the itinerant physician on what to look out for as he goes from city to city in his practice. It itemizes the different kinds of diseases to be expected in cities facing winds from different directions, though the quality of the drinking water and the life-style of the inhabitants have also to be taken into account. In a similar vein the *Aphorisms* (III section 5) specifies that south winds cause deafness, dimness of vision, heaviness of the head, torpor, and so on, while the north wind causes coughs, sore throats, constipation, difficulty in passing urine accompanied by shivering, and pains in the sides and chest.

On the sacred disease presents as interesting a mixture of traditional and innovative ideas as does Empedocles. The treatise is famous for its attack on those who claimed to know which deity was responsible for which kind of epileptic seizure and who said that they could cure them by purifications, charms, and incantations.[4] On the other hand the author's own explanation of the condition is pretty fanciful. It is due mainly to the way in which the *phlebes* ('veins': but they contain more than just blood) in the brain become blocked by phlegm. Chapter 16 then announces that it is particularly at the changes in the winds that patients are attacked, most often when the south wind blows, then the north, then the other winds. The north wind is said to precipitate the moisture in the air and to make it clear and bright: it is the healthiest of winds. But the south wind has the opposite effect, making everything dull instead of bright, warm instead of cold, damp instead of dry. It acts on everything that grows, indeed everything that has moisture in it. As evidence for this, following a methodology that is common among the new investigators of nature,[5] the author cites what happens to jars containing wine or other liquids stored indoors or even underground: they are all affected similarly by the south wind. That gives him his conclusion: '[T]his disease arises and flourishes from the changes that come and go: it is no more difficult to treat or to understand than other diseases, and is no more divine than the others are'.

Both internal and external air have their parts to play in the highly heterogeneous theories we lump together as Hippocratic pathology and therapeutics, but in both cases we are dealing with *material* objects. Proof that air *is* a body had indeed been undertaken by both Empedocles and Anaxagoras, using tests with clepsydras and inflated bladders (to show that air is resistant) – though their contemporaries presumably would not have needed much convincing that even though you do not *see* the air, you can certainly feel the wind. But the problems begin to get much trickier and more interesting when we consider early Greek ideas of life. In Homer *psuche* is one of the words (along with *thumos*, *phrenes*, *kardie* and others) that is used to describe human's cognitive, conative, and affective faculties,[6] but on death, the *psuche* leaves the body and goes off to Hades. It is obviously not incorporeal, but it is certainly insubstantial. When Odysseus goes to interview his mother and others in the underworld (*Od.* 11.90ff.), the ghosts can converse with him only once they have drunk the blood from the sacrifices he makes.

When we get to the Presocratic philosophers and Hippocratic writers we find a number of basically materialist accounts of life and mind. Theorists tended to identify soul-stuff with whatever they made the primary or basic constituent or origin of physical objects, air for Anaximenes, fire for Heraclitus, earth, water, air, and fire for Empedocles. Aristotle offered the view that his predecessors were mainly interested (1) in soul as the cause of motion and (2) in soul as cognitive. But he complained that if you made soul out of water, say, or air, that did not explain why some things are alive, others are not. Why does water explain life in the living, if water elsewhere (in rivers or the sea) is inanimate? Thales himself, for his part, with his idea that 'all things are full of gods' or 'of soul', may have been unhappy with any categorical distinction between living and non-living, if, that is, the question had been put to him in the first place. Truth to tell, however, we do not really know what he *did* believe on this subject.

But take the Hippocratic treatise *On regimen*, where we have a whole treatise to work with, not isolated citations that attracted the interest of later authors. All animals, the writer says (I chap. 3), humans included, consist of fire and water, fire being hot and dry (with a little of the moist) and water being cold and wet (with a little of the dry) (chap. 4). That gave a definite answer as to the material constituents of living creatures, but he uses the same pair of elements to account not just for their bodies, but also for their souls (chap. 6). Soul, *psuche*, too, he says (chap. 7), is a blend of fire and water, where he allows certain differences between the blending in the case of males and females, for example.

The problem was: wherein lies the difference between the ordinary water we see or drink, and the ordinary fire that burns wood, and the fire and water that are supposed to account for vital activities? When in chapters 35f. the author associates intelligence, *phronesis* (or the lack of it), with the mixture or blend, he says that what you need for the highest intelligence is the moistest fire and the driest water. That enables him to make certain suggestions about how to adjust diet and regimen to become more intelligent. But we are left without any explanation of how the blending is supposed to account for thinking, or of the difference between psychic and ordinary, other, physical blends.

One way of resolving the problems (up to a point) was to suggest that soul/mind is quite different from body. That was Plato's solution. Soul is ontologically distinct from body, the one incorporeal, the other corporeal. Yet that immediately posed the converse problem to that facing the materialist. The materialist had soul made of physical elements which enabled a straightforward account to be given of their interactions, but did not explain what was distinctive about psychic functions. The dualists, like Plato, ensured that distinctiveness, for sure. But if the soul is incorporeal, how does it affect or interact with the body at all? Ryle (1949) dubbed the dualist view the 'Ghost in the Machine'. How does the incorporeal ghost flick the switches in the physical machine it inhabits?

Let me backtrack for a moment. The Presocratic philosopher Anaxagoras, who got good marks from Plato for having introduced *nous*, reason, as the source of order in the cosmos, described it as the 'thinnest and purest of things' (fr. 12), though it is 'mixed with nothing'. That illustrates the dilemma: it is as if he wanted, on the one hand, to have mind to be a quite separate kind of thing, and yet, on the other, to keep it in touch with everything else by locating it at one extreme end of that spectrum of thinness and purity.

Plato produces some notable statements of the extreme dualist position – and he certainly needs to insist on that ontological divide between soul and body for the sake of his idea of the immortality of the soul. But he introduces, from time to time, complicating factors that serve to qualify that dualism. One problem, as I mentioned, was to explain how the soul controls the body or interacts with it in any way whatsoever. The converse difficulty was how what happens to the body can affect the soul. Yet Plato evidently allows that it can. In the *Timaeus*, where he distinguishes, in any case, surprisingly, between the immortal and the *mortal* – lower – parts of the soul, he develops a theory of diseases that starts with those of the body but then proceeds to those that affect the soul 'through the body' (86b). The humours can run amok in the body and cause all sorts of problems, including rashness and cowardice. Even such an arch-dualist as Plato has to find a way of building a bridge between the two ontologically distinct entities he so emphatically separated.

Aristotle's solution to the mind/body problem is very different, and he has *pneuma* play a distinctive part in his story about life. He will have nothing to do with any theory that treats soul and body as two distinct entities. Rather, the soul is the activity of the body – as vision is of the eye. So it is pointless, he says, in a famous passage (*On the soul* 412b6f.) where he clearly has Plato in mind, to ask whether the soul and the body are one – or two – as pointless as asking whether the wax and the mark of the signet ring in it are one or two.

Yet while that resolved the problem of psychic activity brilliantly – as the activity not of a separate entity but simply of the body while it is alive – it leaves another major difficulty further down the line. The ordinary sublunary elements, earth, water, air, and fire, are not themselves alive. Aristotle rejects, as we saw, what we call hylozoism, the doctrine that matter is alive. But then why are some material compounds capable of those psychic functions, but others not? When dealing with Aristotle we have to be careful about what he takes to be brute fact, not explicable in terms of other factors. In a famous rebuttal of the denial of change, he asks what the existence of change could conceivably be demonstrated from. Explanation has to be in terms of some causal factor that is clearer than what it explains. But there is nothing clearer than change from which it could be shown. Similarly as regards the natural world, the properties of many things can and should be explained – in terms of their causes – but other properties have to be taken as given. In the final analysis maybe this is so with life.

Even so Aristotle is faced with some severe problems where he does attempt explanations. One is that he believes in the spontaneous generation of animals and plants.[7] Tackling this in *GA* (762a18ff.), he says that 'animals and plants are formed in the earth and in the moist, because in earth, water is present and in water, *pneuma* is present, and in all *pneuma* vital heat (*thermotes psuchike*) is present'. He even concedes that 'in a way' all things are full of *psuche* (life). *Pneuma*, which starts off in its semantic range just meaning wind or breath does service for the breath of life and ends up being said to be analogous to the stuff of the stars (*GA* 736b34ff.), which are made of *aither* and are eternally alive. It is at work in ordinary animal reproduction (semen has *pneuma*), but it is also invoked to account for the various kinds of animals and plants generated in decaying matter, in mud and simply in the earth. Those materials need to be worked on by the sun or by vital heat, present, Aristotle claims, in all *pneuma* (though he presumably means potentially). He is clear that *fire* cannot generate living things, but 'the hot' comes in various modes. Sometimes hot is just hot, but sometimes it is or contains vital heat, not that Aristotle gives a hard-and-fast distinction between the two; they are distinguished, rather, by their effects.

So Aristotle is closer to the hylozoists that one might imagine from his explicit rejection of their position.[8] He does not, like Plato, have two substances, soul and body, but he is still faced with the problem of distinguishing what is alive from what is not, and, given that some animals and plants are not generated by their parents, but spontaneously, that seems to imply that the inanimate can, in the right conditions, generate the animate. *We* may think of matter as inert, but for Aristotle matter is always relative to form. The matter of which living creatures are made is certainly not inert. The matter from which animals are spontaneously generated is not either. There are gradations and gradations of matter, then. We see that *pneuma* and vital heat act as mediating terms in the intermediate area between regularly reproducing species of animals and the totally inanimate.

The early Stoics elaborate *pneuma* theory even further. They may or may not have known the Aristotelian treatises we have (some of which are seldom referred to, and some scholars think many were lost, in the period between Aristotle's death and the 'edition' of his works by Andronicus in the first century BCE). But they reverted to a full-blooded corporealism closer to that of some of the Presocratics than to either Plato or Aristotle. They distinguished two fundamental principles, the active and the passive. The passive is quality-less substance or matter. The active is variously identified as the cause, god, reason, fate, soul, or *pneuma*. *Both* these principles are corporeal, but the two are in total mixture (the theory of *krasis di'olon*). *Pneuma* as the active principle pervades everything, but, as I noted, the Presocratics distinguished different modes of unity. 'Tenor', the state of being held together, is the kind of unity exemplified by stones. There there is 'physique', *phusis*, nature, as in plants capable of growing and reproducing themselves. Thirdly there is *psuche*, soul, exemplified by animals capable of perception and movement. But in each case what holds the unity together is *pneuma*, conceived not as a static external constraining force, but as a dynamic internal tension. The cosmos as a whole is just such a living creature, pervaded with *pneuma*, life and reason.[9]

The Stoic solution to the problem of the distinction between the animate and the inanimate was to deny there is a *fundamental* divide here. Everything is instinct with *pneuma*. When we distinguish animals, and plants, and stones, we should understand that the reality is that they exemplify different modes of pneumatic unification.

The Stoics were not especially interested in the detailed investigation of natural phenomena, let alone in medical theory (physics, in their view, is undertaken for the sake of moral philosophy). But if we turn back now to medicine, we find both influences from contemporary philosophy and independent developments, especially where *pneuma* is concerned. In a problematic passage in a treatise of Galen that is not extant in Greek – only in Arabic and Latin versions – he speaks of Athenaeus of Attaleia as the founder of the Pneumatists (*On sustaining causes*, 1, Long & Sedley 1987: I, 335), and in histories of late ancient medicine one reads a great deal about this 'school'; indeed whole monographs have been written on the subject (see, e.g., Wellmann 1895). But we have to be careful. Greek terms for medical groupings are notoriously slippery, and Galen's usage is often pretty free. The 'Dogmatists', for instance, were in no sense a 'school'. They shared a belief in the possibility of investigating unseen causes and hidden reality, but they disagreed fundamentally on what should be said about those causes and reality.

Galen tells us that Athenaeus was influenced by Stoic causal theory (which is what he, Galen, is concerned with in this context). Yet his ideas on *pneuma* may have owed as much to another possible source of influence, namely the work of those in the early Hellenistic period who had begun investigating the properties of air in the field of mechanics known as 'pneumatics' – direct evidence for which we have in Philo of Byzantium and later in Hero of Alexandria. In particular the principle of *horror vacui* seems to have played an important part in the theories of both Asclepiades and Erasistratus. This is not to say that the vitalist associations of *pneuma* were any less important in their pathologies, but it is to add to the existing fund of ideas certain new ones that treated physiological processes in mechanical terms.

Galen was no Stoic, and he rejected Erasistratean mechanical explanations, but he offered a synthesis of earlier ideas that draws on a number of sources. Adapting a Platonic tripartite division of the soul, he distinguishes the rational, the spirited, and the appetitive, with principles in the brain, the heart, and the liver, respectively. While the nature of the vital faculties in question is clear enough, and Galen does a masterly job of work on the anatomical description of the organs where he locates those faculties, the major problems he was faced with were to explain how these faculties operated, and the relationship between them. Once again *pneuma* has the key role to play, in two guises. Galen distinguishes the vital *pneuma* in the arterial system from the psychic *pneuma* responsible for the activities of the brain and the nervous system.

On the one hand Galen wants a unified account, explaining how the various *pneumata* relate to and are derived from one another. On the other, he has considerable difficulty in producing a coherent story. He thinks that the vital *pneuma* is produced in the heart and arteries from a combination of the air we inhale and 'exhalations' from the humours (mainly blood), where he recycles a term that Aristotle had much used in his *Meteorology*. This *pneuma* in turn is further changed in the rete mirabile at the base of the brain into psychic *pneuma*, though the external air we breathe has a part to play in the production of this *pneuma*, too. Rocca (2003) has recently repeated Galen's dissections on the brain of an ox and has shown that the description of what Galen saw is very largely correct, including in the account given of the convoluted structures at the base of the brain. Galen has been much criticized for making inferences to the human brain from the ox – though he had no real option but to proceed by analogy with other animals. But he has also been often taken to task for his account of the ox brain itself – where some of his critics may be guilty of analogizing in the reverse direction.

In both types of *pneuma* production Galen gives a complex account, and indeed does so in some of the most convoluted prose in his corpus. He does not have a single origin in either case, but hedges his bets, involving external air in both but combining that with exhalations in the one case, and the vital *pneuma* itself in the other. He is absolutely clear about the effects he wants eventually to be able to account for – the various vital functions that he associates with the heart and the brain. As noted, he has detailed and accurate knowledge of the anatomy of animals that he felt were sufficiently close to humans to enable him to base his account on them. Certainly he had no reason to suppose that the functions of the sensory and locomotive nerves differed in humans and other animals. He was convinced that the nerves had lumina – indeed he claims to have verified that in the optic nerve – and that they operated not by transmitting a signal, but by transporting a substance. But when he faces the question of what that corporeal substance is, he falls back on *pneuma*. Everyone knew that air is necessary for life; like other theorists, the speculation Galen prefers is that other vital activities, too, can be assigned to further functions of *pneuma* as it gets to be changed, modified, or elaborated in the body.

Let me stand back now and take stock of this remarkable conglomeration of Greek theories. From a comparative standpoint one of the most striking features is indeed their variety, the lack of agreement among theorists who approached the problems from different perspectives, or even from the same one. From some points of view, Greek *pneuma* resembles Chinese *qi*, in its close association with breath and with vital activities. But while Chinese doctors, philosophers, cosmologists, music theorists, and others certainly used *qi* in different ways, they did not radically disagree on what *qi* was or on its importance, even though there are, to be sure, certain significant developments in its use.

What we find in Greece is a far more sustained and overt polemic. The Greeks did not just continue to disagree about the answers to the questions, of what soul is and of how it affects the body; they went on disagreeing also on the basic senses and references of many of the key terms, especially *aither* and *pneuma*. Many of the philosophers and medical writers were highly critical of others' ideas and prided themselves on their methodological and epistemological sophistication. Yet in their own solutions to the problems, particularly in the vitalist images and analogies they used both in cosmology and in their accounts of specific phenomena, they often recycled ideas that had had a long history in traditional beliefs.

Partly the difficulties stem from the very ambition with which they explored the issues. Once someone (Plato) had suggested that soul, or mind, and body are fundamentally different, then saying how the one influenced the other was extremely difficult. If you treat them as different kinds of entity, as Plato did, then the problem became how to explain how there could be any interaction between them. But if you treated them as two aspects of the same entity – the living creature – as Aristotle did, you still had to give an account of why some material bodies are alive, others not. If, thirdly, you treated all bodies as in some sense alive, as the Stoics did, the problem was relocated and became one of saying how different entities differ.

Some of those who engaged on speculations concerning psychological functions had little if any detailed anatomical knowledge, of animals or humans. But if you went in for sustained anatomical investigations, as Galen did, that meant you were in a far better position to localize vital functions, including perception and movement and other activities of the nervous system. But what was responsible, in the nerves, for those different activities remained a matter of speculation. Galen knew it was not blood, or (just) air, but he was convinced that the nerves transported not just an impulse but also a substance, and he opted for *pneuma*, in some form, as his solution to the main problem about what that substance was. However, his answers about how the different types of *pneuma* are produced are opaque. The more one knows about the brain – and Galen knew a great deal – the harder it becomes to say what the relationship between brain and mind is. But then, as I noted at the outset, this is still a problem for us today.

NOTES

[1] The secondary literature on the subject is very extensive. See, for example, Nussbaum (1978), Osler (1991), Putscher (1974), Verbeke (1945; 1978), especially. Vermeir (2004) has recently followed up some later influences of Greek ideas.

[2] Compare Zysk's discussion in this volume of the different theories proposed in different sources concerning *prāṇa*, *apāṇa*, *samāna*, *vyāna*, and *udāna*, where it appears that the vocabulary in which those different views are expressed is stable.

[3] Plato's own complex position with regard to the use of mythological images (in the *Phaedrus* itself) is discussed by Ferrari (1987: chap. 1).

[4] I analysed the polemic in the opening chapters of *On the sacred disease* in Lloyd (1979: chap. 1).

[5] The slogan for this method was: *opsis adelon ta phainomena*, 'things that are apparent are the vision of things that are unclear' (see Diller 1932; Lloyd 1966: chap. 5; Regenbogen 1930-1).

[6] Snell's account of Homer on the soul (Snell 1953 [1948]) has now been superseded by Padel (1992).

[7] I have discussed this problem in Lloyd (1996: chap. 5).

[8] He even says at *GA* 778a2ff. that the winds have 'a life of a sort and a genesis and decay', and like many Presocratics he invokes air in his explanation of several natural phenomena. Where Anaximander was reported by Aetius (III 3 1; Kirk, Raven & Schofield 1983: 137) to have said that lightning and thunder as well as whirlwinds all happen as a result of wind, Aristotle's own theory of the dry exhalation is that it is the same substance that causes wind on the earth's surface, thunder in the clouds, and even earthquakes below the earth (*Meteorology* 370a25ff.). To back up his explanation of earthquakes he cites an analogy between the effect of air compressed within the earth and what happens in our own bodies when pent-up air in us has the force (so he says) to cause tremors, tetanus, and spasms (*Meteorology* 366b14ff.). Yet the *Meteorology* is full of criticisms of others' views, especially those who want to make a name for themselves for cleverness, as Aristotle says of some theorists who argued that all the winds are one (349a20ff.). Basing himself on his own theory of a spherical earth, he classifies them according to their cardinal direction, noting both symmetries and asymmetries between those in the northern and southern hemispheres (*Meteorology* II chaps 5-6).

[9] The idea that the cosmos is formed and grows by 'breathing in' the air around it is attested for several early philosophers. At *Physics* 213b22ff. Aristotle attributes some such idea to the Pythagoreans, and at *On the Soul* 410b27ff. he reports that he has found a similar idea in certain 'Orphic' verses. On occasion, however, when our evidence is late, it may sometimes be suspected of reading back Stoic ideas into much earlier thinkers. One case in point is what may purport to be a quotation from Anaximenes 'fragment 2', in Aetius (I 3 4; Kirk *et al.* 1983: 158f.): 'Just as our soul, being air (*aer*), holds us together, so does *pneuma* or air (*aer*) enclose the whole world'. Elsewhere, I analyse the extensive evidence for vitalist images in early Greek cosmologies (Lloyd 1966: 232ff.).

BIBLIOGRAPHICAL NOTE

The most readily accessible editions with translations of most of the Greek authors I cite are those in the Loeb Classical Series (London and Cambridge, Mass.: Heinemann). This applies to Homer (*Iliad* and *Odyssey*),

Hesiod (*Theogony*), Herodotus, the Hippocratic treatises (*On breaths, On the nature of man, On airs, waters, places, On regimen, Aphorisms,* and *On the sacred disease*), the dialogues of Plato (*Phaedrus, Timaeus*), the treatises of Aristotle (*History of Animals, On the Generation of Animals, On the Soul, Physics,* and *Meteorology*) and Diogenes Laertius.

The fragments of the Presocratic philosophers (Anaximenes, Empedocles, Anaxagoras) are cited according to the numbering in the edition by H. Diels, revised by W. Kranz, *Die Fragmente der Vorsokratiker*, sixth edition (Berlin: Weidmann, 1952), where the most readily accessible English translations are in G.S. Kirk, J.E. Raven & M. Schofield, *The Presocratic philosophers*, second edition (Cambridge: University Press, 1983). Testimonies for Hellenistic philosophers are cited according to A.A. Long & D.N. Sedley, *The Hellenistic philosophers*, 2 vols (Cambridge: University Press, 1987).

REFERENCES

BERRYMAN, S. 2002. Aristotle on *pneuma* and animal self-motion. *Oxford Studies in Ancient Philosophy* **23**, 85-97.

DILLER, H. 1932. Opsis adelon ta phainomena. *Hermes* **67**, 14-42.

FERRARI, G.R.F. 1987. *Listening to the cicadas.* Cambridge: University Press.

KIRK, G.S., J.E. RAVEN & M. SCHOFIELD 1983. *The Presocratic philosophers.* (Second edition). Cambridge: University Press.

LLOYD, G.E.R. 1966. *Polarity and analogy.* Cambridge: University Press.

——— 1979. *Magic, reason and experience.* Cambridge: University Press.

——— 1996. *Aristotelian explorations.* Cambridge: University Press.

LONG, A.A. & D.N. SEDLEY 1987. *The Hellenistic philosophers.* 2 vols. Cambridge: University Press.

NUSSBAUM, M.C. 1978. *Aristotle: De motu animalium.* Princeton: University Press.

OSLER, M.J. (ed.) 1991. *Atoms, pneuma and tranquillity: Epicurean and Stoic themes in European thought.* Cambridge: University Press.

PADEL, R. 1992. *In and out of the mind.* Princeton: University Press.

PUTSCHER, M. 1974. *Pneuma, Spiritus, Geist; Vorstellungen vom Lebensantrieb in ihren geschichtlichen Wandlungen.* Wiesbaden: Steiner.

REGENBOGEN, O. 1930-1. *Eine Forschungsmethode antiker Naturwissenschaft.* (Quellen und Studien zur Geschichte der Mathematik, Astronomie und Physik B 1: 2). Berlin.

ROCCA, J. 2003. *Galen on the brain.* Leiden: Brill.

RYLE, G. 1949. *The concept of mind.* London: Hutchinson.

SNELL, B. 1953 [1948]. *The discovery of the mind* (trans. T.G. Rosenmeyer). Oxford: Blackwell.

VERBEKE, G. 1945. *L'évolution de la doctrine du pneuma du Stoïcisme à Saint Augustin.* Louvain: Éditions de l'Institut Supérieur de Philosophie.

——— 1978. Doctrine du pneuma et entéléchisme chez Aristote. In *Aristotle on mind and the senses* (eds) G.E.R. Lloyd & G.E.L. Owen, 192-214. Cambridge: University Press.

VERMEIR, K. 2004. The 'physical prophet' and the powers of the imagination. Part I: a case-study of prophecy, vapours and the imagination 1685-1710. *Studies in History and Philosophy of Biological and Biomedical Sciences* **35**, 561-91

WELLMANN, M. 1895. *Die pneumatische Schule.* (Philologische Untersuchungen 14). Berlin.

10
Gruff boreas, deadly calms: a medical perspective on winds and the Victorians

VLADIMIR JANKOVIC *University of Manchester*

In this paper I propose to reflect on the medical meanings of the nineteenth-century winds. I am not prepared to say anything about their qualities as meteorological phenomena nor am I equipped to judge on whether Victorian winds differed from the winds of today. Perhaps no amount of weather modelling and past data interpretation would do to complete such a project. My intention is rather to look at the period in which the cultural and medical understanding of wind came to reflect the role of scientific knowledge in shaping both the traditional and scientific understanding of health and environment. The Victorian period in particular witnessed a series of negotiations on the limits, meanings, and purposes of the natural knowledge as it came to be increasingly institutionalized (Levine 2002; MacLeod 1982; Yeo 1993). Scientific authority, utility, and cultural status have been brought to bear on the forms of traditional knowledge and, in particular, on medical practices. Where previously a multiplicity of environmental meanings coexisted in epistemic competition, the nineteenth-century public appreciation of science effected an exclusivist hierarchy of knowledge that opposed rational truth to mere opinion and 'folklore'. Increasingly the public and the state acquiesced to the idea that the 'everyday nature' was a 'scientific nature'. What was once a knowledge available to the majority was appropriated by an expert clique speaking esoteric tongues. This bifurcation, of course, was not a new development. Ever since natural philosophy had gathered institutional momentum in the early eighteenth century, nature had been systematically deprived of emblematics and accessibility, the result of which was a trend culminating in the naturalism of the mid-Victorian period. This redefinition is apparent in the history of atmospheric sciences (Favret 2004; Jankovic 2002; also general discussion in Anderson 2005; Friedman 1993; Reed 1983). In the natural philosophy textbooks, the many sentimental and spatial meanings of the eighteenth-century 'atmosphere' gave way to the notion of a grand chemical 'laboratory' (Adams 1798: 474; Ferriar 2004). The nineteenth-century medical aetiology of diseases pursued an analogous reductionist turn (Hamlin 1992).

What follows is an examination of the wind's medical significance within neo-Hippocratic medical thinking and environmentally inflected discourses, including medical topography (Cantor 2002; Harrison 1999; Jordanova 1979; Livingstone 1999;

Riley 1987). The examination will scrutinize the meandering meanings of the wind as a public meteor. As with other public meteors – the atmospheric phenomena that could be observed regardless of the status and education of an individual – the wind had often been described as an agency whose qualities included those of breath, omen, fertilizer, or destructor. The wind had also been known as a carrier of smoke, smell, miasma, and death, but also, as a power that propelled ships, scattered seeds, fertilized mares, ventilated rooms, and mixed gases. In literary tradition winds howled, whistled, roared, and moaned. They changed people's opinions, confined them indoors, and taxed their lungs. They altered outcomes of horse races. But despite these roles and presences, wind was also regarded, quite simply and since at least Seneca, as the air in motion. The anemometer and weather-vane measured its speed and direction. Like other public events, winds were shared across communities and discourses, and it is pointless to provide an absolute rationale for isolating its medical meaning on the basis of medical theory only. Indeed, medical meanings of wind emerged from the situational logic of daily lives that comprised travel, economic transactions, exploration, colonial epidemiology, and anecdotal evidence. Yet it should be noted that the creation of medical space in these realms often depended on a 'poetics of pathology' rather than medical maps or experimental knowledge (Wrigley 1996; 2000).

The purpose of this paper, however, is not to engage with the many medical connotations of the wind. Rather, it is to explore the ways in which wind has been constructed as a medical force, the ways whereby it could acquire a 'pathogenic' agency, that is, the ability to act as a cause of disease. I conceive wind's agency as a crossing of the boundary between the non-medical and the medical. Historically, such crossing could take numerous manifestations – from nuisance to pain, from discomfort to debility, from chronic exposure to acute condition – and one of the aims of this paper is to show how such changes took place in relation to medicalization of wind in a period of European history known for its pervasive interest in 'exteriority' and, more generally, the polarization of social space (Pilloud & Louis-Courvoisier 2003). The goal is to examine what might be termed a *meteorological pathogenesis*, that is, the understanding of how the pre-pathological elements of the 'environment' occupied medical attention and public anxiety as a disease-bearing agency. How did winds, rains, and sunlight enter medical research and regimen? As later sections demonstrate, such research involved a deconstruction of the wind and, in effect, the removal of its 'blowing' from medical problematics.

Winds of risk and death

The medical meanings of winds have been known since antiquity. Hippocratic tradition put emphasis on the city's exposure to winds; the winds specific to places and seasons represented the elements of an 'atmospheric constitution' that defined the nature and intensity of the prevailing diseases (Miller 1962; Sargent 1982). Yet the Hippocratic opus did not strive to assemble a causal theory of environmental influence; it merely prepared a physician for practice in a new town. A new physician was required to know that, for example, the inhabitants in a city exposed to hot winds suffered from bodily flabbiness, had humid heads, and irritable bowels unsupportive of wine; that women suffered from excessive menstruation, infants from asthma, and other adults from dysentery and haemorrhoids. Whether such conditions stemmed from the hot wind itself or were merely coincidental to it remained outside the physician's purview. Following the writings of the seventeenth-century doctor

Thomas Sydenham – called the 'English Hippocrates' for his interest in disease as an environmental imbalance – Enlightenment medics continued to pursue this route and opened up a possibility of thinking about diseases as naturally reoccurring phenomena (see Bisset 1762; Dolan 2002; Huxham 1759; Lee 1973; Murray 1774; Poynter 1973; Rusnock 2002; Rutty 1770; Short 1749; Weindling 1985; Wintringham 1727).

Early modern European culture, however, witnessed an intense cultural exposure to the non-European world. Travellers, colonists, and explorers published accounts about diseases and environments not felt in European lands. Like plants, people, diseases, and topography, foreign winds elicited interest for their odd and unsuspected qualities that captured the European imagination regardless of their relevance for philosophical or other forms of knowledge (Barnes & Mitchell 2002; Knellwolf 2002; Rousseau & Porter 1990). The French scholar Chardin publicized an account of people killed by a sudden blow of the African 'mortifying' *samiel*. They seemed asleep, with limbs separated from their bodies. Volney observed that the victim of the *khamsin* wind remained warm, swollen, and blue for a long time, as if killed by thunder (Robertson 1808: 305). Harmattan, the dry African wind, had attracted attention for its desiccating and healing properties. It killed plants and parched the skin, but cured fevers and the bleeding fatigue; it could put a stop to smallpox and diarrhoea and exert preventive powers against infections, ulcers, and skin eruptions (Dobson 1782-3: 261-2). Yet if it reached Europe, it became pestilential through the 'adventitious' qualities that it soaked up from the underlying soil.

The influence of soil gave some winds a terrifying notoriety. This was the case with the easterly wind in Senegal 'with which those who are suddenly met ... are scorched up as by a blast from a furnace', or of the notorious Falkland Island winds that attacked fowl with cramps and stopped the perspiration of the locals (Adams 1798: 541-2). Known for their suffocating, depressing, and 'relaxing' qualities were the Sirocco and the Levant (Jugo in the Adriatic), which badly affected Minorca and Gibraltar but which originated over the burning expanses of Libya and Egypt. Sirocco in Naples and Palermo stopped digestion and killed over-eaters; city folks shut their houses and stayed in until the end of its onslaught. The identification of the geographical origin of these winds (often African) is an indication that learned Europeans thought of the tropics as a place of 'elementary contention and violence', of luscious vegetation and putrefaction, shaken by the geological convulsions and winds that 'vary their terrors: sometimes involving all things in a suffocating heat, sometimes mixing all the elements ... and sometimes destroying all things in their passage'. Given the mildness of mid-latitude Europe, it seemed necessary that infectious diseases had to be 'imported from some sultry climate' (Brown 1797: 52, 53).

Crucial in these disquisitions was physicians' tacit expectation that a physical place should exhibit a stable homeostasis between its inorganic features, such as winds, soil and precipitation, and human life and health. This reciprocity has been debated in the context of climatological determinism and natural theology (Gates 1967; Glacken 1973). Into the nineteenth century, it even became possible to speak about 'hereditary climates': 'Has not Nature adapted the constitution of man to his hereditary climate?', asked Thomas Burgess. 'Is it consistent with nature's laws that a person born in England and attacked by consumption can be cured in a foreign climate?' (1850: 591). An environmental pathology therefore came about only as a *relative* misadaptation to local conditions, which by and in themselves did not cause disease. Sir Walter Scott's

Highlanders were reported to sleep outdoors, unperturbed by the hoarfrost in their hair (1996 [1817]: 76). The notorious quack James Graham claimed to have achieved robust health by keeping his windows open for the maximum wind impact during Scottish storms (1793: 5).

While some of these feats were explained by a sympathy between the body and its native exteriors, no precise formulations had been advanced on the physiological responses to weather and climate:

> We see then that the insalutary impressions of the atmosphere transmitted from the surface to the central parts of our bodies, may be reproduced and transmitted from organ to organ, by means of the sympathies ... [t]ill various and complicated maladies, accompanied by a tribe of obscure and complicated symptoms have arisen, that are as embarrassing to the Physician as they are distressing to the patient (Johnson 1818: 12; see also Vila 1997).

Keeping unperturbed the sympathetic exchanges between the 'in and out' was tantamount to good health.

Such views were the medical orthodoxy during the Enlightenment (Rosenberg 1992). In 1785, Andrew Hamper, the author of a health treatise, phrased it thus: 'All things considered to act immediately upon the Body, or make Impression on it, at a Distance, through the Medium of the Senses, the changes that happen in the Atmosphere which surrounds us, and the Air we breath, constitute the general, *external causes* that affect Health' (1785: 1).[1] The wording is significant: the external causes of disease – what the Augustan physician John Arbuthnot (1733) had called the 'powers without' – could act even 'at a Distance' and through 'the Medium of the Senses', rendering the body a vital barometer recording the alteration of its surrounding milieu. These associations testified to the common use of 'influence' among eighteenth-century physicians, who often met with patients with extreme atmospheric sensibility (Castle 1995; Golinski 1998; Phelps 1743; Shuttleton 1995). These 'human barometers' suffered from a 'nervous' disease which made them exceptionally attuned to the 'vicissitude' of the weather. They gave emphatic meaning to being 'under the weather'. In the age of sympathetic sensibilities this condition was virtually self-evident and a subject of moral analysis: '[I]t was a damn'd bad thing to have a constitution subject to squalls of weather' (Bage 1796: 88).[2]

As for the medical views, the condition was diagnosed as a result of under-exposure to fresh air. Eighteenth-century sociability (salons, libraries, lectures, card routs, dancing, clubability) was related to environmental improvements designed to provide thermal equability in interiors whose calms and comfort contrasted with the wind-bruised English outdoors. In these environmental technologies, the domestic space was the haven of calms. This accorded a greater value to the cosiness of private space, which favoured a low-metabolism and high-caloried sedentariness, and which were in turn tainted by traditional fears of draughts and the miasmatic night air. The specifically medical reasons for this over-protection were to do with the perceived risks of sudden changes caused not only by the alterations in outside weather or instant exposure to winds, but by a careless night life (Gregory 1815: 40). Thermometric equability and regulated exposure ruled the medical enlightenment, which, as was pointed out by contemporaries, bred a peculiar type of citizens, pale, out of shape, pampered and unreasonably shielded from the bracing outdoors (Johnson 1839).

Anthony Florian Madinger Willich wrote in 1800, for example, that such trends created an acute medical condition. Next to gout, he wrote, there is the 'still more general malady of the times, ... an extreme sensibility to every change of the atmosphere; or, rather, constantly sensible relation to its influence'. Willich noted the sensibility of some of his patients to identify the direction of the wind while even inside their apartments. He was struck by the 'talent so peculiar to our age' and acquired in a climate that defined English health as 'dependent, frail and transitory'. Even the question of whether political strife itself owed to people's 'secret dependence on the weather' was legitimate because 'beings so organized cannot warrant, for a single hour, their state of health, their good-humour, or their physical existence' (Willich 1800: 58-9). For the British, this dependency also became crucial for the colonial project (Curtin 1964).

As the analyses and criticisms of the New World, tropics, and the otherwise popular Mediterranean health resorts amply illustrate, foreign climates were practically equivalent to (and judged in terms of) the harm they wrought on their visitors (Arnold 1996; Bolton-Valencius 2002; Hoolihan 1989; Wrigley 2000). The Mediterranean, for example, came under negative scrutiny increasingly because its local climates violated the hereditary argument. Medical commentators claimed that even though the British enjoyed rather chilly, windy, and rainy weather for the most part of the year, its bleak uniformity none the less spared consumptives from adjustments to the violent changes in temperature known to affect the European South. In some of the Mediterranean resorts, local winds were claimed to be especially morbid: the Sirocco, Liebeccio, and Leste depleted the vitality with blasts followed by copious dews. These were conditions unknown to the unsuspecting British invalid. In Malta, cold winds ('bracing' in the British climate) were too piercing to allow one to venture outdoors: 'I do not remember ever to have felt the sensation of cold so acutely in this country [England] as I have done in Malta during a dry, north-westerly, or north-easterly wind' (Burgess 1850: 592). For contrast, in England, Charles Kingsley paraphrased Shelley's 'Ode to the West Wind' with his own 'Ode to the North-east Wind', to celebrate its hardening qualities suited to Victorian robust moral ambition: 'Welcome, blackNorth-easter! O'er the German foam, the Danish moorlands, thy frozen home. Tired we are of summer, Tired of gaudy glare' (Kingsley 1909-14 [1889]).

In medical theory and topography, however, the fear of Southern, non-European winds was further heightened by their supposed miasmatic qualities (Cipolla 1992; Hannaway 1993; Pelling 1978). 'Miasma' was the generic term used to describe the allegedly material agency that spread epidemics: the 'anticontagionists' contended that epidemics had almost nothing to do with bodily contact between the infected and the healthy, because the magnitude, spread, and speed of the pestilence could be explained only by the wind-blown miasmas (Ackerknecht 1948). Winds were foul insofar as they pushed infectious material across national, even continental, borders. Wind was a vehicle of transmission and a medium of pollution – in a broadest possible sense, a carrier of 'matter out of place' (Douglas 1966; Hamlin 1994). But this also made it a ventilating force, a harbinger of health. Authorities and the medical profession of eighteenth-century Europe grappled with these two meanings in a variety of ways. The environmental medicine assumed that air could become corrupted by subterranean processes, organic decomposition, re-breathing, and urban waste (Hannaway 1972; 1974; Jordanova 1981). It was asserted that in unfavourable conditions (never fully specified) adulterated air caused cholera, fevers and typhoid, and even death itself by the 'mortiferous exhalations' that sometimes spurted out from pits, mines, and coffins (Laqueur 2002; Robertson 1808).

The wind here was a purifier and a polluter. How did such qualifications influence the works of mid-nineteenth-century medics? How were they prompted to investigate the inner workings of wind's purifying or polluting powers? In the remainder of the paper, I show that the answers to these problems also bear on popular versus professional readings of public meteors and on the epistemic status of the almost universal belief in the refreshing powers of wind and pure air generally.

The winds electrical; the winds of ozone

Eighteenth- and nineteenth-century physicians, geographers, town planners, medical authorities, meteorologists, and common folk often referred to winds as having unique ventilating powers capable of supplying unlimited amounts of fresh air to a space of any scale, from privies to churches, from streets to industrial districts, from the sea coast to the Scottish moors. The litany of fresh air and ventilation established itself as the moral basis of the British public health movement, transfixed as it was by the paradigm of environmental purity at the expense of other socially and economically created vectors of misery and disease: 'What habitation in the British empire can have an excuse for a stagnant atmosphere?' asked a reviewer of Thomas Bateman's article on contagion in 1820. 'If such places there be, they ought not to be permitted to exist' ('Review' 1820; see also Hamlin 1992; Rome 1996; Wohl 1983). The zeal for ambiental purity that such information fomented was recorded in the fact that between 1800 and the 1860s, the estimated need for indoor fresh air soared from four to sixty cubic feet per person (Bruegman 1978: 153)!

This culture of 'fresh air' did not go uncriticized for its exaggerated claims and unreasonably high expectations. One of its most prominent critics was London practising physician and author John Charles Atkinson, the authority on the 'change of air', and a member of the Royal College of Surgeons with long-standing interests in environmental epidemiology and health. The fad of 'fresh air', he claimed, was of the same nature as those to do with Elixirs, Drops, Waters, mesmerism, hydropathy, homeopathy. 'Change of air' is the last of these and 'is forced upon everyone', as the public and the professionals advise visits to spas, places with special healing powers, and those with a good exposure to prevailing winds (Atkinson 1848: 8). Atkinson's early works focused on the role of atmospheric electricity during cholera epidemics, while in his later years he researched the therapeutic aspects of wind, sleep, and fear. Writing in 1849 in the medical journal *The Lancet*, he noted a lack of exact knowledge into the effects of winds on the national morbidity. Of his own research he found no precursors and only a 'domestic and proverbial' knowledge: 'When the wind is in the east / It's neither good for man nor beast'. This he thought was puzzling given the role of winds in Hippocrates' *Airs, waters and places*, where the author urged physicians to pay attention first to the seasons and 'Then the winds, the hot and the cold, especially such as are common to all countries, and then such as are peculiar to each locality' (2004: 3).

Atkinson set to cut the Gordian knot of causality on the premise that most of winds' medical effects owed to imagination and 'common voice' rather than their real action. Neither was the direction nor the action of winds observed properly: telescopes could be used to observe the motion of clouds and thus determine the direction of wind at higher altitude. The action of winds was not properly discussed, because not all patients were affected similarly during the same wind: some had ailments in which the afflicted organ showed more susceptibility to a particular wind's influence regarding the amount of damaged tissue. Furthermore, observing that chemistry could not differentiate between the airs found in different locations – valleys or plains, one country or another, the ratio of its constituents remained the same – Atkinson queried as to 'what can we attribute the variable influences of different winds, if not to something yet undiscovered something which has wholly escaped observation?' (Atkinson 1849*a*: 208).

Patients, in particular, guessed the change in wind when 'closely shut up or imprisoned in a room, not exposed even to the whispering of the wind' because there was something 'in the atmosphere which, by change of wind, causes a simultaneous action on all living substances and structures', this something being 'the actions and decomposition, attraction and repulsion', that is, the properties of electromagnetism (Atkinson 1848: 318). This fact explains the truth of animals' and plants' prognostication of the weather because – like the hypersensitive and the sick – these 'poor-man's barometers' (pimpernel, chickweed, leeches, horses) instinctively respond to the stimuli of atmospheric electricity. As far as the human body was concerned, the changes of wind, temperature, and electricity were sufficient to disturb the body's secretion and excretion and thus cause 'a loss of the balance of the proper and health functioning of life'. But winds in particular determine local conditions. For Atkinson, without a comprehensive anemometry that took into account electrical states of the weather, no full understanding of epidemics was forthcoming (Atkinson 1843: 323). But because such work had not been done, medical writers struggled to determine the exact nature of wind's pathogenicity by other means and considerations. The discussions were structured according to the dichotomy between the wind as a polluter and as a purifier.

The dichotomy was indirectly tackled by Alfred Haviland (1853), a self-confessed Hippocratist educated at St Thomas's Hospital in London and a practising surgeon in Cannington, Somerset. His works give an indication of the shared anxiety with regard to the 'foreignness' of pestilential winds but also the scale of the Victorian quest to assess the medical co-ordinates of a place (Barret 1998; Freeman 1978-9; Harley 2003). Haviland in this respect belongs to the vibrant tradition of medical topography and regional geography that had thrived in the British Isles since the early 1800s, following the work of Leonhard Ludwig Finke, James Lind, James Johnson, and James R. Martin.[3] For our purpose what is important is, first, Haviland's apparent rejection of the wind's miasmatic character in favour of its ozonic content. In this reduction of wind's medical properties to wind's chemical composition, Haviland was, like his contemporaries in other field sciences, effectively putting an end to a common-sensical understanding of 'public nature'. Introducing analytical chemistry to replace empirical diagnostics based on an anecdotal evidence of the wind's properties announced a parting of the ways between mundane and esoteric winds, between shared and analytically circumscribed natures.[4] This is significant in that such parting went directly against the entrenched psychological identification with the environment that had been repeatedly inscribed in the many manifestation of the Victorian medical geography (Bewell 1996).

Haviland's professional involvement with wind started during the 1849 English cholera outbreak when he looked after patients in his native Bridgewater. In four months he witnessed over 200 deaths. Pondering over the circumstances that might have contributed to such mortality, he entertained the possibility that the number of new cases varied according to the wind patterns. This led him to take weather observations, not least important of which were his avant-garde experiments with atmospheric ozone, the results of which were compiled in *Climate, weather and disease* (1855). While the idea to correlate weather with cholera was not uncommon (Atkinson

1849*b*; 1850), the book aimed at a broader if erudite audience by offering a one-of-a-kind pastiche of ancient history-cum-climatology and the statistical data gleaned from the recently available tables of the Royal Observatory at Kew Gardens.[5] Most relevant for our purpose was the discussion on the 'pestilential constitution', a Hippocratic concept defined as a mix of environmental circumstances thought to be conducive to an epidemic (Ackerknecht 1982). The notion served as the framework within which meteorological elements could cause pathogenic effects. The pestilential constitution was thus the notional site of pathogenesis, a site in which the wind could cross the threshold of its medical identity within the learned discourse of Victorian science.

Haviland's method of discussion and analysis involved the use of both meteorological and historical sources. These helped him move from the colloquial and descriptive to what seemed medically validated. No sympathetic theory ever got involved. In this he self-avowedly remained faithful to Hippocrates. His method is illustrated in his dealing with the malignity of the south wind. He opens the discussion by the doxographic reference to the ancients and follows it up by the modern opinions of Fodéré (1813), who, in discussing the wind's origins, relied on plague's Egyptian provenance: 'There only is it engendered; in the other regions it is always alien' (Haviland 1855: 92-3). From then on Haviland plunges into mortality data and the views of the eighteenth-century epidemiologist Joseph Browne. Browne thought that as the plague deaths typically peaked during the periods marked by south winds, those must have been passing over the deserts in southern Egypt, where they became 'loaded with putrid emanations exhaled from the animal and vegetable substances which are decomposed in the lakes formed by the retiring' of the Nile and its surrounding cemeteries. Thus impregnated, the wind 'blasted' the inhabitants of the Mediterranean and their northern neighbours (quoted in Haviland 1855: 122-3). The picture thus emerges of a wind as a bearer of exogenous material, but in a way in which the content and the medium cannot easily be separated.

Haviland takes these views with a grain of salt. The wind as a carrier cannot really explain the geography of the plague. For if the above is correct, every country would have to have its own Egypt! Instead, it might be the case that the south wind itself, regardless of its poisonous content, is responsible for creating a set of conditions in a given place that gives rise to a positively pestilential atmosphere. While any given location can be prone to the plague, it is the south wind that triggers it by its warmth and humidity (Haviland 1855: 123). Indeed, he notes that Galen believed that heat was the active, and humidity the material, cause of putrefaction – a view he thinks amply confirmed in the annals of plague, which show their unfailing concomitance. The annals of influenza, sweating sickness, catarrhs, and cholera indicate a 'southern constitution' of elements such as wet and warm conditions accompanied with 'great gluts of rain' and 'stinking fogs' (Haviland 1855: 125). What remained unclear was the precise nature of the south wind's harmfulness. Is it in its general 'hemispheric' flow, which enables humidity and warmth to generate a specific disease? Is it through its stimulation of putrefaction and miasmas? Is it by bringing them already formed? Or is it by some other means, perhaps entirely mechanical? The language is not straightforward. Sometimes, the south wind is 'favourable' or 'conducive' to cholera, suggesting its predisposing or exciting but not immediate role in its causation. In other places its 'morbific property' as an active agent has to do with some quality like the haziness of air: '[W]hat is this haze?,' Haviland asks. 'In the West of England a hazy day in spring is called a blight' (Haviland 1855: 127).

In other places, to further complicate the picture, Haviland suggests that instead of the south wind, one might need to concentrate on the northerly, or even on no wind at all, but on its absence, the calms. In this he follows the results of the doctor J.A. Hingeston connecting the highest mortality during the 1832 Asiatic cholera to the 'fearful atmospheric stillness and that seemingly interminable moistness', combined with the 'gloomy and cloudy' weather and a certain grey mist which painters call 'scumbling' (Hingeston 1853). The calms might have been deadly simply because they let miasmas hover for longer and instigate the creation of local poisons. Atkinson called these 'disease mists' that dissipated with the wind (1848: 17). In such situations, human habitations exercise an influence on the 'supernatant air of a district, especially during the prevalence of calms, when whatever rises from them accumulates and concentrates in such a manner as seriously to affect the health of those who inhale the poisoned atmosphere' (Haviland 1855: 109; see also Allison 1839). With regard to endemic disease, Haviland finds that 'bronchocele' (i.e. goitre or the enlargement of the thyroid gland) reigns in the deep, dark, and humid valleys of Switzerland, 'where the atmosphere is seldom ruffled by a breeze of sufficient power to remove the accumulate poison ... Were this valley beneath a tropical sun, it would be the seat of pestilence and death' (Haviland 1855: 92). The tropics re-emerge as the baseline of morbidity.

This reasoning had implication for climatotherapy. By Haviland's time the practice had all but reigned supreme among those able to take a Mediterranean or Continental *tour de bagnes* to imbibe the qualities of fresh air.[6] Haviland, for instance, considers it inadvisable to shut the windows in a hospital under the pretence of protecting patients from the cold east winds because 'the atmosphere thus pent up gets loaded with animal emanations' and becomes positively poisonous (1855: 118). The 1832 cholera was the most lethal during the calms, the dead calms, what the soldiers call 'cat's paws' – and the disease began to decline only when the wind rose. This view, parenthetically, seems to have been widely spread: many noted the coincidence of highest mortality and the sickly, sticky calms during the periods of an unusually luxuriant growth of plants, greasy appearance of window glass, and numerous dead flies circled by their solidified faeces (Cross 1857). Charlotte Brontë's *Shirley* captured the role of wind in dispelling these morose times:

> So long as the breath of Asiatic deserts parched Caroline's lips and fevered her veins, her physical convalescence could not keep pace with her returning mental tranquillity; but there came a day when the wind ceased to sob at the eastern gable of the Rectory, and at the oriel window of the church. A little cloud like a man's hand arose in the west; gusts from the same quarter drove it on and spread it wide; wet and tempest prevailed a while. When that was over the sun broke out genially, heaven regained its azure, and earth its green: the livid cholera-tint had vanished from the face of nature: the hills rose clear round the horizon, absolved from that pale malaria-haze (1849: 34).

The importance of calms is indicative of Hingeston's and Haviland's interest in considering winds as purifiers, not polluters. But does this purifying happen in virtue of mere ventilation (mechanical removal of filth and miasmas) or in virtue of some positive property inherent to wind? And which wind? Haviland rejects the former possibility and introduces ozone as the agency. Ozone was a newly discovered mid-century gas that was just about beginning to rule among public health officials due to its alleged disinfecting powers (Fox 1873; Schönbein 1845). With ozone, purification was easier to explain: the wind was now imagined to supply a region with fresh amounts of ozone, but when it stopped blowing, the gas dissipated and was replaced by the putrid emanations from the locale, eventually giving rise to epidemics. When somewhat later Thomas Moffat from Hawarden, Flintshire, the early English ozone authority, showed that the cholera-free atmosphere contained ozone only when three concomitant conditions were met (high pressure, low temperature, and wind from the north), it became plausible to imagine that the healthy place can be defined as exposed to a steady (north) wind (Moffat 1860). Haviland asks: 'May not the almost perpetual calms that obtain in lowest valleys of the earth, be powerful encouragers of the endemics which prevail therein?' (Haviland 1855: 130). To say this is to say that the pathogenicity of wind equalled the pathogenicity of its absence, the calm; but also, with the ozone as the measure of a place's healthiness, the wind itself lost its proper medical role except that of a dynamic container of a chemical agency.

The mucous membrane and the ontology of winds

Victorian men of science and medicine increasingly saw wind as a medium of transfer, not a phenomenon *per se*. The studies undertaken by Atkinson and Haviland showed that the change of environmental scrutiny meant a shift from the notoriously unhealthy south quadrant to the newly discovered north quadrant of bracing purity. Not all would agree with this trend, however. In fact, the north (and the east) wind came under repeated scrutiny for their notorious unhealthiness. Haviland himself admitted that the eastern and northeastern *aspect* of land was unfavourable for British agriculture, referring to a report of a Fellow of the Royal Agricultural Society on how the shepherds on the Wiltshire and Sussex downs exercise caution on the approach of northeasterlies, making sure 'when their flocks are in a situation having easterly aspect, to remove them at once ... to prevent "the shotting of the blood" ' (1855: 93), an inflammation resulting from exposure in an easterly aspect. Similarly, the popularity of health resorts in South Wales, the Isle of Wight, the south Hams of Devon, and the neighbourhood of Penzance almost entirely derived from their situation being sheltered from the 'chilly influence of the northerly winds' (1855: 93).

This would ring true with most contemporaries, who saw the north and northeasterly winds as the epitome of discomfort and disease, but in the epithets different from those they would use to describe the southern winds of lassitude. A medical periodical reported that 'our coldest, north east winds occasion croup, soar throat, swelled glands, pulmonary ailments' (*Collactenea* 1834: 190). Medical statisticians found that they increased the levels of urban mortality; others noted their prevalence during paralytic attacks (Drummond 1849: 410). The business commentary in *The Times* was replete with reports on shipping disruptions and accidents occasioned by the north wind's gusts. The literary take of its influence ranged in nature and seriousness. In Jane Austen's *Emma* one reads that, 'though you will never own being affected by the weather, I think everybody feels a North-west wind' (1816: 258). Non-medical depiction of the north wind as cold, piercing, and snowy was common: Charlotte Brontë's Jane Eyre described how it had been 'whistling through the crevices of our bed-room windows all night long, had made us shiver in our beds, and turned the contents of the ewers to ice' (1847: 91). Others experienced distraction or mood changes, like a late Hanoverian novel hero, Baron Phillips, who, on hearing that the wind veered to the northeast, immediately realized why he felt 'not know how-ish' (Bage 1796: vol. 3, 88). The critic Leigh Hunt commented that we cannot answer 'for what a north-east wind or a fall of snow may do to us. I have myself, before now, had a whole host of fine ideas blown away by the one; and have been compelled to retreat from the other, mind and body, with my knees almost into the fire' (Hunt 1817: 11). The northeaster howled, roved, moaned, crept, cut, froze, and did all these things loudly enough to elicit a poet's supplication:

> Silence, oh North-East wind thy saddening cry
> Silence, oh wind thine everlasting moan!
> Is the child Innocence all naked thrown
> Out on the freezing earth, is the great sky
> Now made of lead for ever, nor again
> May the heart cheer up nor sweet lips be curled?
> Silence oh deadly wind!
>
> (W.B. Scott 1854)

The more damning judgment still came from medical professionals. Dr C.B. Garret of the Royal Human Society, a medical officer based in a dispensary in Kingston, Surrey, outlined a ghastly gallery of afflictions that his countrymen suffered during the onslaught of this grand 'Aeolian enemy'. He sketched an image of a fictitious London pedestrian caught in the February northeaster, faltering in step, forced to frequent stoppages to draw full breath, and with a nervous glance:

> Observe how he elevates his shoulders and supports his hands on his side as he stops to inhale, and accomplish a husky raking clearance of the windpipe by a cough. This is an endurer of no common an affliction with a sense of impending suffocation, and the most pitiable feebleness, his very look is that of trepidation and supplication for assistance (Garret 1855: 4).

From Garret we learn that the wind causes a range of physiological debilities, from private to national: a sense of heaviness, swelling, and tightness in the head that was accompanied by sudden flashes of giddiness. People feel faint, short of breath, without strength and appetite. Some suffer from a short-term memory loss; many have restless sleep wetted by uncontrollable salivating; in time, the whole nation is apt to lose temper, become fidgety, fretful, and excitable, and eventually to plunge into a great depression of spirits (Garret 1855: 78).

Clearly this was not the miasmatic and sticky south wind packed with infectious particles from African deserts and tropical marshes. The north wind's signature was in its dynamic aggression – sometimes thought of as a 'lazy' wind in going 'through' rather than 'around' the person – combined with its parching dryness that attacked the throat's mucous membrane and from where it triggered further symptoms. Not all people suffered from the condition, however, and Garret explained this differential in an analysis of digestive function, concluding that the northeaster's victims include those who share the so-called 'lactacidic' constitution, or a form of gastritically induced susceptibility. Garret identified that it was the thermo-physiometric quality of wind's air that was pathological, not its chemical, electrical, or dynamic composition. Neither was he interested in epidemics; this allowed him to avoid any involvement with miasmas. The pathogenicity arose only through the 'gruff Boreas's' desiccating powers, which worked their way through the mucous membrane of the nose. The latter had already been investigated for its important physiological role as the first interface, with the skin, between the body and the ambient air. Although Garret does not specify other researchers, he must have been aware of the research on the subject by the French tissue pathologist Xavier Bichat and that of François Magendie in which the nose's membrane appears as an 'air conditioning system' (Proctor 1974: 360). This explains Garret's discussion on the wind-shielding role of the recently introduced ventilators by Julius Jeffreys (1842; 1850).

As Proctor (1974) explains, by the 1880s, the importance of the mucous membrane in wind-related diseases (including the common cold) gained widespread currency. *The Lancet* published a commentary that exemplified this by explicitly rejecting the impressionistic discourse and putting forward the *real* explanation:

> [That] the 'east wind' has from the earliest times been credited with evil influence is apparent in the fact that Ephraim was described in one of the most ancient of the Jewish traditions as feeding upon it. What a repast! Modern science has determined that what we call the east wind is *really* a current of air from the north, its direction being modified by the rotatory movement of the earth. This is not difficult to understand. The avidity with which the dry cold wind takes moisture, and particularly that from the mucous membrane lining of the air passages, inpissating the mucus, and as it were, gluing together the cilia of the epithelium, is the *real* cause of the malignancy of the 'east wind'. We have repeatedly explained this fact, and pointed to the use of a succulent jujube or something which will give off moisture in the mouth to be carried into the air-passages with the inspired air as the best of practicable measures of protection. We believe that if only the habit of keeping a morsel that gives off aqueous vapour – not one that dissolves by taking up moisture – in the mouth during the time of exposure to the east wind were formed, there would be a very few colds from that cause (*The Lancet* 1886: 559).

The important consequence of this rebuttal of wind's 'popular' ontology was that it invalidated the notion of wind as a medical phenomenon in its own right. It also questioned the credibility of the public understanding of 'nature' insofar as it reduced the health risks of exposure to a 'wind' to the risks of exposure to the qualities of air, regardless of their association with the wind. It is not in the nature of *winds* to be healthy or harmful, but in the nature of the concomitant *conditions* of electricity, ozone, and other meteorological qualities such as rain or humidity. Later investigation took this point seriously and avoided doing anything other than correlating the wind's direction to the prevailing weather condition and the statistics of morbidity (Gordon 1903; 1905; 1910). If the twentieth-century volumes of the pre-eminent *Lancet* are anything to go by, the medical importance of wind has all but lost relevance for the profession. The only researches published on the topic included that on the 'wind of explosives' during the First World War (*The Lancet* 1915), the minor effects of wind in the treatment of tuberculosis (Girdlestone 1925), the (questioned) role of wind in the spread of foot-and-mouth disease (Burne 1969), the Foehn and myocardial infarction (Ambach, Tributsch, Mairinger, Steinacker & Reinegger 1992), wind-related injuries (*The Lancet* 1992), and wind noise when motorcycling (McCombe, Binnington, Donovan & McCombe 1992).

We should not conclude from this declining interest in medical analyses of wind (*qua* motion) that there has been a corresponding decline in interest in the phenomenon on the modern public, spiritual, industrial, energy-sector, or personal level. The above analysis does not contend that these processes brought about anything like a 'redefinition' of the natural world. Instead, the different generic engagements with the wind indicate for us an unstable coexistence within the nineteenth-century medical space, even when a reductionist Hippocratism sought to purge this space of the naïvety of colloquial meteorology. But regardless of the relative merit which this and other weather idioms enjoy in contemporary society – and they can be prophetic, prognostic, theoretical, naval, agricultural, or racial – they all seem to outline something resembling a modern *climatological citizenship* within putative polity boundaries which are fixed by the physical impact of the weather on local people's lifework.

NOTES

[1] On smell, see Corbin (1986); on medical police, see Rosen (1957); on eudometry, see Schaffer (1990).

[2] On sensibility, see Barker-Benfield (1996), Frye (1990), and Rousseau (1976).

[3] Local topographers included Burrows (1814), Coldstream (1833), Hastings (1834), Hooper (1837), Royston (1809), Smith (1816), and Walker (1818). For history, see Jankovic (2000) and Rupke (2000).

[4] For uses of chemistry in the analysis of spa waters, see Porter (1990).

[5] On meteorology and public health, see Burton (1990).

[6] Medical texts on the qualities of foreign and domestic climates were numerous, e.g. Bennet (1861); Bright (1854); Burgess (1850); Clark (1820; 1841); Cullen (1852); Dalrymple (1861); Davis (1807); Farr (1841); Francis (1853). For history, see Turner (1967).

REFERENCES

ACKERKNECHT, E. 1948. Anticontagionism between 1821 and 1867. *Bulletin of the History of Medicine* **22**, 562-93.

——— 1982. Diathesis: the word and the concept in medical history. *Bulletin of the History of Medicine* **56**, 317-25.

ADAMS, G. 1798. *Lectures on natural and experimental philosophy*. London: J. Dillon.

ALLISON, S.S. 1839. *An inquiry into the propagation of contagious poisons, by the atmosphere; as also into the nature and effects of vitiated air*. Edinburgh: MacLachlan and Stewart.

AMBACH, E., W. TRIBUTSCH, T. MAIRINGER, R. STEINACKER & G. REINEGGER 1992. Fatal myocardial infraction and Tyrolean winds (the Foehn). *The Lancet* **339**, 1362-3.

ANDERSON, K. 2005. *Predicting the weather: Victorians and the science of meteorology*. Chicago: University Press.

ARBUTHNOT, J. 1733. *An essay concerning the effects of air on human bodies*. London: Thonson.

ARNOLD, D. (ed.) 1996. *Warm climates and Western medicine: the emergence of tropical medicine, 1500-1900*. Amsterdam: Rodopi.

ATKINSON, J.C. 1843. Meteorology and cholera. *The Lancet* **62**, 322-3.

——— 1848. *Change of air: fallacies regarding it*. London: John Ollivier.

——— 1849*a*. On the effects of different winds on the human constitution. *The Lancet* **53**, 207-8, 318, 410, 533-35; **54**, 91-3.

——— 1849*b*. Electricity in cholera. *The Lancet* **54**, 50.

——— 1850. On the connection of meteorological phenomena with cholera, influenza, and other epidemic diseases. *The Lancet* **1**, 240.

AUSTEN, J. 1816. *Emma: a novel, vol. 3*. London: J. Murray.

BAGE, R. 1796. *Hermsprong; or, man as he is not. A novel. In three volumes. By the author of Man as he is*. London: William Lane.

BARKER-BENFIELD, G.J. 1996. *The culture of sensibility: sex and society in eighteenth-century Britain*. Chicago: University Press.

BARNES, G. & A. MITCHELL 2002. Measuring the marvelous: science and the exotic in William Dampier. *Eighteenth-Century Life* **26**, 45-7.

BARRET, F.A. 1998. Alfred Haviland's nineteenth-century map analysis of the geographical distribution of disease in England and Wales. *Social Science and Medicine* **46**, 757-81.

BENNET, H.J. 1861. *Menton and the Riviera as a winter climate*. London.

BEWELL, A. 1996. Jane Eyre and Victorian medical geography. *English Literary History* **63**, 773-808.

BISSET, C. 1762. *An essay on medical constitution of Great Britain to which are added observations on the weather*. London: A. Millar and Wilson.

BOLTON-VALENCIUS, C. 2002. *Health of the country: how American settlers understood themselves and their land*. New York: Basic Books.

BRIGHT, J. 1854. *A practical synopsis of diseases of the chest and air-passages*. (Second edition). London: J. Churchill.

BRONTË, C. 1847. *Jane Eyre*. London: Smith, Elder & Co.

——— 1849. *Shirley*. London: Smith, Elder & Co.

BROWN, S. 1797. *An inaugural dissertation on the bilious malignant fever. Read at a public examination, held by the medical professors, before the Rev. Joseph*. Boston.

Bruegman, R. 1978. Central heating and forced ventilation: origins and effects on architectural design. *Journal of the Society of Architectural Historians* **37**, 143-60.

Burgess, T. 1850. Inutility of resorting to the Italian climate for the cure of pulmonary consumption. *The Lancet* **1**, 591.

Burne, J.C. 1969. Not blowing in the wind. *The Lancet* **294**, 901.

Burrows, G.M. 1814. Medical topography of London. *London Medical Repository* **1**, 80-90.

Burton, J.M.C. 1990. Meteorology and the public health movement in London during the late nineteenth century. *Weather* **45**, 300-7.

Cantor, C. (ed.) 2002. *Reinventing Hippocrates*. Ashgate: Aldershot.

Castle, T. 1995. *The female thermometer: eighteenth-century culture and the invention of the uncanny*. Oxford: University Press.

Cipolla, C.M. 1992. *Miasmas and disease: public health and environment in the pre-industrial age*. New Haven: Yale University Press.

Clark, J. 1820. *Medical notes on climate, disease, hospitals, and medical schools in France, Italy, and Switzerland*. London: T.G. Underwood.

——— 1841. *The sanative influence of climate*. (Third edition.) London: J. Murray.

Coldstream, J. 1833. An account of the topography, climate, and present state of the town of Torquay (Devonshire). *Edinburgh Medical and Surgical Journal* **40**, 351-64.

Collactenea, 1834. The hardening System. *Collactenea. Medical Quarterly Review* **1**, 190-3.

Corbin, A. 1986. *The foul and the fragrant: odor and the French social imagination*. Leamington Spa: Berg.

Cross, E. 1857. Cholera and diarrhœa. *The Lancet* **70**, 180-1.

Cullen, W.H. 1852. *The climate of Sidmouth*. Sidmouth.

Curtin, P.D. 1964. Promise and the terror of the tropical environment. In *The image of Africa: British ideas in action 1780-1850* (ed.) P.D. Curtin, 58-87. Madison: University of Wisconsin Press.

Dalrymple, D. 1861. *Meteorological and medical observations on the climate of Egypt*. London.

Davis, J.B. 1807. *The ancient and modern history of Nice*. London: Tipper & Richards.

Dobson, M. 1782-3. An account of the Harmattan, a singular African wind. *The British Magazine and Review* **3**, 259-84.

Dolan, B. 2002. Conservative politicians, radical philosophers and the aerial remedy for the diseases of civilization. *History of the Human Sciences* **15**: **2**, 35-54.

Douglas, M. 1966. *Purity and danger*. London: Routledge & Kegan Paul.

Drummond, H. 1849. On the effects of winds etc. in the production of disease. *The Lancet* **53**, 410.

Farr, W. 1841. *A medical guide to Nice*. London: John Churchill.

Favret, M.A. 2004. War in the air. *Modern Language Quarterly* **65**, 531-59.

Ferriar, D. 2004. The erotics of empiricism. Unpublished paper, University of Leeds.

Fodéré, F.E. 1813. *Traité de médecine légale et d'hygiène publique ou de police de santé adapté aux codes de l'empire français et aux connaissances actuelles*. Paris.

Fox, C.B. 1873. *Ozone and antozone: their history and nature. When, where, why, how is ozone observed in the atmosphere?* London: J. and A. Churchill.

Francis, D.J.T. 1853. *Change of climate considered as a remedy in dyspeptic, pulmonary, and other chronic affections*. London: John Churchill.

Freeman, T.W. 1978-9. Alfred Haviland: 19th-century medical geographer. *Geographical Magazine* **51**, 90.

Friedman, F. 1993. *Appropriating the weather: Vilhelm Bjerknes and construction of a modern meteorology*. Ithaca, N.Y.: Cornell University Press.

Frye, N. 1990. Varieties of eighteenth-century sensibility. *Eighteenth-Century Studies* **24**, 157-72.

Garret, C.B. 1855. *East and northeast winds, the nature, treatment, and prevention of their distressing morbid effect on the respiratory and other organs, especially the larynx*. London: Samuel Highely.

Gates, W.E. 1967. The spread of Ibn Khaldun's ideas on climate and culture. *Journal of the History of Ideas* **28**: **3**, 415-22.

Girdlestone, G.R. 1925. The sun, the wind, and the skin. *The Lancet* **205**, 1227-8.

Glacken, C. 1973. *Traces on the Rhodian shore: nature and culture in Western thought from ancient times to the end of the eighteenth century*. Berkeley: University of Californian Press.

Golinski, J. 1998. The human barometer: weather instruments and the body in eighteenth-century England. Paper at the American Society for Eighteenth-Century Studies Annual Meeting, Notre Dame.

Gordon, W. 1903. The influence of wind on phthisis. *British Medical Journal*, **23** May.

——— 1905. On the influence of rainy winds on phthisis. *The Lancet* **165**, 10-16, 77-82.

——— 1910. *The influence of strong, prevalent rain-bearing winds on the prevalence of phthisis*. London: H.K. Lewis.

GRAHAM, J. 1793. *A new and curious treatise of the nature and effects of simple earth, water, and air*. London: Richardson.

GREGORY, J. 1815. *A dissertation on the influence of change of climate in curing diseases* (trans. and notes by W.P.C. Barton). Philadelphia: Thomas Dobson.

HAMLIN, C. 1992. Predisposing causes and public health in early nineteenth-century medical thought. *Social History of Medicine* **5**, 43-70.

——— 1994. Environmental sensibility in Edinburgh, 1839-1840: the 'fetid irrrigation' controversy. *Journal of Urban History* **20**, 311-39.

HAMPER, A. 1785. *The economy of health*. London.

HANNAWAY, C. 1972. The Société Royale de Médecine and epidemics in the Ancient Regime. *Bulletin of Medical History* **46**, 257-73.

——— 1974. Medicine, public welfare, and the state in eighteenth-century France: the Société de Médecine de Paris (1776-1793). Ph.D. dissertation, Johns Hopkins University.

——— 1993. Environment and miasmata. In *Companion encyclopedia of the history of medicine*, vol. 1 (eds) R. Porter & W.F. Bynum, 292-308. London: Routledge.

HARLEY, T. 2003. 'Nice weather for the time of year': the British obsession with the weather. In *Weather, climate, culture* (eds) S. Straus & B. Orlove, 103-20. Oxford: Berg.

HARRISON, M. 1999. *Climates and constitutions: health, race, environment and British imperialism in India*. Oxford: University Press.

HASTINGS, C. 1834. *Illustrations of the natural history of Worcestershire*. London.

HAVILAND, A. 1853. The iatro-meteorology of Hippocrates. *Association Medical Journal* **1**: **44**, 961-4.

——— 1855. *Climate, weather and disease: being a sketch of the opinions of the most celebrated antient and modern writers*. London: John Churchill.

HINGESTON, J.A. 1853. Atmospheric phenomena in relation to the prevalence of Asiatic cholera. *Association Medical Journal* **42**, 927-9.

HIPPOCRATES 2004. *Airs, waters and places*. Whitefish, Mont.: Kessinger.

HOOPER, G.S. 1837. Observations on the topography, climate and prevalent diseases of the island of Jersey. *The Lancet* **2**, 900.

HOOLIHAN, J. 1989. Health and travel in nineteenth-century Rome. *Journal of the History of Medicine and Allied Sciences* **44**, 462-85.

HUNT, L. 1817. Essays. In *The round table: a collection of essays on literature, men and manners* (ed.) W. Hazlitt. Edinburgh: Archibald Constable and Co.

HUXHAM, J. 1759. *Observations of the air and epidemical diseases, made at Plymouth from 1728-1737* (trans. from Latin). London: J. Hinton.

JANKOVIC, V. 2000. *Reading the skies: a cultural history of English weather 1650-1820*. Chicago: University Press.

——— 2002. The politics of sky battles in early Hanoverian Britain. *Journal of British Studies* **41**, 429-59.

JEFFREYS, J. 1842. On the artificial climates for the restoration and preservation of health. *London Medical Gazette* **1**, 27-30.

——— 1850. *A word on climate and atmospheric influences*. London: Longman, Brown, Green & Longmans.

JOHNSON, J. 1818. *The influence of the atmosphere*. London: T. & G. Underwood.

——— 1839. *Change of air or Pursuit of Health*. London: Highley.

JORDANOVA, L.J. 1979. Earth sciences and environmental medicine. In *Images of the earth: essays in the history of the environmental sciences* (eds) L.J. Jordanova & R. Porter, 119-46. Chalfont St Giles: British Society for the History of Science.

——— 1981. Policing public health in France, 1780-1815. In *Public health* (ed.) T. Ogawa, 12-32. Tokyo: Taniguchi Foundation.

KINGSLEY, C. 1909-14 [1889]. Ode to the North-East Wind. In *English Poetry III: from Tennyson to Whitman*, vol. **XLII**. New York: P.F. Collier & Son.

KNELLWOLF, C. 2002. The exotic frontier of the imperial imagination. *Eighteenth-Century Life* **26**, 10-30.

THE LANCET 1886. *The east wind*. **127**, 559.

——— 1915. *Nervous manifestation due to the wind of explosives*. **186**, 348-9.

——— 1992. *Ill winds*. **340**, 171.

LAQUEUR, T.W. 2002. The places of the dead in modernity. In *The age of cultural revolutions: Britain and France, 1750-1820* (eds) J. Jones & D. Wahrman, 17-32. Berkeley: University of California Press.

LEE, W.R. 1973. The emergence of occupational medicine in Victorian Britain. *British Journal of Industrial Medicine* **30**, 118-24.

LEVINE, G. 2002. *Dying to know: scientific epistemology and narrative in Victorian England.* Chicago: University Press.

LIVINGSTONE, D. 1999. Geographical inquiry, rational religion and moral philosophy: Enlightenment discourses on the human condition. In *Geography and Enlightenment* (eds) D.N. Livingstone & C.W.J. Withers, 93-120. Chicago: University Press.

MCCOMBE, A., J. BINNINGTON, D. DONOVAN & T.S. MCCOMBE 1992. Motorcyclists and wind noise. *The Lancet* **340**, 911-12.

MACLEOD, R. 1982. The 'bankruptcy of science' debate: The creed of science and its critics, 1885-1900, *Science, Technology, & Human Values* **7**, 2-15.

MILLER, G. 1962. Airs, waters, and places in history. *Journal of the History of Medicine and Allied Sciences* **17**, 129-40.

MOFFAT, T. 1860. *Medical meteorology and atmospheric ozone.* London: J. Churchill.

MURRAY, J. 1774. Journal containing daily meteorological and monthly medical observations. Wellcome Trust Library Manuscripts MS.7840.

PELLING, M. 1978. *Cholera, fever and English medicine, 1825-1865.* Oxford: University Press.

PHELPS, Mr. 1743. *The human barometer: or the living weather glass. A philosophic poem.* London: M. Cooper.

PILLOUD, S. & M. LOUIS-COURVOISIER 2003. The intimate experience of the body in the eighteenth century: between interiority and exteriority. *Medical History* **47**, 451-72.

PORTER, P. (ed.) 1990. *The medical history of waters and spas, medical history,* supplement no. 10. London: Wellcome Trust.

POYNTER, F.N.L. 1973. Sydenham's influence abroad. *Medical History* **17**, 223-34.

PROCTOR, R. 1974. The nose, ambient air and airway mucosa: a pathway in physiology. *Bulletin for the History of Medicine* **48**, 352-76.

REED, A. 1983. *Romantic weather: the climates of Coleridge and Baudelaire.* Hanover, N.H.: University Press of New England.

'Review' 1820. *Bateman's* A succint account of the contagious fever. *Medico-Chirurgical Journal,* **372**.

RILEY, J. 1987. *The eighteenth-century campaign to avoid disease.* New York: Knopf.

ROBERTSON, H. 1808. *A general view of the natural history of the atmosphere and of its connection with the sciences of medicine and agriculture.* 2 vols. Edinburgh: Abernethy & Walker.

ROME, A.W. 1996. Coming to terms with pollution: the language of environmental reform, 1865-1915. *Environmental History* **3**, 6-28.

ROSEN, G. 1957. The fate of the concept of medical police. *Centaurus* **5**, 99.

ROSENBERG, C. 1992. *Explaining epidemics and other studies in the history of medicine.* Cambridge: University Press.

ROUSSEAU, G.S. 1976. Nerves, spirits and fibres: towards defining the origins of sensibility. *The Blue Guitar* **2**, 125-53.

——— & R. PORTER (eds) 1990. *Exoticism in the Enlightenment.* Manchester: University Press.

ROYSTON, W. 1809. Hints for a medical topography of Great Britain. *Medical and Physical Journal* **25**, 13.

RUPKE N. (ed.) 2000. *Medical geography in historical perspective. (Medical History,* Supplement **20**). London: Wellcome Trust Centre for the History of Medicine.

RUSNOCK, A. 2002. Hippocrates, Bacon, and medical meteorology at the Royal Society, 1700-1750. In *Reinventing Hippocrates* (ed.) D. Cantor, 136-53. Aldershot: Ashgate.

RUTTY, J. 1770. *A chronological history of the weather and seasons and of the prevailing diseases in Dublin.* London.

SARGENT, F., II 1982. *Hippocratic heritage: a history of ideas about weather and human health.* New York: Pergamon Press.

SCHAFFER, S. 1990. Measuring virtue: eudimoetry, enlightenment and pneumatic medicine. In *The medical enlightenment of the eighteenth century* (eds) A. Cunningham & R. French, 281-318. Cambridge: University Press.

SCHÖNBEIN, C.F. 1845. *Ueber die langsame und rasche Verbrennung der Körper in atmosphärischer Luft.* Basel: Schweighauser'sche Buchhandlung.

SCOTT, SIR W. 1996 [1817]. *Rob Roy.* London: Everyman.

SCOTT, W.B. 1854. The wind in the casement. In *Poems.* London.

SHORT, T. 1749. *A general chronological history of the air, weather, seasons, meteors etc. in sundry places and different times.* London: T. Longman.

SHUTTLETON, D.E. 1995. 'A modest examination': John Arbuthnot and the Scottish Newtonians. *British Journal for Eighteenth-Century Studies* **18**, 47-62.

SMITH, H. 1816. A brief sketch of the medical topography of Salisbury. *London Medical, Surgical and Pharmaceutical Repository* **6**, 108.

TURNER, E.S. 1967. *Taking the cure*. London: Joseph.

VILA, A.C. 1997. Beyond sympathy: vapours, melancholia, and the pathologies of sensibility. *Yale French Studies* **92**, 88-101.

WALKER, J.K. 1818. Medical topography of Huddersfield. *London Medical Repository* **10**, 1-14.

WEINDLING, P. (ed.) 1985. *The social history of occupational health*. London: Croom Helm.

WILLICH, F.M. 1800. *Lectures on diet and regimen: being a systematic inquiry into the most rational means of preserving health and prolonging life*. London: Strahan.

WINTRINGHAM, C. 1727. *Commentarium nosologicum morbos epidemicos et aeris variationes in urbe Eboracenci locisque vicinis, ab anno 1715, usque ad finem anni 1725*. London: J. Clark.

WOHL, A. 1983. *Endangered lives: public heatlh in Victorian Britain*. London: Dent.

WRIGLEY, R. 1996. Infectious enthusiasms: influence, contagion and the experience of Rome. In *Transports: travel, pleasure and imaginative geography* (eds) C. Chard & H. Langdon, 75-116. New Haven: Yale University Press.

——— 2000. Pathological topographies and tourist itineraries: mapping malaria in eighteenth- and nineteenth-century Rome. In *Pathologies of travel* (eds) R. Wrigley & G. Revill, 207-28. Amsterdam: Rodopi.

YEO, R. 1993. *Defining science: William Whewell, natural knowledge and public debate in early Victorian Britain*. Cambridge: University Press.

11
An ill wind: the Foehn in Leukerbad and beyond

Sarah Strauss *University of Wyoming*

An ethnography of the wind – indeed, this is a most unlikely topic. But in the case of a special wind, a named wind like the Foehn, such an effort seems possible and perhaps even necessary. The entwining of the outside winds, those understood to be part of the 'environment', with the winds that animate human bodies, and help them interact with that environment, offers one window into the relationship between humanity and the natural world. Tim Ingold's reflections on this relationship are legion, but particularly relevant to this discussion is his comment that '[a]n environment surrounds, and therefore presupposes something – an organism to be surrounded' (2003: 303). In German, the word *Umwelt* is literally 'the world around', and the assumption of a subject interacting with the world is one of the things that differentiates *Umwelt* from *Natur*, nature in a more pure sense, with no interaction of subject and world around implied. By suggesting that we should consider time and process in the development of human knowledge of and responses to local conditions, Ingold advocates for recognition of 'the mutual constitutive engagement between persons and environment in the ordinary business of life' (2003: 307). Such an approach is useful for thinking about how people make sense of wind and weather, and how they incorporate local knowledge of these processes into the fabric of their lives.

> Everyone knows this – during the night, the Foehn arrives, and scarcely as it has covered the ground on the following day have the numerous troubles begun: not a few people had sleep disturbances during the night, finding themselves dull and 'under the weather' in the morning, unable to concentrate. The tally for automobile accidents in the morning commuter traffic has climbed sharply. Other people feel depressed, restless, or edgy. Migraines set in for some. The sicklist for office and factory workers is large. 'Yes, yes, the Foehn,' it is then named, and this explanation suffices for all. Yet many do not feel these negative effects at all, and are pleased to have the mild and dry heat of the Foehn. They ignore the illnesses it brings, or laugh about them, thinking that these are products of the imaginations of others (Weingaertner 2000: 95).

As the quotation above suggests, some winds help define the places in which they reside; often, these winds have names – testaments to the strength of their identities, each recognizable from afar by internal or external indicators, such as a 'feeling in the bones' or a particular pattern of cloud cover. Ordinary winds may inspire poetry and prose, or instill fear and loathing in those who experience them, but perhaps not quite to the same degree. Such privileges are reserved for the predictable winds that visit or inhabit certain locales, intruding deeply into personal space and becoming a part of the identities of the residents, while at the same time asserting their status as entities unto themselves. The Foehn is one of these winds, and my goal here is to present a brief natural history and biography of it. More particularly, I will talk about the Foehn that resides in the Swiss canton of Valais and occasionally visits the village of Leukerbad. In order to place this ethnographic account of the Valaisan Foehn in a broader context, I will also present some examples of how the Foehn and similar winds around the world have been experienced through literary traditions and meteorological/biomedical analyses. Through the use of such a wide-ranging array of representations, my goal is to bring into focus one example of the co-construction of nature and culture through the infusion of a local wind in the hearts and minds, both literally and figuratively, of the people who live through them.

The Foehn in Leukerbad

Imagine that you have received in the mail a beautiful postcard of the Swiss Alps. What do you see? Surely there is a bright blue sky, either cloudless or containing non-threatening wisps of white here and there at the margins of the picture, high above the sharp grey-black ridges of the mountains and the gentler slopes of the green pastures below. Perhaps your vision includes patches or flows of shimmering white or blue water in its many forms: glaciers, rushing waterfalls and rivers, placid lakes, steaming thermal springs. Beautifully kept houses might colour the lower borders of the postcard, with flower boxes dripping carnations if it is summer, or piles of snow overhanging the rooftops if it is winter.

Waking up of a winter's day in Leukerbad, I have found myself in the middle of just such a postcard, with a clear, sunny sky and a warm wind blowing (Fig. 1). Watching a few high clouds drift past the Torrenthorn, I recognize that Leukerbad is feeling the effects of the Foehn. To someone like me, who grew up in the grey and slushy winters of the mid-Atlantic coast of the United States, such a day is bound to bring smiles of anticipation – what glorious opportunities await! But had I been instead a *wetterfühlig* person – someone who can sense changes in the weather, usually through feelings of poor health – I would have likely known about the advent of the Foehn long before looking outside to see the colour of the sky or the existence of the clouds.

Leukerbad, a community of about 1,500 residents, belongs to the bilingual Swiss canton of Valais (French)/Wallis (German). The village lies pressed against the back of a 10-mile-long valley – a box canyon, it would be called in the American West. A journey to Leukerbad takes a traveller as far into the main spine of the Alps as he or she can go without coming out again on the other side. The Dalatal (named for the river Dala that runs through Leukerbad) is a place where the forces of nature have clashed dramatically with the efforts of culture for quite a long time. Archaeological evidence exists for Iron Age habitation by the Celts throughout the region, followed later by Roman occupation. More recent finds in neighbouring valleys take us back into the Neolithic. Weather-dependent threats to home and livelihood have always been central concerns for the inhabitants of this valley. Surrounded by steep shale cliffs, Leukerbadners live in the shadow of a thousand avalanche chutes, and indeed the history of the village is one of repeated destruction by thundering rock and snow slides. The first

Figure 1. Leukerbad (VS) Switzerland: Gemmipass (author photo).

protective walls against avalanches were erected in the eighteenth century, and the subsequent 250 years have seen the implementation of increasingly sophisticated systems of fences and other avalanche management techniques. The geography is dramatic; many people find it threatening and oppressive (a reasonable response to the continued, very real avalanche danger), though others have told me that they feel safe in Leukerbad, enclosed and protected by what a middle-aged German woman who owns a holiday home calls the 'womb of mother earth'. Because of the nearly north-south orientation of the valley, the Foehn effect mostly bypasses the Dalatal, though it is felt very strongly in the Simplon region of the Rhone Valley and near Zermatt. Still, the Foehn is well known to people in Leukerbad, and features in everyday discourse there, as it does throughout Switzerland.

The economy of Leukerbad depends entirely on its varied water resources, which include thermal springs, used commercially since the sixteenth century, a ski area, and a small hydroelectric system fed by the Dala, which provides power for all of the community's summer electrical needs, and more than a third of the winter power. Until the late 1950s, every family in Leukerbad had a cow or two, a few goats, and a large garden plot. Subsistence was supplemented by wage labour, often available only by seasonal (winter) outmigration, and perhaps by some summer tourist income. As with other Swiss Alpine communities (cf. Friedl 1974; Netting 1981; Niederer 1996; Wiegandt 1977), grazing land, as well as forest- and water-use rights, were held in common, and access distributed across families designated as *einheimische* (native – with the connotation of having settled there well prior to the nineteenth century). Since 1958, when a large rheumatology clinic capitalizing on the thermal springs was built with funding from the northern cities of Zurich, Winterthur, and Lucerne, an influx in foreigners (defined not only as those from other countries, but *Uesserschwiiz* or non-Valaisan Swiss as well) has been accompanied by a rapid decline in subsistence-level smallholdings. Now, there are very few stock animals left; a handful of families make their living at farming, and almost no one else maintains animals year-round.

Over the past eight years, I have spent a total of about eleven months conducting field research on water and weather in Leukerbad, in two long trips of six weeks and six months, and several shorter trips of a few weeks each. Because of its water-based economy, Leukerbad is an excellent location to study weather, climate, and water resources. Despite the shift from a subsistence-orientated economy, weather and climate have continued to be important concerns for the economic health of the valley, due to the short- to mid-range consequences of altered precipitation patterns for the ski area, as well as the long-term impact of global environmental change on the glaciers that permit a stable flow of water through the Dalatal.

While Leukerbad is situated at the back of deep valley, it has never been a particularly isolated community. At first glance, the geography might appear to deflect travellers rather than attract them. But the Gemmipass, which connects Leukerbad to the Berner Oberland, was in fact one of the earliest north-south routes across the Alps. This pass is noteworthy for its singular steepness and for the poor quality of the rock from which it is made, in comparison with the many glacier-smoothed granite passes to the east of the Gemmi. What must be recognized is that such glaciation made the other passes, now ice-free, poor candidates for a crossing of the Alps, while the Gemmi, certainly more dangerous then than now, offered relatively dry passage with the prospect of hot baths at the end of the crossing. For the purpose of this paper, it is also important to know that it is the source of the special Gemmiwind, a cold north wind or *Bise* frequently occurring in Leukerbad. The combined impact of the ease of travel on the Bernese side, the hot springs, and the fact that the valley on the Leukerbad side had not been as heavily glaciated as many of the other side valleys of the Valais helped promote the pass despite the outrageously steep climb required on the south side.

Literary representations of the Gemmiwind and the Foehn

Over the centuries, many authors have described both the Gemmipass and the Foehn wind as it is experienced in the Valais and in Switzerland more generally. Leukerbad was a stop on the Grand Tour of the nineteenth century, and from this period we have many literary renderings that resonate still. Guy de Maupassant's short story 'The inn' (1886) describes both the remoteness of the pass and the ferocity of the wind as a nearly living entity that can sweep away a man's mind, leaving only a shadow in its wake. In the middle of winter, while out looking for his companion caretaker who had not returned to the inn after what was intended to be a brief sojourn into the cold, the unfortunate protagonist, young Ulrich, experiences the full force of the Gemmiwind: 'The wind had risen, the icy wind that breaks the stones and leaves nothing living on these deserted heights. It passes in stiff gusts more dessicating and deadly than the fiery wind of the desert'. After passing a tortured winter alone, hearing voices in the wind, Ulrich is finally retrieved by the owners of the inn upon their return in the spring, but it is too late; he has gone mad.

Mark Twain visited Leukerbad in 1878 and described the trip over the Gemmipass from Interlaken in *A tramp abroad* (1880), writing not with horror but with his customary wry humour. His depictions of both the harrowing trip over the Gemmipass on a mule, and the sights to be seen in the therapeutic baths of the village, are striking. Of the place described by de Maupassant, he says,

> We stopped for a nooning at a strongly built little inn called the Schwarenbach. It sits in a lonely spot among the peaks, where it is swept by the trailing fringes of the cloud-rack, and is rained on, and snowed on, and pelted and persecuted by the storms, nearly every day of its life. It was the only habitation in the whole Gemmi Pass.

In his fairytale *The Ice Maiden* (1862), Hans Christian Andersen described the same passage across the Alps from the Berner Oberland to the Valais via the Gemmipass, noting the frequency of the Foehn at several points throughout the tale:

> The sun had gone down, and the clouds lay low in the valley of the Rhone between the tall mountains; the wind blew from the south, an African wind; it suddenly sprang up over the high summits like a foehn, which swept the clouds away; and when the wind had fallen, everything for a moment was perfectly still. The scattered clouds hung in fantastic shapes between the wooded hills skirting the rushing Rhone; they hung in the shapes of sea monsters of the prehistoric world, of eagles hovering in the air, of frogs leaping in a marsh; they settled down on the swift river and seemed to sail on it, yet they were floating in the air (Andersen 1949 [1862])

Here, the mention of the Foehn as 'an African wind' derives from the theory current at the time that such a warm, dry, wind could only come from the Sahara (Hann 1989 [1866]; cf. Jankovic, this volume), though by two decades later, this notion had been displaced by a variant on the current scientific explanation of adiabatic compression and local topographic configuration (Seibert 2004), which forms the basis for current theory. A complete history of the theoretical shifts in understandings of the Foehn (Dürr 2000) points out that the technical understanding of the phenomenon has been one of the most contested issues in meteorology over the past 150 years, and even today, practising meteorologists demonstrate that their assumptions about the Foehn are derived from a pastiche of these competing theories rather than adhesion to any particular one.

Equally compelling is Romain Rolland's description of the intensity of the Foehn's impact, bringing vitality instead of insanity to his protagonist – quite the opposite of de Maupassant's vision. In the climactic ninth section of an extraordinary ten-part novel sequence entitled *Jean-Christophe* (completed in 1911), for which Rolland gained world-wide recognition with his receipt of the Nobel Prize for Literature in 1915, the Foehn figures prominently. Rolland tells in detail how Jean-Christophe, a depressed musician and composer who has come to the Jura mountains of Switzerland to regain his health, experiences a Foehn storm:

> Suddenly, in the distance, there came a storm. A premonitory gust of wind blew up from the depths of the forest. Like a galloping horse it rushed over the swaying tree-tops. It was like the God of Michael Angelo passing in a water-spout. It passed over Christophe's head. The forest rustled, and Christophe's heart quivered ... All Nature seemed dead. The forests which covered the sides of the mountain were sleeping, lying heavy beneath a weight of sadness. The still air was magically clear and transparent. There was never a sound. Only the melancholy music of a stream – water eating away the rock – sounded the knell of the earth ... Night. He had dozed off. In the silence the distant storm arose once more. The wind returned, like a hurricane now, the *foehn* of the spring, with its burning breath warming the still sleeping, chilly earth, the *foehn* which melts the ice and gathers fruitful rains.
>
> It rumbled like thunder in the forests on the other side of the ravine. It came nearer, swelled, charged up the slopes: the whole mountain roared. In the stable a horse neighed and the cows lowed.

> Christophe's hair stood on end, he sat up in bed and listened. The squall came up screaming, set the shutters banging, the weather-cocks squeaking, made the slates of the roof go crashing down, and the whole house shake. A flower-pot fell and was smashed. Christophe's window was insecurely fastened, and was burst open with a bang, and the warm wind rushed in. Christophe received its blast full in his face and on his naked chest. He jumped out of bed gaping, gasping, choking. It was as though the living God were rushing into his empty soul. The Resurrection! ... The air poured down his throat, the flood of new life swelled through him and penetrated to his very marrow. He felt like to burst, he wanted to shout, to shout for joy and sorrow ...

This moving text so inspired Rolland's friend, the French composer Charles Koechlin, that he wrote a symphony, *Le Buisson Ardent* (The Burning Bush), based on the ninth book of the sequence, through which the theme of the Foehn pervades. Koechlin comments in correspondence with Jacques Lonchampt that writing the music of the Foehn was extremely difficult, and that 'he feared himself incapable of living up to the descriptive genius of Rolland' (Orledge 1989: 190), but this wind was too important to leave out. As this passionate text makes clear, the Foehn can serve many functions; its effects on individuals may be positive or negative, and may change with the seasons.

Snow-Eaters and Santa Anas

While the Foehn of the European Alps is the type-wind for this category, local names for similar winds in other locations vary greatly. A well-known North American Foehn-type wind is the Chinook of the northern United States and Canadian plains. The Chinook covers a wide geographic area in the Rocky Mountain region; it has localized names and meanings for particular peoples, but the phenomenon is recognized as similar across a broad slice of the continent. In the oral traditions of the Blackfeet people of Montana and Alberta, the Chinook is called Snow-Eater; as a ferocious wind, it is dangerous, but can also be extremely beneficial, warming up the landscape dramatically in the middle of winter, melting away the snow, bringing in game to hunt, and making things just a bit easier for nomadic people whose exposure to the cold and snow is otherwise unrelenting for much of the year. One Blackfeet story tells of how the bear stole the Chinook wind, putting it in a bag to hug and warm himself, while the other animals and people froze. A co-ordinated effort to release the wind from captivity so that it could warm everyone left the bear very angry, and for this reason, bears hibernate each winter, isolating themselves from the rest of animal society (Wagner 2004). In Boulder, Colorado, the effects of the Chinook are also legendary; reports of howling gusts of wind, racing down to the plains at speeds of up to 160 km/hour are not uncommon, and destruction in the past few decades has ranged from loss of roofs to downed power-lines.

Another famous and quite local North American expression of the Foehn is the Santa Ana wind of southern California. Author Joan Didion was inspired to describe the palpable influence of this wind on the people of the Santa Ana area:

> There is something uneasy in the Los Angeles air this afternoon, some unnatural stillness, some tension ... I have neither heard nor read that a Santa Ana is due, but I know it, and almost everyone I have seen today knows it too. We know it because we feel it. The baby frets. The maid sulks ... To live with the Santa Ana is to accept, consciously or unconsciously, a deeply mechanistic view of human behavior (1990 [1968]: 217).

In the case of Didion, who herself claims to be strongly influenced by the onset of this particular wind, it is worth noting that we can see both the infusion of the wind in the personality characteristics of the individual, and the pervasive social impacts of such an intertwining of environment and humanity. In the case of the Santa Ana, as in those locales where the Swiss Foehn is particularly strong, the emotional response to the wind is driven not only from the inside, by the cumulative effect of multiple individuals who are experiencing unease, but also from the outside, where the very real potential for environmental damage looms large in the community's collective consciousness. In addition, the Santa Ana – much like the Gemmiwind as a local form of the Bise/ Northwind in Leukerbad – offers one form of identification that allows community members to situate themselves in a local landscape, for better or for worse. The Gemmiwind is not seen as having specific body- or mind-altering properties like the Foehn or Santa Ana, but it is clearly an element of the environment that helps people feel embedded in their place.

Environmental hazards of the Foehn

While these literary representations can provide a visceral sense of the extremely negative or positive ways in which the Foehn can influence people, it is also important to examine the more pragmatic and depersonalized manifestations of this type of wind. In considering the impact of the Foehn on everyday life in Switzerland, we can begin with the environmental problems associated with Foehn winds. First, in certain regions, especially the Vierwaldstädtersee area of central Switzerland, the windstorms associated with the Foehn effect create very dangerous conditions on the lake, and some portions of the shore have special 'Foehn Docks' for the ferries to pull into port for emergency shelter under such conditions. This problem has been memorialized in one of the dominant myths of the Swiss federation, that of Wilhelm Tell. In the first act of Schiller's eponymous play, a man who is trying to escape the governing authorities finds that Tell is the only person willing to take him onto the Lake of Lucerne, the Vierwaldstädtersee.

Tell was familiar with the Foehn as a typical local weather event, which Gessler, the Austrian governor of Tell's Swiss canton, and his men are not, and is able to use his knowledge to advantage, and take the refugee to safety. In Theodore Martin's English translation of Schiller's epic drama, one of the men in the boat calls out 'The South Wind's up! See how the lake is rising!' And in footnote 4 of the English translation, it is explained further that in the original text, the name for the south wind was Foehn; further,

> 'When,' says Mueller, in his History of Switzerland, 'the wind called the Foehn is high the navigation of the lake becomes extremely dangerous. Such is its vehemence that the laws of the country require that the fires shall be extinguished in the houses while it lasts, and the night watches are doubled. The inhabitants lay heavy stones upon the roofs of their houses to prevent their being blown away' (Schiller 1804).

Later in the play, Tell uses the Foehn as a metaphor for keeping quiet and not stirring up trouble:

> When the fierce south wind rises from his chasms, Men cover their fires, the ships in haste Make for the harbor, and the mighty spirit Sweeps o'er the earth, and leaves no trace behind. Let every man live quietly at home; Peace to the peaceful rarely is denied.

But, Tell continues, if others will start the fight, they can count on him to hold true to the cause.

Second, because Foehn winds are very dry, they have historically been associated with high risk of forest fire, and many communities in Switzerland post a fire watch when the Foehn is predicted, especially if it occurs in summer or autumn. The dessicating effect is one reason for this, and the windspeed as a contributor to the spread of fire, if it occurs, is another. During certain periods of combined dryness and Foehn, even in the winter, forest fires have been reported on a daily basis (Conedera, Marxer, Ambrosetti, Della Bruna & Spinedi 1998). Another negative Foehn impact in winter, quite the opposite of forest fires, is the increased risk of avalanche hazard. When a warm wind is followed quickly by precipitation, like winter rain or heavy, wet snow, the frequent result is that the snow already on the steep slopes becomes quite unstable. The avalanche hazard increases tremendously, then, as was the case in the Alps during the notorious winter of 1999. Clearly, the concerns that the Foehn generates in relation to potential threats to homes and livelihoods are both real and experienced regularly. It is not a large step to make the connection between these external threats and the internal storms most familiarly associated with the Foehn.

Wind, life, health: the biometeorology of the Foehn

The continuity between inside and outside air is one of the themes of this volume, and the Foehn provides an excellent example of this linkage between self and environment. For the origins of biometeorological discussions of health problems, specifically in relation to the wind, one need look no farther than Hippocrates, who in 400 BC used his treatise *On airs, waters, and places* to address directly the impact of specific local warm and cold winds on the health of human populations. Michel Foucault reminds us of 'the study of topographies (location, terrain, water, air, society, the temperaments of the inhabitants), [and] meteorological observations (pressure, temperature, winds)' (1994 [1973]: 28; cf. Jankovic, this volume) and of its importance for the emergence of modern medicine in the latter half of the eighteenth century in France. One of the earliest mentions of Foehn illness in the Swiss literature was made by a Dr Zolliker in 1819, at the founding of the St Gallen Natural History Society (de Rudder 1989 [1948]). For the century and a half following, there was a steady flow of papers and discussion of the health problems posed by Foehn winds in various locations. By the 1970s, however, this line of research had diminished nearly completely, only to be revived a few decades later, most visibly by work done in Canada on the negative health impacts of Chinook winds on migraine sufferers (Cooke, Rose & Becker 2000). Other recent work made possible by advances in technology has allowed measurement of atmospheric ion concentrations that show significant influences on biological processes in humans and animals as they change according to larger atmospheric shifts. Both of these lines of research have brought the Foehn into the realm of contemporary popular scientific and medical discourse, about which more below.

Among the public health problems associated with Foehn periods in the popular imagination is an increased rate of traffic accidents, whether due to increased stress and nervousness, or some other unspecified reason. One of my discussants in Leukerbad, a highly educated professional man in his fifties who had grown up near Brig in the Valais, reminisced about his time living near Lucerne, also located on the Vierwaldstädtersee, saying that:

> The Foehn brings mostly warmth, it also brings dry air and then it keeps the rain from falling, and it also has effects on various people in terms of their comfort level ... I was in Lucerne for three years and

> I could always say, by 6 or 7 a.m., in my room, 'today is Foehn' – this because I had already heard the police and ambulance sirens at least two to three times, and then one could reliably say, oh, today is Foehn weather. It must somehow also have an effect on the people ... it's also just unpleasant because it's wind. Wind is always, somehow, having an influence on people, when they are out in the wind. But for me personally, I am very healthy, or at least I feel healthy, and neither fog nor rain nor snow nor sleet nor summer heat nor cold nights bothers me, not at all, nothing makes me feel better, really the weather plays very little role in my life. I think I'm pretty weatherproof!

From one of the best-known Leukerbad weather aficionados, a man in his eighties whom I call here Matti, who also collects weather data for the Swiss meteorological agency, MeteoSwiss, comes a description of the Foehn locally:

> Yes, when there is a strong Foehn in the valley, with a windspeed of 120 or 100 [km/hr], then we feel the influence here [in Leukerbad], but minimally, we have the feeling of pressure in our ears, strongly, and then the Foehn comes over the Torrent and presses down under here. The warm air then encounters our cold air, and that then makes for very strange situations. And when the Bise comes afterward, that makes everything cold, [blows] everything away, that is interesting ...

When asked about the winds in Leukerbad, many people offered statements about the health effects of the Foehn, whether on themselves or others. One middle-aged woman, who did not grow up in the Valais, said,

> I don't feel the effects of the Foehn myself, and so I can't really say if it comes here often or not. I am not *foehnfühlig* – sensitive to the Foehn – like they say, and I don't know much about the forms of wind. For me, it's all the same, whatever kind of wind blows, I just call it wind, but I couldn't tell you what kind of wind it is. But they say here in Wallis that the Foehn is very important, and I see that is specifically true in the sense of the importance to the vineyards. The grapes then get something extra, one might say, a special sugar content through the sun and through the wind, but aside from that, I don't know anything about the Foehn. For me, it's not important.

Others connect the Foehn to broader issues of climate change, suggesting that its frequency has increased in recent years, and making reference to the capacity of the Foehn, like the Chinook of the northern Plains of North America, to be a 'Snow-Eater', making snow sublimate in its wake, without passing through the melting stage at all. Said one native of Leukerbad,

> I think the Foehn has, sad to say, been here more often in the last few years. We have more Foehn now than five years ago. The people who say that it's the Foehn's fault when they have a headache or are in a bad mood, I don't believe them. But the Foehn is unpleasant; when it comes in winter it makes the snow disappear, it cleans it right away. And when the snow is gone, we have fewer tourists. That's clear.

In this example, the relationship between internal moods and external environmental conditions is seen to be measured by the pocketbooks of those impacted by the change in the wind. Whether one is willing to accept the biometeorological effects on human health and well-being, clearly experienced only by a minority of the population, it is patently obvious that the Foehn can have an adverse effect on Valaisan society, where wealth is now primarily determined by the number of tourist beds in a town and the percentage of days that those beds are filled.

The science of the Foehn: of meteorologists and men

The Foehn has counterparts in many different mountainous regions of the world. Other winds similar to the Foehn, already discussed above, are the Chinook in the north-central part of North America, and the Santa Ana in southern California, though there are many more of these autumn winds that demonstrate the warming effect of adiabatic compression: the Zonda in Argentina, the Koembang in Java, the Sirocco in North Africa, or the Samiel in Turkey. The Foehn is a local or regional wind, as opposed to one that is generated by the global circulation of air currents. It is orographic in origin, meaning that the very shape of the mountains, as well as their orientation to the prevailing wind pattern, generates this particular wind effect. As Descartes noted in the seventeenth century, '[W]e must consider that the vapors rise very unequally from the diverse sections of the earth; for the heavenly bodies heat the mountains differently from the plains, the forests differently from the prairies, cultivated fields differently from deserts' (2001 [1637]: 295). Even earlier, the Greek Theophrastus, student of Aristotle, pointed out that when clouds were forced by the wind into the side of a mountain, rain was the result. Rain on the windward side of a mountain range, as described, is one prerequisite for assignment of Foehn conditions; another is a minimal temperature increase of 0.5 degrees centigrade per 100 metres of drop on the leeward slope, though the average is about 1 degree centigrade, and it can be as high as 3 degrees. The *Foehnmauer*, a wall of cumulus clouds that is pushed up against the windward side of a range by the rising and cooling air mass, drops a large amount of rain on that side. But as the air mass pushes over the summit, the air dries and warms rapidly – a fact which quite puzzled Theophrastus, but is now explained by the process of adiabatic compression.

It is a strange notion, really – we know that cold air should fall, and hot air rise. That is the basic principle. So downslope, or katabatic, winds should be, by definition, cooling since cold air is denser and heavier than warm air. And there are many such winds: the Mistral in France, and the Bora in the Adriatic are two cold downslope winds. These winds start out very cold, and though they are compressed as they move downwards (the adiabatic process) and should therefore be heated, the amount of heating is not sufficient to turn the thermal gradient, and so they still provide a cooling effect. The amount of moisture in the air is part of this determination.

> Imagine a parcel of air containing no moisture at all crossing the Alps or the Rockies. It would cool on climbing – because it expands – and then would warm at the same rate in coming down the other side – because it is compressed by the greater atmospheric pressure. Result: The parcel of air would have the same temperature at the same elevation on either side of the mountains.
>
> Now follow another parcel of air across the ... Alps ... As it climbs, it again cools. Soon its temperature reaches the dew point. Clouds form. Higher up, it rains. By the time the air parcel reaches the crest of the mountains, all its water vapor has returned to the liquid state. And all the sun's energy that originally evaporated the water ... is liberated, and heats the now-dry air parcel. That's quite apart from the heating by compression as the air descends. Result: At the same elevation, the air parcel is considerably warmer on the far side of the mountains (Kals 1977: 56-7).

The sky is very different on the two sides of the Foehn boundary. On the windward side, as noted, there is a wall of clouds that pours down rain. On the leeward side, the air and sky are clear, and thin, high, lenticular clouds are formed (see Fig. 2).

The Foehn is most common in the winter and spring, least often felt in the summertime. While the Foehn brings mild and dry weather, when it breaks, the weather turns quite wet and nasty. The *Bauernregel*, or 'farmer's rule', is '*Der Foehn macht das Wetter schoen, wenn er vergohd, faellt es ins Kot*' (Malberg 1999: 67): loosely, 'The Foehn makes the weather good, but when it fades away, the weather turns rotten'. Foehn winds are one of the most commonly 'named' winds, identified by their physical characteristics as well as by the effects on living beings attributed to them. Talk of the Foehn in Switzerland is ubiquitous; it is blamed for all manner of individual and societal problems, and an attorney I know says that it has been claimed successfully as a reasonable cause for insanity in a legal defence. In a recent publication designed by the Swiss Federal Office for Migration to assist people who would like to move to Switzerland for work, the section on climate notes that large portions of the country 'suffer occasionally from the "Foehn" (an oppressive warm, dry, wind from the south)' (2005: 3); this seems an interesting but unnecessary disclosure for prospective immigrants.

Another official Swiss representation of the Foehn is included on the Health pages of the MeteoSwiss federal weather service website.[1] There, the daily forecast for weather-sensitive people is made available, along with a general diagram that explains the impact of different types of weather patterns on human health. Specific advisories are given, not only for those with seasonal allergies, but also for joint pain, headache, cardiac and circulatory problems, and mental health status; the medical literature has reported direct weather correlations to these particular complaints. For example, the strong, cold north wind (Bise) conditions of 22 November 2005 generated a health advisory for those prone to general headaches and migraines, to heart and circulatory ailments, and to 'nervous unrest', while the forecast for Foehn on 4 December 2005 warned against possible migraine, restlessness, concentration disturbances, and depression. The Foehn in Leukerbad is often contrasted with the Gemmiwind, a local north wind in the Bise family, as in this comment by a member of one of the families whose ancestors came from Italy, but have none the less become one of the most prominent families in Leukerbad:

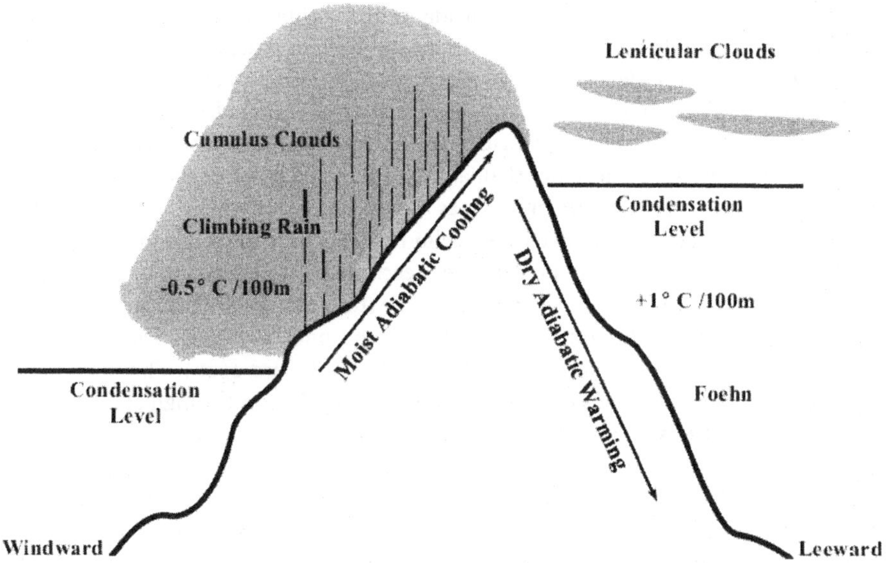

Figure 2. The Foehn.

> In Wallis we have a great deal of Foehn – Leukerbad feels it a bit less, but then we have the north wind, that we call the Gemmiwind, a very cold and strong wind ... We have the Gemmiwind up here, when it comes it is also very strong, and blows for three to four days; it can be associated with rain showers as well, so it isn't very pleasant. When there is so much wind, it makes for an uncomfortable time. That wind comes right off the Gemmi, it is the wind that is unique to Leukerbad.

And, referring to the relative health values of the Gemmiwind and the Foehn, apropos the research on positive and negative ion concentrations, another local man pointed out that

> It's certainly true that the Gemmiwind blows really strong, and one notices it here in Leukerbad very clearly. The Foehn also comes, but less strongly, and then more up on the Torrent is where people really notice the Foehn. But there is Foehn here in Leukerbad too, just less ... There is a pediatrician in Brig who always said that Leukerbad had healthy weather, because we have the proper Gemmiwind so often, and it blows away all the pollution, that's what he always said. [But when the Foehn comes,] we don't have the healthy air here, that's true, but it is very infrequent, much less than the Gemmiwind.

Leukerbad has, indeed, for well over a century been characterized by geographers and meteorologists, as well as physicians, as having a so-called *Reizklima*, that is, a healthy mountain climate, neither too high nor too low, receiving a great deal of sun, but not too much, being high enough to be above the fray, but not too low in atmospheric pressure to make for difficulty in breathing (Ward 1906).

Internalizing the wind

Some of the reported effects of Foehn winds include psychological symptoms of depression or anxiety; feelings of general unease or irritation are also often mentioned. Beyond these, however, is the range of complaints linked to the circulatory system: migraine headache, stroke, and heart attack (Field & Hill 2002; Piorecky, Becker & Rose 1997). In the 1950s and 1960s, a number of studies on the health effects of the Foehn, addressing increases in incidence of suicide, traffic accidents, 'female problems', and non-specified neuralgia, were conducted, mostly by researchers in Germanic Alpine Europe (e.g. Frey 1965; Hartweger 1956; Moos 1964; Vogel & Neubeiser 1955). The classic description of Foehn illness by de Rudder (1989 [1948]) includes headache, nausea, insomnia, and intensification of arthritis. In the 1970s, Hans Richner (1989) updated the findings, looking for causal rather than associative relations for Foehn sensitivity, and identifying shifts in barometric pressure as significant.

More recent studies have linked the Foehn to a variety of ailments, including heart problems and asthma attacks (Villeneuve, Leech & Bourque 2005; von Mackensen, Hoeppe, Maarouf, Tourigny & Nowak 2005). One study even examined the relationship between the Foehn and Sudden Infant Death Syndrome (SIDS/Cot Death), though ultimately no association was found (Macey, Schuter & Ford 2000). The main factor that has been claimed as causal in these various health effects is the high concentration of positive ions that is produced in the atmosphere as a result of a large air mass moving rapidly over land, which strips electrons from the air. In laboratory studies and field studies of the Sharav in Israel (Sulman 1980), an equivalent to the Foehn, it was found that high concentrations of positive ions can lead to the formation of serotonin in animals and people. The hormone serotonin controls mood, and in low levels can be calming. High serotonin levels are associated with migraine and insomnia, among other things, as well as an increase in platelet aggregation in the blood, which can be an aggravating factor for stroke, although the studies conducted to ascertain stroke risk in relation to the Foehn have been conflicting.

For example, severe weather of any kind tends to produce an adrenaline response in just about everyone, and this classic 'fight or flight' response to environmental stress could easily explain some of the circulatory ailments under those conditions (Gensler 1972), but not necessarily under the pre-Foehn and less palpable wind conditions. While many regions report higher incidence of stroke during the winter months, when the Foehn is also prevalent, many questions remain. Counter-studies demonstrating the positive effects of high concentrations of negative ions have also been conducted; places that historically have been seen as having 'healthy' air, like the seaside and specific mountain resorts – including Leukerbad – have been shown to have high negative ion levels, and these are generative of a relaxation response. The other physical attribute of the Foehn effect that has been linked with health problems is the existence of sferics, or very-low-frequency atmospheric pulses; these are also associated with lightning storms, and generate pulse-shaped alternating electromagnetic fields (Vaitl, Propson & Stark 2001); in the context of the Foehn, they are present as precursors, before any other measurable meteorological effects can be detected. Sferics have been conclusively demonstrated to produce pain in amputees, whose stumps were noted to be highly sensitive to weather changes.

The situation regarding migraine headache has received a great deal of attention since the publication of a study based in Calgary, Canada (Cooke *et al.* 2000). In that case, two subsets of individuals who were patients of the headache clinic at the University of Calgary reported higher frequency of migraine headache on either the day preceding a Chinook occurrence, or the days of Chinook occurrence. While most people did not demonstrate sensitivity to Chinook conditions, these two subsets showed marked differences on Chinook/non-Chinook days. And, while only two people showed sensitivity to both conditions, a sizeable group was afflicted by one or the other, suggesting different mechanisms of action in each case.

The meaning of the Foehn

So why do people keep talking about the Foehn? It is by now a commonplace among many social theorists that modern identities, whether of individuals, communities, or nations, are not fixed, but fluid, shape-shifting as new forces from both within and without generate ever-changing patterns. In Switzerland, the fixing of identity is if anything more problematic than in many other Western European contexts. Switzerland is often viewed as an anomaly, especially in terms of its politics (Bendix 1992); historically, Switzerland is a crossroads, a place where many borders meet. Swiss identity must be understood within the context of this anomalous location. Using Renato Rosaldo's definition of the term, Switzerland is a borderland: 'Borderlands surface not only at the boundaries of officially recognized cultural units, but also at less formal intersections, such as those of gender, age, status, and distinctive life experiences' (1989: 29). For Rosaldo, such experiences could range from particular uses of time and space, to bereavement, eating habits, or political practices; 'such borderlands,' he says, 'should be regarded not as analytically empty transitional zones but as sites of creative cultural production that require investigation' (1989: 208). There are many levels and kinds of borderlands in Switzerland, as everywhere. In this paper, I have begun to address the ways in which a particular Swiss town sees itself and is seen by others as reflecting certain features of what may be called a Swiss national identity, which is predicated simultaneously on a kinship with the natural world (involving a bond that, desired or not, like family and nation, one is simply stuck with) and a craving for the cultural fruits of modernity, including medical and meteorological science.

'Formed by the mountains': Leukerbad's nature

Leukerbad generates a kind of ambiguity that is in many ways characteristic of Switzerland more broadly; its *einheimische* people, residents who are born to that place, simultaneously see themselves as typical traditional mountain folk and also urbane moderns who have made their small town into a destination for others by virtue of their business acuity and attention to trends and opportunities in the marketplace. They feel that they have taken the natural resources of their valley and strategically transformed this raw nature into a desirable cultural commodity, just as they have transformed themselves from 'simple mountain people' to sophisticated managers. There was an ad campaign a few years ago for Swiss Gruyere cheese, which showed the Matterhorn with an overlay of a wheel of cheese, and a slogan to the effect of 'The mountains shaped (*gepraegt*) its character'. Recognition of the ferocity of the Gemmiwind and the ill effects of the Foehn are two other ways in which Leukerbadners demonstrate that they, too, have been formed by nature. The winds, ephemeral but ever-returning, also offer a resource for building Swiss identity, making even (or especially) city-dwellers in the flatlands a part of the locally produced landscape. This also demonstrates the importance of being located within the landscape as well as being identified with its features. The story about Wilhelm Tell is one way of showing how important local knowledge of place is to the formation of identity, as it separates insiders from outsiders. Likewise, the discussants who detailed the ways in which the winds are expressed in Leukerbad versus how they play out in the rest of the Valais or the flatlands were showing how the demarcation of local boundaries helps to secure people in their places, generating a sense of belonging in many cases.

Finally, the discourse surrounding the Foehn demonstrates the limits of knowledge, both local and universalizing. The gap between the scientific and 'folkloric' understandings of wind in Leukerbad is sometimes wider, sometimes narrowing. It is clear that understandings of technical processes have improved over the last century, but also that the local perceptions of these winds remain important. The *wetterfühlig* among us, those who are so sensitive to the smallest shifts in ionic concentration or air pressure, have been labelled crazy by many who claim a higher capacity for rationality, viewing these claims as beyond the realm of sensible phenomena. Yet as our technological capacities in scientific and biomedical research have improved, so too has the socially accepted range of plausible explanations for the personal experience of the effects of the wind. And with acceptance comes marketing; new meteorological products, like the *Wetterfühligkeit* forecast on the MeteoSwiss website and the many ionic air purifiers available for purchase, attest to the values now attached to these sensitivities and their solutions.

How can a wind become so important to the identity of a people? Many questions remain, and the answers to these could well close the gap, leaving both views with equal claims to credibility and helping to demonstrate, once again, the value of discursive formations instead of monologic domination of singular explanations. Air may be a singular entity, diffuse, amorphous, blending distinctive qualities into a pastel smear of essences; winds, however, are many and distinct. Wind is part of the landscape, an oxymoronic moveable fixture of the environment, here and gone, and back again. It permeates rather than surrounds. Accepting that the Foehn is important to Swiss identity helps clarify Ingold's suggestion that we view people and their environments in a mutually constitutive way. As we belong to a place, are citizens with civic rights and responsibilities, we are also meteorological citizens (Jankovic, this volume) with varying degrees of privilege in insulating ourselves from or exposing ourselves to the winds and weather, and the place in which we dwell leaves its mark on us, infusing us with strength or sucking that strength away, as surely as we inhale and exhale.

NOTES

The author gratefully acknowledges research support in the form of grants from the National Science Foundation (BCS-0078891), the University of Wyoming (International Travel Grant, A & S Basic Research Fund, and Faculty Grant-in-Aid), and ETH-EAWAG. Thank you to Rick Weathermon, University of Wyoming Department of Anthropology, for the design of Figure 2. The opportunity to present this material at the University of Oxford for the initial workshop organized by Elisabeth Hsu and Chris Low was greatly appreciated; this paper has been strengthened by their comments, as well as by those of the anonymous reviewers. In particular, this paper benefited greatly from extended discussion with Vladimir Jankovic.

[1] *http://www.meteoschweiz.ch/web/de/wetter/gesundheit/wetterfuehligkeit.html.*

REFERENCES

ANDERSEN, H.C. 1949 [1862]. The Ice Maiden. In *The complete Andersen* (trans. J. Hersholt; available on-line: *http://www.andersen.sdu.dk/vaerk/hersholt/TheIceMaiden_e.html*, accessed 2 December 2005).

BENDIX, R. 1992. National sentiment in the enactment and discourse of Swiss political ritual. *American Ethnologist* **19**, 768-90.

CONEDERA, M., P. MARXER, P. AMBROSETTI, G. DELLA BRUNA & F. SPINEDI 1998. The 1997 forest fire season in Switzerland. *International Forest Fire News* **18**, 85-8.

COOKE, L.J., M.S. ROSE & W.J. BECKER 2000. Chinook winds and migraine headache. *Neurology* **54**, 302-7.

DE MAUPASSANT, G. 1886. *L'Auberge* (available on-line: *http://un2sg4.unige.ch/Athena/maupassant/maup_aub.html*, accessed 25 December 2005).

DE RUDDER, B. 1989 [1948]. Das Medizinische Foehnproblem. In *Foehnstudium* (ed.) M. Kuhn, 425-84. Darmstadt: Wissenschaftliche Buchgesellschaft.

DESCARTES, R. 2001 [1637]. *Discourse on method, optics, geometry, and meteorology.* (Revised edition, trans. with an Introduction by P.J. Olscamp). Indianapolis: Hackett.

DIDION, J. 1990 [1968]. *Slouching toward Bethlehem.* New York: Farrar, Straus & Giroux.

DÜRR, B. 2000. *Föhn Heute und Gestern – ein interdiziplanäres Forschungsbericht.* Diplomarbeit am Institut für Atmosphäre und Klima. ETH-Zürich.

Federal Office for Migration, Swiss Confederation 2005. Living and working in Switzerland (available on-line: *http://www.swissemigration.ch/imperia/md/content/elias/r-z/SCHWEIZ_AK_E.pdf*, accessed 25 December 2005).

FIELD, T.S. & M.D. HILL 2002. Weather, Chinook, and stroke occurrence. *Stroke* **33**, 1751-8.

FOUCAULT, M. 1994 [1973]. *The birth of the clinic* (trans. A.M. Sheridan Smith). New York: Vintage.

FREY, W. 1965. On the problem of the Foehn disease. *Wiener Klinische Wochenschrifte* **77**, 125-8.

FRIEDL, J. 1974. *Kippel – a changing village in the Alps.* New York: Holt, Rinehart.

GENSLER, G. 1972. Föhn und Wetterfühligkeit. *Klimatologie der Schweiz, Teil II.* Heft zu den Annalen der Schweizerischen Meteorologischen Zentralanstalt, 121-34.

HANN, J. 1989 [1866]. Zur Frage über den Ursprung des Föhn. In *Föhnstudien* (ed.) M. Kühn, 103-9. Darmstadt: Wissenschaftliche Buchgesellschaft.

HARTWEGER, E. 1956. Treatment of weather sense and weather sensitivity: Foehn disease. *Medizinische Klinik (Munich)* **51**: **12**, 274-6.

INGOLD, T. 2003. Two reflections on ecological knowledge. In *Nature knowledge: ethnoscience, cognition, and utility* (eds) G. Sanga & G. Ortalli, 301-11. Oxford: Berghahn Books.

KALS, W.S. 1977. *The riddle of the winds.* New York: Doubleday.

MACEY, P.M., P.J. SCHUTER & R.P.K. FORD 2000. Weather and the risk of Sudden Infant Death Syndrome: the effect of wind. *Journal of Epidemiology and Community Health* **54**, 333-9.

Malberg, H. 1999. *Bauern-regeln aus Meteorologischer Sicht.* (Third edition). Berlin: Springer Verlag.

Moos, W. 1964. The effects of 'Foehn' weather on accident rates in the city of Zurich, Switzerland. *Aerospace Medicine* **35**, 643-5.

Netting, R.McC. 1981. *Balancing on an Alp: ecological change and continuity in a Swiss mountain community.* Cambridge: University Press.

Niederer, A. 1996. *Alpine Alltagskultur zwischen Beharrung und Wandel.* Bern: Verlag Paul Haupt.

Orledge, R. 1989. *Charles Koechlin (1867-1950): his life and works.* Luxembourg: Harwood Academic Publishers.

Piorecky, J., W.S. Becker & M.S. Rose 1997. Effect of Chinook winds on the probability of migraine headache occurrence. *Headache* **37**, 153-8.

Richner, H. 1989. Neuere Erkentnisse über die physikalischen Ursachen der Föhnbeschwerden. In *Föhnstudien* (ed.) M. Kühn, 485-96. Darmstadt: Wissenschaftliche Buchgesellschaft.

Rolland, R. 1911. *Jean-Christophe: journey's end* (available on-line: *http://www.gutenberg.org/dirs/etext05/8jend10.txt*, accessed 25 December 2005).

Rosaldo, R. 1989. *Culture and truth.* Boston: Beacon Press.

Schiller, F. von 1804. *Wilhelm Tell* (available on-line: *http://www.gutenberg.org/files/6788/6788-h/6788-h.htm*, accessed 15 December 2006).

Seibert, P. 2004. Hahn's Thermodynamic Foehn Theory and its presentation in meteorological textbooks in the course of time. Presented at International Commission on the History of Meteorology Conference, Polling, Germany, 5-9 July (available on-line: *http://www.meteohistory.org/2004polling_preprints/docs/abstracts/seibert_abstract.pdf*, accessed 15 December 2006).

Sulman, F.G. 1980. Migraine and headache due to weather and allied causes, and its specific treatment. *Uppsala Journal of Medical Science, Supplement* **31**, 41-4.

Twain, M. 1880. *A tramp abroad* (available on-line: *http://www.gutenberg.org/files/119/119.txt*, accessed 25 December 2005).

Vaitl, D., N. Propson & R. Stark 2001. Natural very low frequency sferics and headache. *International Journal of Biometeorology* **45**, 115-23.

Villeneuve, P.J., J. Leech & D. Bourque. 2005. Frequency of emergency room visits for childhood asthma in Ottawa, Canada: the role of weather. *International Journal of Biometeorology* **50**, 48-56.

Vogel, H. & D. Neubeiser 1955. Hypersensitivity to weather and Foehn. *Hippokrates* **26**: **2**, 62-4.

von Mackensen, S., P. Hoeppe, A. Maarouf, P. Tourigny & D. Nowak 2005. Prevalence of weather sensitivity in Germany and Canada. *International Journal of Biometeorology* **49**, 156-66.

Wagner, C.B. 2004. How the bear stole the Chinook winds (available on-line: *http://www.wisdomoftheelders.org/prog208/transcript_tis.htm*, accessed 25 December 2005).

Ward, R. de C. 1906. The classification of climates. *Bulletin of the American Geographical Society* **38**: **7**, 401-12.

Weingaertner, H. 2000. *Wenn die Schwalben niedrig fliegen.* Munich: Piper Verlag.

Wiegandt, E. 1977. Communalism and conflict in the Swiss Alps. Ph.D. dissertation, Department of Anthropology, University of Michigan.

Index